BIG BROTHER
BIG BANKER

ALL SEEING - ALL KNOWING - ALL LYING

The Disturbing True Story of the *'Money Lenders'*
and their Deliberate Plans to Create the New World Order

By
Steven M. Bishop
Copyright © 2011, All Rights Reserved.

Published by
Thought Crime Publishing
www.ThoughtCrimePublishing.com

First Edition published 2011
© Steven M. Bishop 2011

A catalogue record for this book is available from
The British Library
ISBN: 978-1-908374-02-8

TABLE OF CONTENTS

Chapter Fifteen: War on the Family

Chapter Sixteen: United Nations of Religion

Chapter Seventeen: Greatest Scientific Fraud in History

INTRODUCTION

Plato writes of a group of prisoners enslaved from birth to death in a dark underground cave, with heads in chains the prisoners are prevented from turning their heads - they can only look in one direction. All the prisoners had seen for their entire lives was the interior of the same one wall. Projected on the wall were shadowy images from a fire lit behind them. The prisoners had long since agreed on the meanings of the shapes and images on the wall and what they represented. All new prisoners from birth born into the 'system' would be taught to believe in the same values and ideas, real or imagined gained from the wall of the collective prisoners.

One of the prisoners eventually escapes, venturing above ground to find the truth for himself of how the world really works. He had a rude awakening when realizing things were not quite as they seem. Heading back to the cave to tell his friends of the amazing news of what he had discovered, he was sure they would be astonished at what he had to say. Unfortunately the other prisoners did not quite see things in the same manner, and not wanting to believe what he had to say, they killed him.

In the movie *The Matrix*, Morpheus explains the above scenario when referring to the matrix or the system that people are born into: "Most of these people are not ready to be unplugged, and many of them are so hopelessly dependent on the system, [that] they will fight to protect it." Humans will fight mentally and physically to retain their illusions. Prisoners that don't know their prisoners don't think they are prisoners.

Plato's cave is institutional control which people allow themselves to be subjected to. The matrix is the system you are born into that you take for granted; doing what everybody else does because you have been trained just like everybody else and don't know any different. Modern society lives in Plato's cave and doesn't know it, never realizing that what is seen is what has been taught to be seen, not 'what is.' No-one question's the world they are born into, why should they, 'it's just the way things are.' Living is viewed as a sequence of random events that just happen; we make our way in the world and the future unfolds, it never occurs to the average Joe that these 'random' events may not be that random after all. All these events in isolation just seem normal, but as we shall see, nothing happens by chance - these seemingly unrelated events are connected.

Generations of men and women were trained to look in one direction, going to their graves never knowing that most, if not all of the major historical events of the past were pre-planned in secret by men in power, with the sole intent to manipulate and deceive the masses into accepting a society they would otherwise reject. Society has been deceived in every possible way imaginable to prepare the masses for the coming New World Order, a term father Bush used in the 90's - but was quickly dropped as the public didn't like it. The new society being propagated through the media is a progressive authoritarian control system which has slowly crept upon the sleeping public for nearly two-hundred and fifty years.

The New World Order will be a new 'system' of living; set up to eliminate all that is relevant to the 'old' world order. By 'old,' I mean ideas such as family values that generations have fought for and cultivated over millennia, Christian beliefs, fixed moral laws, property rights and human rights, etc. Timeless wisdom of the ages is to be replaced with a new set of values for a more 'tolerant' society.

It is my wish within these pages to highlight some key points over the last couple of centuries that have helped shape our current society; it is by no means complete. Understanding that people act on the basis of what they think, that one must have the right world view in order to make right decisions, I hope to connect-the-dots, to paint a world view that gives men and women a truth of 'what is.' I recommend reading these chapters in succession, each building upon the last, to reveal a very different picture on the wall. Just don't shoot the messenger.

Money Lenders, Usury and Christ

Since the times of Babylonian Nimrod and the Prophet Abraham five thousand years ago, the rulers and controllers at the top have devised and evolved systems to enslave and control the peasants, mentally and physically for their own selfish financial gains. The preferred system of control that has always worked above all others is the monetary system. Money is the control system of choice because we all depend upon it to survive, 'civilized' societies don't hunt for food, we buy from supermarkets, we don't build our own houses, agents source the house for us, and we pay them, etc. We all need, use and want money, and if you're the person who gets to issue the money to the people, you get to put your two cents in once in awhile about where and how that money will be spent.

Prophets of God and other men of conscience have all warned and exposed schemes of the 'Money-Lenders', and all their clever monetary methods of control and manipulation for centuries. Elite Money-Lenders who have worked and manipulated themselves into positions of power through generations have evolved through time to gain control over the modern day monetary systems, i.e. the banking system. The charging of interest or what was once referred to as usury, is one of these systems of control used by banks that has also been a continual source of conflict throughout history. Usury is one of the most important moral and economic dangers that any society ever faces, if not fought, usury will eventually bring a society to a form of economic slavery.

St. Thomas Aquinas, the leading theologian of the Catholic Church argued that the charging of interest on money was wrong because it 'double charged' the people for both the money and the use of the money. His concepts followed the teachings of Aristotle that taught the purpose of money was to serve the members of a society, to facilitate the exchange of goods needed to lead a virtuous life. The charging of interest was contrary to reason

1

and justice because it put an unnecessary burden on the use of money. Thus, Church law in the Middle Ages Europe forbade the charging of interest on loans and even made it a crime. Usury was seen as the act of a parasite or a thief, and most major religions prohibited its use; money should only be used to facilitate goods and services. Christopher Hollis in his book, *The Two Nations*, referring to Disraeli stated '...Deep down in his soul there was the immemorial teaching of his ancient race against usury – the teaching of Moses and the teaching which traditions of the race take back beyond Moses to the identification of usury with the serpent's bite of Eden.'

In 1822, usury was still under formal ban of the Catholic Church, and the Old Testament and the Koran condemn it to this day.[1] A writer named John Whipple performed a little math usury, he calculated; If five English pennies... had been [lent] at 5 per cent compound interest from the beginning of the Christian era until the present time (say 1850), it would amount in gold of standard fineness to 32,366,648,157 spheres of gold each eight thousand miles in diameter, or as large as the earth.[2]

The Emperor Napoleon wasn't a model Christian, but he fought for a Christian society; the society which conquered him was anti-Christian. It was a society whose foundation was usury, the eternal enemy of the Christian faith. The Eighth Commandment even states: "thou shalt not steal." The Heidelberg Catechism question 110 asks the question: "What does God forbid in the eighth commandment?" to which it answers: "God forbids not only such theft and robbery as are punished by the magistrate, but He also brands as theft all wicked tricks and devices whereby we aim to appropriate our neighbour's goods, whether by force or with show of right, as unjust weights, ells, measures, and wares, false coins, 'usury,' or any other means forbidden by God; likewise all covetousness and all abuse and waste of His gifts." This is the reason Christ had shown that he loved *ALL* people except for one particular group. Christ hated the money lenders, the bankers of His day with a passion. Jesus repeatedly condemned the money-lenders for their practice of usury... He said they were of the Synagogue of Satan. (Rev. 2: -9). He emphatically expressed his extreme hatred of the money lenders when he took a whip and drove them out of the Temple... "This Temple was built as the house of God... But you have turned it into a den of thieves." By performing this act of vengeance against the money-lenders, Christ signed his own death warrant... It was the Illuminati and the false priests and elders in their pay, who hatched the plot by which Christ would be executed by the Roman soldiers. It was *they* who supplied the thirty pieces of silver used to bribe Judas. It was *they* who used their propagandist to *miss-inform*, and *miss-lead* the *Mob*. It was the agents of the Illuminati who led the *Mob* when they accepted Barabbas and screamed that Christ be crucified. It was the Illuminati who arranged matters so that the Roman soldiers acted as their executioners.[3]

Only half a century earlier in 48 BC Julius Caesar took back from the money changers the power to coin money and then minted coins for the benefit of all. With this new, plentiful supply of money, he established many massive construction projects and built great public works. By making money plentiful, Caesar won the love of the common people. But the money changers hated him for it which led to his assassination. Immediately after his assassination, and the demise of plentiful money in Rome, taxes increased, as did corruption. Eventually the Roman money supply was reduced by 90 per cent, which resulted in the common people losing their lands and homes.[4]

The benches on which sat the greasy usurers use to trade in the moneys, have now been converted into temples, which stand magnificently at every corner of contemporary big towns.[5]

Private Printing Press

Most people are unaware as to where their money comes from, let alone the struggles that were fought through the centuries as to who gets to issue and control a nation's money supply. The people have no idea that private bankers, through patient, gradual stealth have taken over the creation and control of the money system, and are using that control to bring about a new economic system, or what father George Bush in the 90's termed as the New World Order. Most of the population of any nation are under the impression that a Government prints and issues its own money. The mint does create a tiny fraction of the physical money in circulation, but money is not created by Governments; it is created everyday by the private banking family institutions.

When you or I head into a bank and ask for a loan, not one single new note will be printed, the amount you require is simply typed into a computer screen and credited to your account, money is created the moment you, the borrower decide you want the loan. This money created by the bank is created *out of nothing* and then lent to the borrower - that's you, *at interest*.

This point has to be thoroughly understood, money is created out of thin air by typing numbers onto a computer screen, there is no gold or silver in the vault, money is created the moment the borrower decides he wants the money. Banks don't lend money they have from deposits; banks lend money on the borrowers '*promise to pay.*' The borrower's signature on the loan paper is an obligation to pay the bank the amount of the loan *plus interest* on specific dates or lose the house, the car or whatever assets have been placed at the time as collateral. This is a big commitment from the borrower, but *the bank risks nothing,* except the piece of scrap paper given to you when you leave the bank that states if you don't pay on these dates put forward, the bank gets all your stuff. Money is created the moment a borrower decides he wants the money. Banks can create as much money as we can eat. The *real* value involved in all transactions is the assets placed as collateral at the time of borrowing. Without the signed document from the bank, the bank would have nothing to lend. As Reed Simpson stated in the forward to *Web of Debt*, "In my experience, in fact, the chief source of bank robbery is not masked men looting tellers' cash tills but the blatant abuse of the extension of credit by white collar criminals." International Bankers are parasites, who are slowly sucking up and absorbing the whole wealth of the world.

Origins of Money

Money is a token representation of value. A monetary system is a contractual agreement among a group of people to accept those tokens at an agreed upon value in trade. The ideal group for this contractual agreement is the larger community called a nation, but if that larger group can't be brought to the task, any smaller group can enter into an agreement, get together and trade.[6]

Money is a storehouse and a *measure* of value; it is a measure by which all other things in the economy can be compared. There was a time in history when communities didn't use paper notes or money; the introduction of money was just another name for a medium of exchange. Our Great ancestors didn't need or use money, they use to exchange goods and services directly with each other, direct exchanges of value with something else of equal value, that's how we functioned as a society, we bartered with each other. However, barter or direct exchange of goods had its problems, because I may not want exactly what you have to offer at the time of exchange, or vice versa. So, as a society, we had to develop systems of exchange, and use objects and goods that represented value for an indirect exchange of goods. Most anything could be represented and accepted as an indirect exchange if it had certain characteristics which made it useful or attractive to everyone in the community. This was the arrival of the money system, which we can describe as a *medium* of exchange of value. As long as what was used as money was portable and people had enough faith in it, it could be exchanged within the community for other things of value. Since the medium of exchange was a commodity of intrinsic value, it can be described as *commodity money*. Among primitive people, the most usual item to become a commodity money was some form of food, either produce or livestock.

Edward Griffin tells us in *The Creature from Jekyll Island* of a period in history when other objects became an accepted medium of exchange between people within a community. Such items as nails, lumber, rice, and whisky... but tobacco was the most common. Here was a commodity which was in great demand both within the colonies and for overseas commerce. It had intrinsic value; it could not be counterfeited; it could be divided into almost any denominational quantity; and its supply could not be increased except by the exertion of labour. In other words, it was regulated by the law of supply and demand, which gave it great stability in value. In many ways, it was ideal money... So close was the identity of tobacco with money that the previous fiat currency of New Jersey, not a tobacco growing state, displayed a picture of a tobacco leaf on its face. It also carried the inscription: "To counterfeit is *Death*." Tobacco was used in early America as a secondary medium of exchange for about two-hundred years, until the new Constitution declared that money was, henceforth, the sole prerogative of the federal government.[7]

A more recent example of tobacco as money can be seen in Germany at the end of World War II of using a commodity as money. The German mark had become useless, and barter became common. But one item of exchange, namely cigarettes, actually became commodity money, and they served quite well. Some ...cigarettes were smuggled into the country, but most of them were brought in by U.S. servicemen. In either case, the quantity was limited and the demand was high. A single cigarette was considered small change. A pack of twenty and a carton of two hundred served as larger units of currency. If the exchange rate began to fall too low - in other words, if the quantity of cigarettes tended to expand at a rate faster than the expansion of other goods - the holders of the currency, more than likely, would smoke some of it rather than spend it. The supply would diminish and the value would return to its previous equilibrium. That is not theory, it actually happened.[8]

Money has taken many forms through the ages, objects such as shells, feathers, and tea leaves compressed into bricks which were traded in East Asia during the 1800's have also been used. With the dawning of the Bronze Age, man learned how to refine and craft iron, copper and tin into units of value. Over time we settled on metals as money because they can be precisely measured, and the value of the metals could easily be determined by its weight and purity. Metals became the primary reason used as *commodity money* because it can meet all of the requirements for convenient trading, by melting and reforming they can be divided into smaller units and used for purchases of smaller items. One metal that has been chosen more so than any other is gold with silver running a close second.

Goldsmiths

Trade in seventeenth century Europe was conducted primarily with gold and silver coins.[9] Our modern day bankers were originally referred to as money lenders or money changers and then later became known as gold-smiths. It was the goldsmith that made trade easier by casting gold into the standardized units of measurement called coins, whose weight and purity could be certified. Coins fast became a convenient representation of value which had the convenience of being exchanged at a later time for something of equal value. However, the goldsmith discovered that carrying around all these gold coins was too heavy, and also very dangerous, so he decided to build a vault for safe keeping. Other people, on discovering the vault, soon wanted to deposit their gold inside the vault, so the goldsmith would issue paper receipts in exchange for their gold; he would also charge a small fee for the safe-guarding of the gold. It worked like this, if you deposited ten ounces of gold into the vault for safe keeping, the goldsmith would issue a paper receipt in the amount of ten gold ounces, in which the depositor could redeem his gold instantly at any time. The purpose of issuing paper receipts (*later known as money*) was to facilitate the *exchange of value*; theses paper receipts or money were representations of *goods of value*, in this case, gold.

The goldsmith then made the observation that the depositors rarely came in to remove their actual physical gold, as the paper receipts issued by the goldsmith in exchange for the gold were being exchanged for goods in the market place as if they were the real actual gold itself. The receipts started to be made to the bearer of the receipt, rather than to the individual deposi- tor of the gold, the notes could now be transferred from person to person without the need for a signature. Paper money was fast becoming the accept- ed medium of exchange within society, because paper money was easier and safer to use, this became the origin of bank notes or money substitutes. It is this form of money that has made exchange possible for the global activity of trade on the planet.

The goldsmith, to increase his profits, started to lend out his own gold in the form of loans, charging a small interest for the service. Over time, as paper money was being accepted within the market place, people started to ask for their loans in the form of the paper receipts instead of gold. But the goldsmiths loans were limited by the amount of personal gold he had in his vault, this is when he had the idea to lend out money on his depositors gold, so the goldsmith started to issue paper receipts against the depositor's gold. The banker could now make a far greater profit than just lending from his own personal supply. This was the 'secret' that the Chicago Federal Reserve said was discovered by the goldsmiths: a bank could lend about ten times as much money as it actually had, because a trusting public, assuming their money was safely in the bank, would not come to collect more than about 10 per cent of it at any one time.[10]

Money for Nothin

There came a time when a borrower came into the counting house or bank, and the goldsmith knew he had reached his limit of lending his gold and his depositors gold, which is when he got the idea to take the lending process one step further. He struck upon the idea that he could issue paper money against gold that wasn't actually in the vault, gold he didn't have, who would know what he was up to or how could they find out?

Goldsmiths began to issue loans at interest on money against gold that wasn't in the vault, that didn't exist; this is how the goldsmith's quickly grew incredibly wealthy. This is how it works now, if the goldsmith had 1000 ounces of gold in the vault and issued 1000 ounces of legitimate receipts, the goldsmith then started to print another 1000 ounces of receipts and lend them out; he would now in effect have 50% in reserve gold. Only 50% of the paper receipts in circulation were now backed by gold in the vault. There is no longer a one to one ratio of paper to gold; some goldsmiths even had as much as three or four pieces of paper in circulation for every piece of gold in the vault. This is how the loaning out of fake receipts at interest has become the foundation of today's money system which is referred to as the Fractional Reserve Banking System, there only has to be a fraction of the gold in reserve at any one time.

Receipts are being issued today, except numbers are moving between one bank account and another on a computer screen, today there is nothing in a vault somewhere that backs up this money. It's important to remember that the paper receipts or money were only representations of something of value, like the gold or silver that was in the vault. Paper receipts have no value in and of themselves, the paper receipts or notes were *symbols* of value, they represented something of *real* tangible value, unlike the computer money or chequebook money we have today which is a representation of *nothing*, which is backed by *nothing*. All the accumulated money and wealth on the planet is in just a handful of private banking family accounts. It's important at this point to ask the question: what could you do if you had a private business that gave you the power to print unlimited amounts of money backed by nothing, lend it out at interest and claim real assets back upon default?

The modern day goldsmith's or money-lenders from the early times of Jesus have never gone away; they are still here, devoted to secrecy and the covert use of financial influence in political life. Goldsmiths discovered that their fraudulent money supply has given them immeasurable control over the running of a nation, especially when lending to Kings. The new and improved versions of goldsmith's are literally 'The creators of money', they control the issue of money which now facilitates the control of governments, which facilitates the control of corporations and ultimately filters down to the control of the people. The privilege to create and control a nation's money supply for private profit instead of for good for the common man is how the dynastic banking families of today have seized power, taken control over society and are in the position to govern the planet.

The modern day goldsmith, the King of all money-lenders was Mayer Amschel Rothschild, who knew how usury or credit could be used to control people, governments and nations. Rothschild once stated: "Let me issue and control a nation's money and I care not who writes the laws." Reginald McKenna, a past Chairman of the Board of Midlands Bank of England stated: "I am afraid that the ordinary citizen will not like to be told that banks can and do create money ...And they who control the credit of the nation [and its citizens and corporations] direct the policy of Governments and hold in the hollow of their hands the destiny of the people."

Fiat Money

The *American Heritage Dictionary* defines fiat money as 'paper money decreed legal tender, not backed by gold or silver.' The two characteristics of fiat money, therefore, are (1) it does not represent anything of intrinsic value and (2) it is decreed legal tender. Legal tender simply means that there is a law requiring everyone to accept the currency in commerce. The two always go together because, since the money really is worthless, it soon would be rejected by the public in favour of a more reliable medium of exchange, such as gold or silver coin. Thus, when governments issue fiat money, they always declare it to be legal tender under pain of fine or imprisonment. The only way a government can exchange its worthless paper money for tangible goods and services is to give its citizens no choice.[11]

The banks receive money from interest simply because they issue a piece of paper against the collective credit of the people as collateral. International banks are creating claims against entire countries; through gradualism, the banks will eventually take ownership of everything, it is a systematic manipulation to absorb the whole wealth of the world. Once upon a time money used to represent value, now money represents debt. Since more money is owed than a nation possesses, the wealth of a nation will eventually be siphoned into the banks, into the private bankers pockets while the people of that nation fall ever deeper into debt.

The nation's tax money goes to the banks to pay interest on the Governments money created in this way, this system is called credit, this is the reason Jesus was upset and threw out the money lenders of his day. Debt is control, the bankers knew this when they set up the system to lend unlimited funds to Government at interest. Bankers are lending money they don't have, if you or I were to do the same, we would be put in prison. It is worth noting that most of the money in circulation today is not physical money. Money is represented by credit cards, money transfers and cheque books. The physical money in circulation is decreasing all the time, with the coming future of the cashless society where the RFID chips will be used for everything. This is the ultimate economic system of control that is being expanded and promoted through the United Nations. As the money-lenders absorb all the wealth of the planet, they are planning and financing a new utopia complete with a centralized world government, a police force, military, education department, a media department and a new religion.

Magic Money Machines

The founding of the Bank of England in 1694 is one of the great dates of world history that was to shape the coming future; as the money-lenders wanted to obtain control of England's economy and the Government, in which they succeeded, and institutionalized the fractional-reserve banking system of today. This was by no means an easy task, for nearly half a century wars and rebellions fought from 1640 to 1689 were fomented by the International money-lenders for the purpose of putting themselves in position to control British politics and the economy.[12] They achieved this by using intrigue and cunning to throw Christians at each other's throats.[13] In order to realize their goals of infiltrating the Bank of England, the international money lenders behind the scenes needed to install one of their own as King; (*this is a technique used to this day, installing your own in influential positions within government, media, academia, etc.*) this was to be achieved in the form of the Dutch Prince William of Orange.

The man who would become King William III began his career as a Dutch aristocrat. He was elevated to Captain General of the Dutch Forces and then to Prince William of Orange with the backing of Dutch money-lenders. His marriage was arranged to Princess Mary of York, eldest daughter of the English Duke of York, and they were married in 1677...and in 1689, William and Mary became King and Queen of England.[14] Their first objective was to obtain permission to institute a Bank of England.[15]

England was financially exhausted after half a century of war against France and numerous civil wars fought largely over excessive taxation... Unable to increase taxes and unable to borrow, Parliament became desperate for some other way to obtain the money... There were two groups of men who saw a unique opportunity arise out of this necessity. The first group consisted of the *political scientists* within the government. The second was comprised of the *monetary scientists* from the emerging business of banking... these two came forward to form an alliance.[16] The organizer and spokesman of this group was William Paterson from Scotland.

King William persuaded the British Treasury to borrow £1,250,000 from these money lenders. The International money-lenders agreed to accommodate the British Treasury to the extent of £1,250,000 providing they could dictate their own terms and conditions, of which was agreed.

The terms were in part:
1. That the names of those who made the loan remain secret; and that they be granted a Charter to establish a Bank of England...
2. That the directors of the Bank of England be granted the legal right to establish the Gold standard for currency, by which...
3. They could make loans to the value of £10 for every £1 value of gold they had on deposit in their vaults...
4. That they be permitted to consolidate the national debt; and secure payment of amounts due as principle and interest by direct taxation of the people.[17]

Thus, for the sum of £1,250,000, King William of Orange sold the people of England into economic bondage.[18] The same Fractional Reserve Banking System of control is in operation today, slowly being implemented in every nation.

Referring to 'Great Britain, Banking In' in the Encyclopaedia Americana, it appears that the Bank of England is not subject to any control by any governmental agency of Great Britain, and that it is *above all government*, and despite the fact that it is *privately owned* and its directors are nominated by its proprietors. In the Encyclopaedia Britannica of 1891 it is termed "a great Engine of Government."[19]

The next four years from 1694–1698, the money in circulation had grown from its initial £1,250,000 to £16,000,000, an increase of 1,280%.[20] William Paterson, however, on obtaining the charter of the bank of England in 1694, to use the moneys he had won in privateering, said: "The Bank hath benefit of interest on all moneys which it creates out of nothing." This was repeated by Sir Edward Holden, founder of the Midland Bank, on December 18th, 1907.[21]

By 1815, the debt was up to 885 million pounds, largely due to the compounding of interest. The lenders not only reaped huge profits, but the indebtedness gave them substantial political leverage.[22] The Bank of England had now become the first central banking system to establish the concept of a partnership between the money-lenders and the politicians. The politicians would receive spendable money (*created out of nothing by the bankers*) without having to raise taxes. In return, the bankers would receive a commission on the transaction- deceptively called interest-which would continue in perpetuity.[23] Or in other words, the interest would accumulate for all time without end. Later, this is why Nathan Rothschild, who controlled the Bank of England after 1820, declared: "I care not what puppet is placed upon the throne of England to rule the Empire on which the sun never sets. The man who controls Britain's money supply controls the British Empire, and I control the British money supply."

The Bank of England soon created a 'new class' of moneyed interests in the City, as opposed to the power of the old barons, whose fortunes derived from their landholdings. Of the five hundred original stockholders, four hundred and fifty lived in London. This was the dawn of the pre-eminence of the "City", now the world's leading financial centre. For this reason, the Rothschild's identified their key American banks with the code word "City".[24]

Brotherhood of Death

Anselm Moses Bauer, a Jewish merchant, tired of his wanderings in Eastern Europe, settled down and opened a shop located on Judenstrasse (*Jew Street*), a ghetto in Frankfurt, Germany. He sold new and used goods, which included rare coins; it was also a '*counting house*' in which he was a money-lender to the people. He placed a sign over the door way to his shop, a red hexagon which depicted a red shield, red being the colour of blood for revolution. He had three sons; one of them being Mayer Amschel Bauer (*1743 – 1812*), who at an early age, showed that he possessed an immense intellectual ability. His father would spend much of his time teaching him everything he knew about the money-lending business, the lessons that he had accumulated from many sources over his life. With his father's skills Amschel later became an apprentice at the House of Oppenheimer's bank in Hanover, his superior ability was quickly recognized and he was awarded a junior partnership. I will return to the Oppenheimer bank shortly.

After his father's untimely death, Amschel returned to Frankfurt to take over his father's business and recognizing the significance of the red hexagram over the entrance to the house, decided to change the family name from Bauer to Rothschild, meaning Red (*Rot*) Shield (*Schild*) in German. The red hexagram shield also known as the Star of David would later be used as the symbol for the World Revolutionary Movement and for the Rothschild created nation of Israel some two centuries later.

In 1770, Amschel married seventeen year old Gudule Schnapper, who bore him five sons, in which he trained them all in the art of money creation and the business of money-lending. Around the dinner table, Amschel would warn his sons to keep their wealth in the family and never marry outside of the family. He also had five daughters whose marriage partners would all be selected for them, solely for the purpose of business connections and keeping all the wealth within the family.

Returning to Mayer Amschel's time at the Oppenheimer Bank, Amschel ran errands for one Lieutenant General Baron von Estorff, an aristocrat who would later introduce Amschel to the Landgrave of Hesse-Cassell, Prince William IX, who was closely related to all the various royal families of Europe. Prince William had a reputation as a cold blooded loan shark and a dealer in human flesh, and for a price, would rent out his own trained Hessian soldiers as mercenary troops to any nation who would pay for them (*a practice that continues today in the form of exporting, 'peacekeeping,' troops throughout the world*). His best customer was the British government who needed troops for such projects as trying to keep the American colonists in line. It was a profitable '*blood for money*' business that made Prince William one of Europe's wealthiest men. With this connection, Mayer Amschel was soon acting as the money-lender and agent for Prince William. Through his dealings with the Prince, Amschel soon discovered that loaning money to Governments and Kings was much more profitable than loaning money to private individuals, not only were the loans bigger, but the loans could be secured on the nations taxes.

During this time, Napoleon with his powerful French army was becoming master of Europe. In 1806, Napoleon made it his sole objective to remove Prince William from his ruler-ship and to strike the house from the list of powers. Prince William was eventually forced to flee to Denmark to stay with his Royal relatives, and left £600,000 (*then $3,000,000, which was a huge sum in the early 1800's*) with Amschel Rothschild for safekeeping. This is money that Prince William had embezzled from the British Government; this vast sum was intended for the services of the soldiers who were morally and legally entitled to the money.

Taken from the 1905 edition of the Jewish Encyclopaedia, Volume X, P. 494: 'According to legend this money was hidden away in wine casks, and, escaping the search of Napoleon's soldiers when they entered Frankfort, was restored intact in the same casks in 1814, when the elector returned to the electorate. The facts are somewhat less romantic, and more business-like.'

The true facts are entirely different, the money wasn't hidden in the wine casks to escape detection from Napoleon's troops, and the money was never returned to the electorate. Mayer Amschel Rothschild embezzled the money from Prince William, who had originally embezzled the money from the British Government. This twice embezzled money was the real foundation of the huge Rothschild Empire. There is not an honestly acquired dollar in the hundreds of billions, now trillions, possessed by the Rothschild family. Amschel Rothschild used this '*blood money*' to send Nathan, his son, to London with the entire sum to establish the London branch of the family business. These are the true beginnings of the Rothschild's Empire.

Eustace Mullin's tells us the overwhelming success of the Rothschild's lay in their willingness to do what had to be done. As Frederic Morton writes in the Preface to *The Rothschild's* 'For the last one hundred and fifty years, the history of the House of Rothschild has been to an amazing degree the backstage history of Western Europe.... Because of their success in making loans not to individuals but to nations, they reaped huge profits.... Someone once said that the wealth of Rothschild consists of the bankruptcy of nations.' In its issue of Dec. 19th, 1983, Forbes Magazine noted that 'Half of Germany's top ten banks are Frankfurt based.' The modern world's financial system, an updating of the Babylonian monetary system of taxes and money creation, was perfected in Frankfurt-on-Main, in the province of Hesse.[1]

The Rothschild's were a constant, if weakening, influence for peace, a pattern established in 1830 and 1840 when the Rothschild's threw their whole tremendous influence successfully against European wars... they were almost equally devoted to secrecy and the secret use of financial influence in political life. These money-lenders eventually became known as the 'International Bankers.'[2]

Mayer Amschel knew the power of money and the wisdom of secrecy, at the time of his death on Sept 9th 1812, aged 68, Mayer Amschel Rothschild had become by far the richest man in the world or that had ever lived. In his will he laid out specific laws that the House of Rothschild descendants must adhere too. Mayer Amschel left instructions that the amount of the inheritance must never be made public, but secrecy and ruthlessness must be used in all business practices and that family members must inter-marry with their own blood relatives to keep the family fortunes all in the family and the bloodlines 'pure', (*Of the 18 marriages by Mayer Amschel Rothschild's grandchildren, 16 were between first cousins, a practice recognized today as inbreeding which is the breeding ground for psychopathic traits*). All key positions in the family business were only to be held by family members; only male members of the family were allowed to participate in the family business, no legal action was to be taken with regard to the value of the inheritance and the eldest son of the eldest son was to become the head of the family (*this condition could only be overturned when the majority of the family agreed otherwise*). This was the case with Nathan Mayer Rothschild being elected head of the family following Mayer Amschel's death. Mayer Amschel left one billion francs to his five sons. The eldest, Anselm, was placed in charge of the Frankfort bank. He had no children, and the bank was later closed. The second son, Salomon, was sent to Vienna, where he soon took over the banking monopoly formerly shared among five Jewish families, Arnstein, Eskeles, Geymüller, Stein and Sina. The third son, Nathan, founded the London branch, after he had profited in some Manchester dealings in textiles and dyestuffs which caused him to be widely feared and hated. Karl, the fourth son, went to Naples, where he became head of the occult group, the Alta Vendita. The youngest son, James, founded the French branch of the House of Rothschild in Paris.[3]

Little could Mayer Amschel have anticipated that his sons would in after years come to exercise such an unbounded sway that the peace of nations would depend upon their nod; that the powerful control they exercised on the European money markets would enable them to pose as the arbiters of peace and war, since they could at their pleasure withhold or furnish the pecuniary means required to carry on a campaign. "But this, incredible as it may seem, was what their vast influence, combined with their enormous wealth and unlimited credit, enabled them to do, for no firms existed strong enough to oppose them for any length of time, or rash enough to take up a business which the Rothschild's had refused. To reach this exalted position Mayer Amschel and his sons required the co-operation of the States, but, when once he had climbed over their backs and reached the height of his ambition, he was independent of all aid and could act with the greatest freedom, whilst the States remained in a suppliant attitude at his feet.[4]

The Illuminati Plan

Rothschild wasn't content with being the richest man in the world; he wanted a share of everyone's money, and everything else on the planet. In 1773, Mayer Amschel was ready to put forth his grand ideas for world domination and invited twelve revolutionary minded men to his shop in Frankfurt, together they conceived and formulated a plan to absorb and control *all* of the world's wealth and resources. These men made a pact to secretly pool their money to influence and bankrupt the nations of the world, and create what we know today as the New World Order. The initiates were all convinced; they had no doubt that the Order would one day rule the world through a world system of political and economic control.

The detailed plan below is summarized from William Guy Carr's book *Pawns in the Game:*

1. The speaker unfolded the plot by saying that because the majority of men were inclined to evil rather than to *good* the best results in governing them could be obtained by using violence and terrorism and not by academic discussions. The speaker reasoned that in the beginning human society had been subject to brutal and blind force which was afterwards changed to LAW. He argued that LAW was FORCE only in disguise. He reasoned it was logical to conclude that "*By the laws of nature right lies in force.*"

2. He next asserted that political freedom is an idea and not a fact. He stated that in order to usurp political power, all that was necessary was to preach 'Liberalism' so that the electorate, for the sake of an idea, would yield some of their power and prerogatives which the plotters could then gather together into their own hands.

3. The speaker asserted that the *Power of Gold* had usurped the power of liberal rulers even then, i.e. 1773. He reminded his audience that there had been a time when FAITH had ruled but stated that once FREEDOM had been substituted for FAITH the people did not know how to use it in moderation. He argued that because of this fact it was logical to assume that they could use the idea of FREEDOM to bring about "CLASS WARS." He pointed out that it was immaterial to the success of HIS plan whether the established governments were destroyed by internal or external foes because the victor had of necessity to seek the aid of 'Capital' which "*Is entirely in our hands.*"

4. He argued that the use of any and all means to reach their final goal was justified on the grounds that *the ruler who governed by the moral code was not a skilled politician* because he left himself vulnerable and in an unstable position on his throne. He said: "*Those who wish to rule must have recourse to 'cunning and to make-believe' because great national qualities, like frankness and honesty, are vices in politics.*"

5. He asserted: "*Our right lies in force. The word RIGHT is an abstract thought and proves nothing. I find a new RIGHT ... to attack by the RIGHT of the strong, and to scatter to the winds all existing forces of order and regulation, to 'reconstruct all existing institutions,' and to become the sovereign Lord of all those who left to us the RIGHTS to their powers by laying them down voluntarily in their 'Liberalism.'"*

6. He then admonished his listeners with these words: "*The power of our resources must remain invisible until the very moment when it has gained such strength that no cunning or force can undermine it.*" He warned them that any deviation from the Line of the strategical plan he was making known to them would risk bringing to naught "THE LABOURS OF CENTURIES."

7. He next advocated the use of 'Mob Psychology' to obtain control of the masses. He reasoned that the might of the Mob is blind, senseless, and unreasoning and ever at the mercy of suggestion from any side. He stated "*Only a despotic ruler can rule the Mob efficiently because without absolute despotism there can be no existence for civilization which was carried out NOT by the masses, but by their guide, who-so-ever that person might be.*" He warned: "*The moment the Mob seizes FREEDOM in its hands it quickly turns to anarchy*"

8. He next advocated that the use of alcoholic liquors, drugs, moral corruption, and all forms of vice, be used systematically by their "Agenturs" to corrupt the morals of the youth of the nations. He recommended that the special 'agenturs' should be trained as tutors, lackeys, governesses, clerks and by our women in the places of dissipation frequented by the Goyim (the Masses). He added: "In the number of these last I count also the so-called society ladies who become voluntary followers of the others in corruption and luxury. We must not stop at bribery, deceit, and treachery when they should serve towards the attainment of our end."

9. Turning to politics he claimed they had the RIGHT to seize property by any means, and without hesitation, if by doing so they secured submission, and sovereignty. He pronounced: "Our STATE marching along the path of peaceful conquest has the RIGHT to

replace the horrors of wars by less noticeable and more satisfactory sentences of death necessary to maintain the [War On...] 'terror' which tends to produce blind submission."

10. Dealing with the use of slogans he said: "In ancient times we were the first to put the words 'Liberty', 'Equality' and 'Fraternity' into the mouths of the masses ... words repeated to this day by stupid poll-parrots; words which the would-be wise men of the Goyim (the masses) could make nothing of in their abstractness, and did not note the contradiction of their meaning and inter-relation."
He claimed the words brought under their directions and control 'legions' "Who bore our banners with enthusiasm." He reasoned that there is no place in nature for 'Equality', 'Liberty' or 'Fraternity'. He said: "On the ruins of the natural and genealogical aristocracy of the Goyim we have set up the aristocracy of MONEY. The qualification for this aristocracy is WEALTH which is dependent upon us."

11. He next expounded his theories regarding war. In 1773 he set down a principle which the governments of Britain and the United States publicly announced as their joint policy in 1939. He said it should be the policy of those present to foment wars but to direct the peace conferences so that neither of the combatants obtained territorial gains. He said the wars should be directed so that the nations engaged on both sides would be placed further in their debt, and in the power of 'Our' Agents.

12. He next dealt with administration. He told those present that they must use their wealth to have candidates chosen for public office who would be *"servile and obedient to our commands, so they may readily be used as Pawns in our game by the learned and ingenious men we will appoint to operate behind the scenes of government as official advisers."* He added: *"The men we appoint as 'Advisers' will have been bred, reared, and trained from childhood in accordance with our ideas to rule the affairs of the whole world."*

13. He dealt with propaganda, and explained how their combined wealth could control all outlets of public information while they remained in the shade and clear of blame regardless of what the repercussions might be due to the publication of libels, slanders, or

untruths. The speaker said: "*Thanks to the Press we have got gold in our hands not with standing the fact that we had to gather it out of the oceans of blood and tears... But it has paid us even though we have sacrificed many of our own people. Each victim on our side is worth a thousand Goyim.*"

14. He next explained the necessity of having their 'Agentur' always come out into the open, and appear on the scene, when conditions had reached their lowest ebb, and the masses had been subjugated by means of want and terror. He pointed out that when it was time to restore order they should do it in such a way that the victims would believe they had been the prey of criminals and irresponsibles. He said: "*By executing the criminals and lunatics after they have carried out our preconceived 'reign of terror,' we can make ourselves appear as the saviours of the oppressed, and the champions of the workers.*" The speaker then added: "*We are interested in just the opposite ... in the diminution, the killing out of the Goyim (masses).*"

15. He next explained how industrial depressions and financial panics could be brought about and used to serve their purpose saying: "*Enforced unemployment and hunger, imposed on the masses because of the power we have to create shortages of food, will create the right of Capital to rule more surely than it was given to the real aristocracy, and by the legal authority of Kings.*" He claimed that by having their agentur control the 'Mob,' the 'Mob' could then be used to wipe out all who dared to stand in their way.

16. The infiltration into continental Freemasonry was next discussed extensively. The speaker stated that their purpose would be to take advantage of the facilities and secrecy Freemasonry had to offer. He pointed out that they could organize their own Grand Orient Lodges within Blue Freemasonry in order to carry on their subversive activities and 'hide the true nature of their work under the cloak of philanthropy.' He stated that all members initiated into their Grand Orient Lodges should be used for proselytizing purposes and for spreading their atheistic-materialistic ideology amongst the Goyim. He ended this phase of the discussion with the words. "*When the hour strikes for our sovereign Lord of the entire World to be crowned these same hands will sweep away everything that might stand in his way.*"

17. He next expounded the value of systematic deceptions, pointing out that their agentur should be trained in the use of high sounding phrases, and the use of popular slogans. They should make the masses the most lavish of promises. He observed: "*The opposite of what has been promised can always be done afterwards ... that is of no consequence.*" He reasoned that by using such words as *Freedom and Liberty*, the Goyim could be stirred up to such a pitch of patriotic fervour that they could be made to fight even against the laws of God, and Nature. He added: "*And for this reason after we obtain control the very NAME OF GOD will be erased from the 'Lexicon of life.'*"

18. He then detailed the plans for revolutionary war; the art of street fighting; and outlined the pattern for the 'Reign of Terror' which he insisted must accompany every revolutionary effort "*Because it is the most economical way to bring the population to speedy subjection.*"

19. Diplomacy was next discussed. After all wars secret diplomacy must be insisted upon: "*in order that our agentur, masquerading as 'political,' 'Financial' and 'Economic' advisers, can carry out our mandates without fear of exposing who are 'The Secret Power' behind national and international affairs.*" The speaker then told those present that by secret diplomacy they must obtain such control: "*that the nations cannot come to even an inconsiderable private agreement without our secret agents having a hand in it.*"

20. Ultimate World Government the goal. To reach this goal the speaker told them: "*It will be necessary to establish huge monopolies, reservoirs of such colossal riches, that even the largest fortunes of the Goyim will depend on us to such an extent that they will go to the bottom together with the credit of their governments ON THE DAY AFTER THE GREAT POLITICAL SMASH.*" The speaker then added: "*You gentlemen here present who are economists just strike an estimate of the significance of this combination.*"

21. Economic war. Plans to rob the Goyim of their landed properties and industries were then discussed. A combination of high taxes, and unfair competition was advocated to bring about the economic ruin of the people as far as their national financial interests and

investments were concerned. In the international field he felt they could be encouraged to price themselves out of the markets. This could be achieved by the careful control of raw materials, organized agitation amongst the workers for shorter hours and higher pay, and by subsidizing competitors. The speaker warned his co-conspirators that they must arrange matters, and control conditions, so that *"the increased wages obtained by the workers will not benefit them in any way."*

22. Armaments. It was suggested that the building up of armaments for the purpose of making the people destroy each other should be launched on such a colossal scale that in the final analysis: *"there will only be the masses of the proletariat left in the world, with a few millionaires devoted to our cause ... and police, and soldiers sufficient to protect our interests."*

23. The New Order. The members of the One World Government would be appointed by the Dictator. He would pick men from amongst the scientists, the economists, the financiers, the industrialists, and from the millionaires because: *"in substance everything will be settled by the question of figures."*

24. Importance of youth. The importance of capturing the interest of youth was emphasized with the admonition that: *"Our agents should infiltrate into all classes, and levels of society and government, for the purpose of fooling, bemusing, and corrupting the younger members of society by teaching them theories and principles we know to be false."*

25. National and International Laws should not be changed but should be used as they are, to destroy the civilization of the people: *"merely by twisting them into a contradiction of the interpretation which first masks the law and afterwards hides it altogether. Our ultimate aim is to substitute ARBITRATION for LAW."*

The speaker then told his listeners: *"You may think the people will rise upon us with arms, but in the WEST we have against this possibility an organization of such appalling terror that the very stoutest hearts quail ... the 'Underground'... The Metropolitans ... The subterranean corridors ... these will be established in the capitals and cities of all countries before that danger threatens.*"[5] [All Emphasis in original] Fact or fictions, the spirit of the writings contain monumental amounts of recent and historical truth.

Adam Weishaupt

Mayer Amschel Rothschild entrusted the development and organization of the Master Plan to one Adam Weishaupt (*Founder of the Order of the Illuminati in Bavaria*). Weishaupt was given the task of organizing and modernizing the '*protocols*.' Weishaupt, a Crypto-Jew was outwardly Roman Catholic, a Jesuit trained professor of canon law who taught at Engelstock University. He had developed an intense hatred for the Jesuits. Although he became a Catholic priest, his faith had been shaken by the Jesuits and so he became an atheist. Weishaupt was an ardent student of French philosopher Voltaire (*1694-1778*), a revolutionary insider who knew the plan and held liberal religious views. Voltaire's beliefs were revealed in a letter to King Frederick II declaring… "Lastly, when the whole body of the Church should be sufficiently weakened and infidelity strong enough, the final blow is to be dealt by the sword of open, relentless persecution. A reign of terror is to be spread over the whole earth."

The Illuminati plan is based upon the teachings of the Talmud, which is in turn, the teachings of Rabbinical Jews. They were to be known as the Illuminati (*Illuminati was a name used by a German sect that existed in the 15th century*), which practices the occult and translates as '*Holder of the Light*'. Adam Weishaupt's revised blueprint for the Rothschild's reveals how wars and revolutions are to be used to bring about world domination, culminating in the formation of a One World Governmental system. Secret police were organized and used to assassinate those members who went astray. Weishaupt's task was officially launched on 1st May 1776, the date which can be seen on the back of the U.S. one dollar bill at the base of the pyramid, along with the symbol of the eye above the pyramid.[6]

Weishaupt's Revised Plan

1. Influence men with the use of monetary and sex bribes to obtain control of people already occupying positions in high places of

power, in all the various levels of governments and other fields of human endeavour. Once an influential person had fallen for the lies, deceits, and temptations of the Illuminati, they were to be held in bondage by application of political and other forms of blackmail and threats of financial ruin, public exposure, and physical harm and even death to themselves and their loved ones.

2. To win the common people in every corner. This will be obtained mainly through the schools. They will show toleration of their prejudices of the people, but will at leisure root out and dispel them. They will use every means possible to gain over Reviewers and Journalists; and also to gain the sellers of books. They will acquire the direction of all education... too bring about opinions spread among the masses by the help of young writers for every art. They will put Illuminati members on the faculties of colleges and universities; they will obtain students possessing exceptional mental ability who belong to well-bred families with international leanings for special training in internationalism. This training will be provided by granting scholarships to those selected (*Bill Clinton was a Rhodes Scholar*). They are to be educated (*indoctrinated*) into accepting the '*Idea*' that only a One World Government can put an end to recurring wars and tribulations. (*This is how the League of Nations, and the United Nations was sold to the public – which we will see later*). They are to be first persuaded and then convinced that men of special ability and brains have the *RIGHT* to rule those less gifted because the people don't know what is best for them physically, mentally and spiritually, the '*Right of Might.*'

3. Influential people will be trapped into coming under the control of the Illuminati, and students who have been specially educated and trained are to be used as agents and placed behind the scenes of *ALL* governments as '*Experts*' and '*Specialists*,' so they can advise the top executives to adopt policies which will serve the secret plans of the New World Order and bring about the ultimate destruction of the governments and religions they were elected or appointed to serve.

4. The Illuminati will obtain control of the press and all other agencies which distribute information to the public. News and information will be slanted so that the masses will come to believe that a One World Government is the *ONLY* solution to the many and varied problems. *(the evidence today is the United Nations relentless push for the Environmental Global Agenda)*

5. They will obtain an influence in the military academies... and the printing-houses, in short, in all offices which have any effect, either in forming, or in managing, or even in directing the mind of man, forming his opinions, even to include paintings and engravings with our messages. They will establish reading societies, subscription libraries, and take everything under their direction, and by owning and supplying *ALL* information, can turn the public mind which way they will.

The One World Government plan is also to be established by breaking down and destroying all existing governments and religions, by dividing the masses (*divide and Conquer*) into competing on all forces of political, racial, social and economic issues. The opposing sides are then armed with an '*incident*' that causes the people to fight, weaken and destroy themselves, with National Governments and religions following.

The Illuminati attitude toward religion is to profess Christianity while working to destroy it. They taught, rather than God creating the universe, the universe is creating God and that man is himself God and therefore unaccountable to a higher power, these are also the underpinnings of the modern day 'New Age' doctrine of the 21st century.

Weishaupt infiltrated the Continental Order of Freemasons with the One World doctrine, establishing the lodges of the Grand Orient inside the already secret society of freemasons. In essence, they were hiding a highly secretive organization within an already highly secret organization. To infiltrate these Masonic lodges in Europe, Weishaupt had enlisted the aid of John Robison, who was a high degree Mason in the Scottish rite, and a professor of Natural Philosophy at Edinburgh University in Scotland. On his visit to Germany, he was given Weishaupt's revised conspiracy plans to study, to expand the Illuminate's influence in the British Isles. However, Robison didn't agree with their principles, and after warning American Masons in 1789, published his book *Proofs of a Conspiracy* which exposed the organization. In 1798 Robison stated: "I have observed these doctrines gradually diffusing and mixing with all the different systems of Freemasonry till, at last, an association has been formed for the express purpose of rooting out all the religious establishments, and overturning all the existing governments of Europe."

Proofs of a Conspiracy

During the later years of the 18th Century, Britain and France were the two greatest world powers of the time, Weishaupt ordered the Illuminati to encourage the colonial wars, including the American Revolution to weaken the British Empire, and organize the French Revolution to start in 1789. However; in 1784, an act of God placed the Bavarian government in possession of evidence which proved the existence of the Illuminati. A German writer named Zwack, put the entire Illuminati plan for world domination into book form, and sent a copy to Robespierre, the Illuminists in France, whom Weishaupt had delegated to provoke the French Revolution. On his way, the courier was struck by lightning and was killed as he rode through Rawleston from Frankfurt to Paris. The police found the subversive documents on his body and turned them over to the proper authorities.

After a careful study of the plot; the Bavarian government ordered the police to raid Weishaupt's newly-organized Lodges of the 'Grand Orient' and the homes of his most influential associates. All additional evidence that was discovered convinced the authorities that the documents were genuine copies of a conspiracy by which the Illuminati planned to use wars and revolutions to bring about the establishment of a one-world government; the powers of which the Rothschild's, intended to take over as soon as it was established. This is still the same plan implemented and fulfilled by the United Nation's today. The evidence recovered from the courier could have saved France if they, the French government, hadn't refused to believe it was true. Although Weishaupt and his co-conspirators were banished from Bavaria, and the Order was officially suppressed, the order simply went underground. Just over half a century later the money-lenders would find another man to further their cause under a new name.

League of Just Men

Karl Marx wrote one-hundred volumes of collected works during his lifetime, but only thirteen were ever published. Marx received a Doctorate in Philosophy in 1841, but was turned down for teaching jobs on account of his revolutionary activities. When he was six, his family converted to Christianity, and although he believed in God, something caused him in his later life to avenge himself against '*the One who rules above*'. Marx deeply believed that the Christian religion was one of the most immoral and disgusting of all the religions which led him to join the Satanist Church.

While living in London Marx joined the Communist League; it was here that he was commissioned to write a *Communist Manifesto*, which quickly became the Bible of various Communist movements around the world. Karl Marx was hired to write the *Manifesto* by the League of Just Men, an offshoot of the Parisian Outlaws League, founded by the Illuminati members who had earlier fled Germany. The *Communist Manifesto* was the update of the Illuminati plans and principles set down and updated by Adam Weishaupt in 1776, Illuminati principles and Communism is one and the same plan.

Marx being a Satanist – it naturally followed that the Illuminati-Communist ideology would be intent upon furthering the idea of dethroning God, but that wasn't enough for Marx, he wanted to go even further and annihilate all concepts of Religion and morality. He believed the family unit would have to go as the family would have no place in the new Communist society; people are only seen as units of production that will benefit the State, that's if you are allowed to be born at all. With strong family units finally eradicated, there would be no-one around to back you up in a struggle, the State could finally talk directly down to you.

The New World Order will operate by all the laws contrary to a 'free' society, virtually everything and everyone will belong to the state, the individual will have little to no rights, including property rights, no ability to plan one's own life, told where you will work, what you will do, where and how you will do it, and for how long. There will be no freedom to seek a better lifestyle for yourself or your family. The New World denies religion, degrades and debases man to a machine that lives for and empowers the State. Children will be born into a world with no search for truth, meaning and understanding, a world with no individuality, you will be moulded to fit the machine. Government will write and rewrite the text books, spreading government lies and propaganda to keep people indoctrinated with politically correct ideas of what is right and what is wrong at any particular point in time. Real history and knowledge of humanity will disappear down the 'memory hole.'

The Insignia of the Order of the Illuminati

MDCCLXXVI at the base of the pyramid is not the date of the signing of the declaration of Independence as the uninformed have supposed, it is Weishaupt's completion of the plan for a New World Order on May 1st 1776.

Novus Ordo Seclorum… Order Out Of Chaos.

First American Central Bank

It may just be a coincidence that the founding of the Illuminati and the founding of the American Republic both took place in 1776. For over a hundred years, the Republic stood as a roadblock to Weishaupt's scheme for his order to rule the world. During this period, the American Republic was a shining example of everything that was contrary to what the Illuminati and its followers were bringing upon the world.[1] As James Madison, the 4th President of America stated: "History records that the money changers have used every form of abuse, intrigue, deceit, and violent means possible to maintain their control over governments by controlling money and its issuance." The United States has fought against the same debt control money system that Christ fought against twenty centuries ago, when He chased the money-lenders from the temple.

The American people were relatively poor in the mid 1700's, and a lack of precious metals like gold and silver made it hard for the people to conduct business transactions. The colonialists were forced to experiment with their own paper money; it was called colonial scrip (*This was debt free paper money, printed in the public interest*). Colonial scrip was not backed by gold or silver and therefore the colonies could control its purchasing power, it was a very successful endeavour. Benjamin Franklin became a big supporter of the colonies printing their own paper money. One by one, all the Colonies began to issue their own paper money to serve as a medium of exchange to make trade vibrant in America.

In 1757, Benjamin Franklin (*1706 – 1790*) was sent to England, where he stayed for the next eighteen years. Associates of the Rothschild's asked Franklin how he accounted for the successful state of affairs in the colonies, Franklin replied: "In the colonies we issue our own money. It is called colonial scrip; we issue it in proper proportion to the demands of trade and industry to make the products pass easily from the producers to the consumers, in this manner, creating for ourselves our own paper money, we control its purchasing power, and we have no interest to pay to no one." The Rothschild's realizing an opportunity when they saw one had to exploit the situation. The Rothschild's with considerable influence over the directors of the Bank of England, passed The Paper Bills of Credit Act of 1763, also known as the Currency Act, a British Act of Parliament that prohibited the American colonies from issuing paper currency as legal tender and made it compulsory for the colonist to obtain their money from the banks at interest. Benjamin Franklin later stated: "In one year the conditions were so reversed that the era of prosperity ended and a depression set in, to such an extent that the streets of the Colonies were filled with unemployment." Franklin also revealed that the main reason for the start of the revolution, when stating: "The colonies would gladly have borne the little tax on tea and other matters had it not been that England took away from the Colonies their money, which created unemployment and dissatisfaction." In 2 to 3 years there was 25 to 30% unemployment, drinking, crime, divorces, debtor's prison, and forced child work.[2]

The colonies were drained of gold and silver coin by the British taxes, after that, the government had no choice but to print the money to finance the war. The first '*shot heard round the world*' was fired on April 19th, 1775 at Lexington, Massachusetts. The Colonial wars would carry on for the next seven years and the Rothschild's made millions from the Revolution by supplying the British with Prince William's mercenary Hessian troops. The US money supply at the start of the revolution stood at $12,000,000, by the end of the Revolution, it was nearly $500,000,000, as a result the currency was virtually worthless, and basic commodities like shoes were selling for $5000 a pair. The Colonial scrip used before had worked because it was just enough to facilitate trade. The Colonial people believed that the English government had robbed them; they never realized that the taxation and other economic sanctions being imposed against them were the result of the activities of a small group of *International Banksters* who held no allegiance to any nation.

In 1780, the International Bankers had no intention of letting the American people start printing their own money again, so the Directors of the Bank of England sent their Rothschild agent Alexander Hamilton to America to represent their interests in the United States, to propose the establishment of a national federal bank; which Hamilton conveyed was to be owned by '*private interests*.' The Hamiltonian proposal for a national bank was a charter for private monopoly, a Congressional grant for a privileged few. The Bank of the U.S. had the sole right to issue currency, it was exempt from taxation, and the U.S. government was ultimately responsible for its actions and debts.[3]

The founding fathers of American Independence knew what Christ knew when He drove the money-lenders from the Temple, that if the International Bankers obtained a monopoly over America's money system... as Thomas Jefferson put it: "If the American people ever allow private banks to control the issue of their currency, first by inflation, then by deflation, the banks and corporations which grow up around them will deprive the people of all property until their children wake up homeless on the continent their fathers conquered." Jefferson knew what was shown earlier, that when private banks issue loans to governments; they will seize any money they have lost through the process of claiming the people's farms, houses and businesses that were placed as collateral at the time of the loan. Our modern academics even ignore Thomas Jefferson's chief reason for remaining in politics, i.e., to save the newly born United States from those elitists Jefferson called 'monocrats' and 'monopolists.' It was the banking monopoly that Jefferson considered to be the greatest danger to the survival of the Republic.[4]

Governor Morris also stated in 1787: "The rich will strive to establish their dominion and enslave the rest. They always did. They always will... They will have the same effect here as elsewhere, if we do not, by the power of Government, keep them in their proper spheres." Because they knew the effects of a private bank for a nation, trying to establish a central bank in America and gain control of America's economy, as was formed in England, the net result of the struggle was that Congress refused to grant the Bank of America its Charter.

Benjamin Franklin, having become very familiar with the Bank of England and the fractional reserve banking system, also understood the dangers of a privately owned Central Bank that controls and issues a Nation's money, and managed to resist the charter of a central bank until his death in 1791, but the International money-lenders immediately taking advantage of Franklin's death wasted no time. A few years earlier in 1789, Alexander Hamilton had been made the Secretary to the Treasury, appointed by high ranking freemason George Washington, which gave him the position to put the notion of a bank forward a second time to take control of America's economy; he called for the new privately owned central bank to be named 'The First Bank of the United States,' which was finally granted. The new Bank was capitalized for $35,000,000; of this amount $28,000,000 was subscribed by European Bankers, which the Rothschild's controlled. It is suspected that the International Bankers decided that Hamilton knew too much about what was really going on and couldn't be trusted any longer. He was inveigled into a duel with an expert named Aaron Burr, who acted as his executioner.[5]

The 5000 year old Babylonian debt system was now introduced into the United States with 'The First Bank of the United States,' which was established with a twenty year charter, of which the bank would now be up for review in 1811. The First Bank of the United States name was specifically chosen to hide the fact that it was merely a *privately* owned Bank, named exactly the same way the Bank of England had been named, to deceive the people in thinking it was established by the Government. Incidentally, this is also the same year Mayer Amschel Rothschild stated his now famous quote: "Let me issue and control a nation's money and I care not who writes the laws." A year later in 1792: Jacob (*James*) Mayer Rothschild is born, who will be sent to head the French arm of the Rothschild banking business in the not too distant future. Within five years of establishing The First Bank of the United States, the Government had borrowed $8,200,000, and prices in the country increased by 72%.[6] Thomas Jefferson remarked: "I wish it were possible to obtain a single amendment to our Constitution, taking from the federal government their power of borrowing."

Twenty years later in 1811 the Banks charter came up for renewal, and was violently opposed, even the press openly attacked the bank. Andrew Jackson said: "If Congress has a right under the Constitution to issue paper money, it was given them to use by themselves, not to be delegated to indi-

viduals or corporations." These outspoken comments warned the International Bankers to expect serious opposition when their Charter for the Bank
of the United States ran out in 1811. To prepare for this eventuality Amschel
Mayer Rothschild had obtained absolute control of the Bank of England in
order to strengthen his control of the World's economy.[7] This led to Nathan
Mayer Rothschild issuing his orders from London who didn't want to lose
his American central bank, and so he made the threat, "Either the application for renewal of the charter is granted, or the United States will find
itself involved in a most disastrous war." However, they called his bluff
and along with congressmen, the renewal bill, through much debate was
defeated by a single vote in the house, the Charter was not renewed which
caused Nathan Mayer Rothschild to issue the word: "Teach those impudent
Americans a lesson. Bring them back to colonial status." So, backed by
Rothschild's money, and Nathan Rothschild's orders, the British declared
war on the United States, and England attacked the United States in 1812.
Jefferson was instrumental in Congress's refusal to renew the charter of the
U.S. Bank in 1811. When the bank was liquidated, Jefferson's suspicions
were confirmed: 18,000 of the Bank's 25,000 shares were owned by foreigners, mostly English and Dutch. The foreign domination the Revolution had
been fought to eliminate had crept back in through the country's private
banking system.[8]

    The Rothschild's war was intended to exhaust the United States to such
an extent, that the legislators would have to beg for peace and seek financial
help. Nathan Rothschild was very specific that no financial aid would be
supplied, unless the charter for the Bank of America was renewed. The continuing war led to inflation and heavy Government debt, America couldn't
carry on for much longer. Thomas Jefferson was still protesting against a new
central bank, but Congress gave in and the banks were given another 20 year
charter for a new privately owned central bank, the British debt system was
now back in control of the United States economy with the introduction of
'The Second Bank of the United States.' Nathan Rothschild's plan worked to
perfection. It mattered not to him, how many men were killed and wounded;
how many women were widowed; how many children were made orphans;
how many people were rendered destitute. He and his co-conspirators
rejoiced in the fact that they had achieved their objective and in so doing

they had created more and more dissatisfaction amongst the masses of the people who blamed the blundering policies of their own governments, while The Secret Power behind the scenes remained unsuspected by all except a very few people... There are many authorities who state quite frankly that the members of Congress who were bribed, or threatened into voting legislation, which put the American people back into financial bondage.[9]

Reasons given for the chartering of the Second Bank of The United States as a private national bank to the people were the inability to collect taxes. The twenty year charter was signed by President James Madison in 1816. It authorized the Bank and its branches to issue the nation's money in the form of bank notes, again shifting the power to create the national money supply into private hands.[10] The Second U.S. Bank chartered in 1816 was 80 percent privately owned.[11] These are the real reasons why the war was perpetrated on the American people, an act of revenge because Jefferson refused to renew the charter of the Bank of the United States; these same International Bankers have motivated every war since.

The Kingdom Financing Business

If you are in the kingdom financing business, you can't just lend to one kingdom, you also have to lend to their enemies. You have to make sure that both kingdoms are of about equal strength, so that, in time of conflict, your financing will be the decisive factor.[12]

Across the pond in Europe, Nathan Rothschild had also been busy supplying gold to Wellington's army in England, while his brother Jacob Rothschild was financing Napoleon's army in France, and thus, the Rothschild's were beginning their policy of funding both sides of every war. The Rothschild's through their private wars, were soon discovering a great way to generate risk free debt, and it didn't matter which country lost the war, as the loans were given on the guarantee that the victor will honor the debts of the vanquished.

While financing both sides of a war, the Rothschild's used their banks that were spread across Europe to give them the advantage of an unrivalled postal network of secret routes and fast couriers. The letters that these couriers carried were to be opened and read for any minute detail that could benefit the Rothschild's in business, so they were always one step ahead of current events, which was to have a major impact on the outcome of the next phase of their world domination plan.

On Sunday, 18th June 1815, it was becoming clear that the outcome of the Battle of Waterloo was going to be won by the British; a Rothschild agent named Rothworth took off for the Channel to deliver the news to Nathan Rothschild that Napoleon would soon be defeated, ahead of Wellington's own courier. With this advanced knowledge of the British victory, Nathan Rothschild rushed to the London stock exchange, where he passed out the word that *Wellington* had been *defeated at* Waterloo, *not* Napoleon, and reinforced this news by dumping all his stocks onto the stock market, which caused everybody else to panic and dump their stocks at ridiculously low prices, which caused the stock market to crash. While the English investors panicked and sold their life savings for peanuts, Nathan Rothschild through his agents, were secretly buying up all the shares he could get his hands on, for pennies on the pound. When official news of the British *victory* over Napoleon was announced, the English stock market skyrocketed and gave Nathan Rothschild, in one single act, *complete control of the British economy*, which forced England to set up a new Bank of England, which Nathan Mayer Rothschild would eventually control. Rothschild's have used these types of devious methods ever since, this is how they have amassed their huge fortune.

Nathan Rothschild was also to boast that he had multiplied the family's capital 2500 times in the course of five years. In 1820 with the capital of the English branch of $3,000,000 multiplied by 2500, comes to $7,500,000,000 (*Seven and a half billion*) As Eustace Mullins pointed out ...The House of Rothschild was (and is) the ruling powers in Europe, for all the political powers were willing to acknowledge the sway of the great financial Despot, and, like obedient vassals, pay their tribute without murmur.... Its influence was so all-powerful that it was a saying; no war could be undertaken without the assistance of the Rothschild's. They rose to a position of such power in the political and commercial world that they became the 'Dictators of Europe.' To the public the archives of the family, which could throw so much light upon history, are a profound secret, a sealed book kept well hidden.[13] It is worth noting that during this period, it is estimated that the Rothschild family was in control of half the wealth of the entire world, and proceeded to create the world's first International Bank called N. M. Rothschild's and Sons, and in 1823, the pope became their most famous customer. The Rothschild's now managed the financial operations of the Catholic Church.

Jackson and No Bank!

Twelve years had passed with the Second Bank of the United States manipulating the US economy to the cost of the American people, so in 1828, the American people decided they had had enough. Opponents of the bank nominated Senator Andrew Jackson of Tennessee to run for President. Jackson stated in 1828: "If the American people only understood the rank injustice of our banking system, there would be a revolution before morning." Jackson had a good understanding of the money-lenders plans. To the alarm of the money changers, Andrew Jackson won the Presidency and made it quite clear that he intended to kill the Rothschild bank at the first opportunity.

In 1832 with Jackson's re-election approaching, the bank tried to have their charter renewed early in the hopes that Jackson wouldn't want the controversy of a fight with the bankers just before the election, but they were wrong, although Congress passed the renewal bill, Jackson vetoed it. Nicholas Biddle was head of the Second Bank of the United States; he was brazen with the financial power he wielded over the nation, he even threatened to cause a depression if Jackson's Veto were not overturned.[14] The President's biographer, Robert Remini, says: "The veto message hit the nation like a tornado. For it not only cited constitutional arguments against recharter-supposedly the *only* reason for resorting to a veto-but political, social, economic, and nationalistic reasons as *well*."[15] Jackson devoted most of his veto message to three general topics: (1) the injustice that is inherent in granting a government sponsored monopoly to the Bank; (2) the unconstitutionality of the Bank even if it were not unjust; and (3) the danger to the country in having the Bank heavily dominated by foreign investors. Regarding the injustice of a government-sponsored monopoly, he pointed out that the stock of the Bank was owned only by the richest citizens of the country and that, since the sale of stock was limited to a chosen few with political influence, the common man, not only is unfairly excluded from an opportunity to participate, but he is forced to pay for his banking services far more than they are worth. Unearned profits are bad enough when they are taken from one class of citizens and given to another, but it is even worse when the people receiving those benefits are not even citizens at all but are, in fact *foreigners*.[16]

Congress could do nothing and was unable to over-turn President Jackson's veto. President Jackson then stands for re-election and for the first time in American history he takes his argument directly to the people by taking his re-election campaign on the road. His campaign slogan is "Jackson And No Bank!" Even thou the Rothschild's pour over $3,000,000 into the campaign of President Jackson's opponent, the Republican, Senator Henry Clay, President Jackson is re-elected by a landslide in November. However, President Jackson knows the battle is only beginning, and following his victory he states: "The hydra of corruption is only scorched, not dead!"[17]

President Jackson, during his first term in office in 1832, rooted out the banks many followers from government service. To illustrate how deep this cancer was rooted in government, he fired 2,000 of the 11,000 employees of the Federal Government. President Jackson started to remove the government's deposits from the Rothschild controlled Second Bank of the United States and deposited them into banks directed by independent bankers. This causes the Rothschild's to panic and so they do what they do best, contract the money supply causing a depression. President Jackson knows what they are up to and later states: "You are a den of vipers. I intend to rout you out and by Eternal God I will rout you out."[18]

In 1835 on January 30th, an assassin tried to shoot President Jackson, but miraculously both of the assassin's pistols misfire. President Jackson later claims that he knew the Rothschild's were responsible for that attempted assassination. He is not the only one, even the assassin, Richard Lawrence, who was found not guilty by reason of insanity, later brags that powerful people in Europe had hired him and promised to protect him if he were caught... following his years of fighting against the Rothschild's and their central bank in America, President Andrew Jackson finally succeeds in throwing the Rothschild's central bank out of America, when the banks charter is not renewed.[19]

President Andrew Jackson is the only President in history to ever get rid of the bank. It would take the international money-lenders another seventy five years to establish the next central bank, the Federal Reserve System. To make sure there are no mistakes they install one of their own bloodline to get the job done. They will put one Jacob Schiff in charge of the project.

The New
Banksters

The Rothschild's attracted too much attention in Europe at the turn of the 20th Century, and so retreated to the United States to hide in the shadows. They hid behind various companies on the world's business and banking stage, such as Kuhn Loeb Co, and banking dynasty's J.P. Morgan and the Rockefellers. The Rockefeller and Morgan trust alliances systematically dominated not only Wall Street but, through interlocking directorships, almost the entire economic fabric of the United States.[1] As Carroll Quigley noted: The structure of financial controls created by the tycoons of 'Big Banking' and 'Big Business' in the period 1880 – 1933 was of extraordinary complexity, one business fief being built on another, both being allied with semi-independent associates, the whole rearing upward into two pinnacles of economic and financial power, of which one, centered in New York, was headed by J. P. Morgan and company, and the other, in Ohio, was headed by the Rockefeller family. When these cooperated, as they generally did, they could influence the economic life of the country to a large degree, and could almost control its political life.[2]

William Rockefeller, the original '*daddy oil bucks*' kicked off the Rockefeller Dynasty in America, pretending to be a doctor selling cures for warts, snake bites, and cancer treatment at $25 a pint. He was a bigamist, horse thief and child molester. He had to leave New York for Cleveland in a hurry to avoid prosecution for the rape of a 15 year old girl. While in Cleveland; he deserted his wife and six children to marry a 20 year old girl.

William Rockefeller taught his own unique ethics to his son's. The family's biographer quotes "Old Bill" as boasting: "I cheat my boys every chance I get. I trade with the boys and skin 'em and I just beat 'em every time I can. I want to make 'em sharp."

The sharpest of the sons was John D. Rockefeller, (known as Reckafellow) who was said to be as straight as an arrow in his private life and deeply religious, although it was all said to be fake. The acorn never falls far from the tree, as John D. had learnt many devious tricks from "Old Bill", he was to become known as an utterly ruthless business man, grasping for money and ultimate power. From his earliest business venture, he was a monopolist, proclaiming 'Competition is a sin,' and planned to destroy his competition from the very beginning. The study of *The Rich and the Super Rich*, writes: "As the history of Standard Oil by any author, pro or con, clearly shows, Rockefeller was of a deeply conspiratorial, scheming nature, always planning years ahead with a clarity of vision that went far beyond anything any of his associates had to offer."[3]

Before Reckafellow was out of his teens, he had entered the oil refining business with the backing of the National City Bank of Cleveland, forming Standard Oil. He used the finance to take over his competitors. Standard Oil was just one of 27 other oil refineries at the time, which was 26 too many for John D. The competition was offered cash or stock in Standard Oil for selling their firms to Rockefeller at rock bottom prices. When peaceful means didn't work, he resorted to other means, such as a campaign of intimidation and violence. If a competitor's refinery was seen as a threat, his own brand of intimidation ensued. One example shows a competitor's chief mechanic was approached, there was a whispered conversation on a rowboat in the middle of Lake Erie, and the foreman was told he wouldn't have to worry about his future if he would 'do something.' Later there was an explosion at the competitor's refinery, and the competitor was out of business.

At the turn of the century, J.P. Morgan and Kuhn, Loeb & Co. controlled ninety five percent of the railroads in the U.S. They offered Rockefeller special rebates on shipping oil through his holding company, South Improvement Co. This enabled him to undersell and ruin his competitors. One of them was a Mr Tarbell, whose daughter, Ida Tarbell, later wrote the first expose of Standard Oil and was termed a "muckraker" by Theodore Roosevelt, a term which promptly went into the language.[4]

John D. always worked through agents and other people, which included politicians. "The ability to deal with people is as purchasable a commodity as sugar or coffee... I pay more for that ability than for any under the sun," admitted Rockefeller.[5] With many politicians in his pocket, John D. had Congressmen promote policies favourable to Standard Oil, which gave him national control, protecting his national monopoly along the way. With John D. exercising tremendous leverage over business, banking and the economy, he used his vast economic power to build even greater political power. Nelson

Aldrich of Rhode Island was the Rockefeller mouthpiece within the Senate at the time, but "...when Aldrich spoke; newsmen understood that although the words were his, the dramatic line was surely approved by 'Big John' [D. Rockefeller]..."[6] In those early days, the Rockefellers had expanded operations to do business in more than one hundred countries.

Morgan's financial power came from control of the enormous cash flow of the nation's biggest life insurance companies.[7] This is the same J. P. Morgan who, according to Gustavus Myers in the *History of the Great American Fortunes* controls billions of dollars of the country's resources and started out by successfully palming off upon the Government during the Civil War with five thousand of its own 'unserviceable rifles' at extortionate prices... profiting from arming the nation's soldiers with self-slaughtering guns (*p, 178*)... that would 'blow off the thumbs' of any soldier that tried to use them.

Morgan enterprises were into everything ...steel, shipping, and the electrical industry; they included General Electric, the rubber trust, and railroads. Like Rockefeller, Morgan controlled financial corporations - the National Bank of Commerce and the Chase National Bank, New York Life Insurance, and the Guaranty Trust Company.[8]

Wall Street reporter Lincoln Steffens interviewed both J.P. Morgan and John D. Rockefeller on several occasions. He soon realized that even thou these men were very powerful, they were mere front men. He noted that: "No one ever seems to ask the question 'who is behind the Morgan's and the Rockefeller's?' No one else ever asked the question, nor did anyone answer it!" Steffens knew the money for their operations was coming from someone else, but never managed to trace it... The Rothschild's have always controlled the Morgan and Rockefeller operations, as well as the foundations set up by these front men to control the people of the United States.[9]

Federal Reserve System

The Rothschild's, now re-grouped in the U.S. behind some of America's richest and influential families were positioned for the next assault on the American public, which would come in the form of the Federal Reserve System, which was never designed to serve the American people; it was set up for the benefit of the American private banking families who were interlocked with the International banking families of Europe. Just as the Bank of England, the First and Second Bank of America were formed as private organizations for private interests, so too was the Federal Reserve System to be formed and owned by the same group of private international money-lenders. Eustace Mullins, referring to the Federal Reserve said it would be owned by private individuals who would draw profit from ownership of shares, and who would control the nation's issue of money, it would have at its command the nation's entire financial resources, and it would be able to mobilize credit and mortgage the United States by involving the US in major foreign wars.[10] Louis T. McFadden, when talking about the Federal Reserve, said: "We have in this country one of the most corrupt institutions the world has ever known. I refer to the Federal Reserve Board; this evil institution has impoverished the people of the United States and has practically bankrupted our Government. It has done this through the corrupt practices of the moneyed vultures who control it."

The American public had forgotten their history, ignoring the warning of Thomas Jefferson over one-hundred years previously, who warned: "If the American people ever allow the banks to control the issuance of their currency... banks and corporations that will grow up around them will deprive the people of all property until their children will wake up homeless on the continent their fathers occupied. The issuing power of money should be taken from the banks and restored to Congress and the people to whom it belongs. I sincerely believe the banking institutions are more dangerous to liberty than standing armies." An article from the *International Business Times*, 21st, November 2010 reveals the wisdom of Jefferson's statement: 'Homelessness is skyrocketing, tent cities are popping up everywhere and countless numbers of American families are experiencing the soul-crushing despair that comes from desperately trying to hang on for month after month after month.' The article goes on to say 'if you really want to see some soul-crushing desperation, go check out the flood tunnels under the city of Las Vegas. But do not do this alone – it is very dangerous... Today, there are hordes of 'tunnel people' who call those dark tunnels home. Nobody knows for sure how many people are down there (some people say that it is well into the thousands), but everyone agrees that the number is rapidly growing.'[11] Jefferson knew well his enemies and what they would ultimately bring to the Republic if left to their own devices.

The Federal Reserve that was imposed upon the American people in 1913 is not part of the US Federal Government, and yet has more power than the United States government. The Federal Government of the United States owns no shares in the Federal Reserve and no American citizen can purchase them. The Federal Reserve System is not a system, and it is not Federal, there is no gold on 'reserve' which can be redeemed for real money, and yet it has a total legal monopoly over all of America's money supply. This monopoly of the nation is uncontrolled by anyone and has guaranteed profit built in. The Federal Reserve doesn't have to answer any awkward questions or produce any accounting books or file any annual statements; it is an unrestricted money monopoly owned by private interests. They are the same banking dynasties who conjure money for loans out of nothing, just as the goldsmiths had done in the past, and were granted the power to do so by fraudulent legislation, which they bribed and manoeuvred politicians into passing. It is incredible that in nearly 100 years, Congress has never investigated 'the Fed' and is highly unlikely to do so. No one will ever see the Federal accounts. The fed are not audited, and there are no balance sheets. No one, but no one, ever criticizes the Fed. Yet Fed policy, not *Government* policy, is the dominant factor in economic growth. The Fed can create jobs by loosening credit. The Government talks a lot about creating jobs but in fact can only create bureaucracies which restrict rather than promote enterprise. The private sector creates productive jobs and the private sector is heavily dependent on Fed policy to do this.[12] It must be understood that 'The Fed' is run by a syndicate of criminals, a cartel of private banks that gained control over America's monetary system by fraud, just as the international bankers had done in Europe and America the previous century.

The Federal Reserve is a private company, not listed in any of the blue government pages of the phone book; it is listed in the business white pages, along with other private businesses such as federal express, the mailing company that delivers the post. The Federal Reserve is no more Federal than Federal Pizza, the name was chosen just like all the other banks to deceive the people. As we have seen, the idea to create private banks such as the Federal Reserve is to have the power to create money out of nothing, this is fiat money not backed by gold or silver, and then loaned to the government at interest. With this banking system, governments can never get out of this endless cycle of debt, this central banking system is what allows nations to be controlled and manipulated by the few individuals who designed the system for their own self-serving interests, not for the benefit of the American people, or any nation that has a central bank installed. In nearly one hundred years, the Federal Reserve System has not once benefited the American people, because those were never its true objectives. When one realizes the circumstances under which the 'Fed' was created, when it becomes clear who authored it, it becomes painfully obvious that the Federal Reserve System is merely a cartel with a government facade. The goal of the cartel, as is true with all of them, was to maximize profits by minimizing competition between members, to make it difficult for new competitors to enter the field, and to utilize the police power of government to enforce the cartel agreement.[13]

As Wright Patman, Democratic Congressman from 1928-1976 stated: "I have never yet had anyone who could, through the use of logic and reason, justify the Federal Government borrowing the use of its own money... I believe the time will come when people will demand that this be changed. I believe the time will come in this country when they will actually blame you and me and everyone else connected with the Congress for sitting idly by and permitting such an idiotic system to continue." Everything that has been built and associated with the banking families was built upon lies and deceit.

Money Panics

The money-lenders, to demonstrate their immense power and show the American people that they needed a central banking system such as the Federal Reserve, (*the 'Money Trust' used a proven method of revolution, that of creating a crisis and then offering a solution, the solution being what the perpetrators wanted in the first place*)[14] the Banksters, namely the Rockefeller's, the Morgan's and the Schiff's deliberately created and precipitated the money panics of 1873, 1893, and 1907.[15] In the case of the 1907 panic ...this was a money panic which had been called by Morgan to wipe out the competition of the Heinz-Morse group in banking, shipping, and iron industries.[16] Because of these panics, J. P. Morgan became known as '*the most powerful banker in the world,*' although he was still just a front for the House of Rothschild.

In conversation with the *New York Times* correspondent, Lord Rothschild paid a high tribute to J.P. Morgan for his efforts in the present financial juncture in New York. "He is worthy of his reputation as a great financier and a man of wonders. His latest action fills one with admiration and respect for him." This is the only recorded instance when a Rothschild praised any banker outside of his own family.[17] The Morgan-Rothschild connection explains the mystery of why J.P. Morgan who died in 1913, famed as '*the most powerful banker in the world*' left only $11 million after his debts were secured revealing he was just another Rothschild pawn.

As a result of the manipulated Morgan panic of 1907, one year later in 1908, President Theodore Roosevelt signed into law the bill creating a National Monetary Commission, which was the result of public outcry that the nation's monetary system must be stabilized to prevent these money panics from ever happening again. Senator Nelson Aldrich was appointed to head the new Monetary Commission, and tour Europe to discuss and study European central banks, especially the German Reichsbank system. Aldrich was a wealthy businessman linked to the Rockefeller family through marriage of his daughter Abby to John D. Rockefeller Jr (*Grandfather of Nelson Aldrich Rockefeller... four times Mayor of New York and the vice president of the United States under President Ford*). Aldrich emerged from his tour as the Congressional expert on bank planning, but not many noticed his close ties to the banking industry.

After some two years of touring Europe, the Commission filed an exhaustive report of more than four thousand pages, which was never read by anybody. In the meantime the bankers and the various commercial bodies and the farmers and the labourers in their conventions, and the politicians and the press were all with one voice demanding a banking and currency system that would make future panics and depressions impossible.[18] What the American people didn't realize was that the panic of 1907 was engineered by the banking families that stood to benefit from a central bank - had created the panic to persuade the voting public that a bank was necessary in the first place!

It is interesting to note what sort of a man Nelson Aldrich was viewed as by the public, in an article that appeared in the *Harper's Weekly* of May 7th, 1910: Mr Aldrich is endeavouring to devise, through the National Monetary Commission, a banking and currency law. A great many hundred thousand persons are firmly of the opinion that Mr Aldrich sums up in his personality the greatest and most sinister menace to the popular welfare of the United States.[19]

Jekyll Island Club

To implement the Federal Reserve System of America, Senator Nelson Aldrich, together with Paul Warburg and other International Bankers put together one of the most important secret meetings in the history of the United States. This was confirmed by Rockefeller agent Frank Vanderlip who admitted many years later in his memoirs: "... I do not feel it is any exaggeration to speak of our secret expedition to Jekyll Island as the occasion of the actual conception of what eventually became the Federal Reserve System."

The secret trip Rockefeller agent Vanderlip was referring to which led to the formation of the Federal Reserve System started at the railway station of Hoboken, New Jersey on the 22nd November, 1910, where a group of newspaper reporters watched a delegation of the nation's leading financiers, headed by Senator Nelson Aldrich, leave the train station on their secret mission. They were to head for the J. P. Morgan owned retreat; one of America's most private institutions known as Jekyll Island in Georgia, a private retreat for wealthy families away from prying eyes. For nine days the financiers discussed how to bring about the central private bank to the United States. Jekyll Island was chosen for the site of the preparation of the central bank because it offered complete privacy and because there was not a journalist within fifty miles.

Accompanying Senator Nelson Aldrich on this secretive trip was one Paul Warburg, a representative of the Rothschild family in England and France. The person who played the most significant part in getting the Federal Reserve adopted was Paul Warburg, who had come to the United States with his brother, Felix Warburg from Germany in 1902. They left their brother Max in Frankfurt to run the family bank (M. N. Warburg and Company). In due time, Paul married Nina Loeb of Kuhn, Loeb and Company, America's most powerful International banking firm, while Felix married Jacob Schiff's daughter, Frieda Schiff. Both brothers became Kuhn-Loeb partners and Paul was awarded a yearly salary of $500,000 to go up and down the country preparing the climate for a central banking system in the United States.[20]

Also accompanying Aldrich was Benjamin Strong – Head of J. P. Morgan's Trust Company (*Later became the first Head of The Federal Reserve System*), Abraham Piatt Andrew – Assistant Secretary of the US Treasury, Frank A. Vanderlip – President of the Rockefeller owned National Citibank of New York (*The largest and most powerful banks in America, and also representing the Kuhn Loeb Company*) and Charles D Norton – President of the First National Bank, New York and Henry P. Davison, partner in J. P. Morgan and Chairman of the Bankers Trust Company. These six men dominated wealth and financial power in the U.S. and also had considerable political influence. Even thou these men were the most influential financiers in the U.S., they were present at Jekyll Island merely as the emissaries of Baron Alfred Rothschild, who had commissioned them to prepare legislation establishing a central bank in the U.S., modelled on the European fractional reserve central banking organizations of the Reichsbank, the Bank of England, and the Bank of France, all of which were controlled by the House of Rothschild.[21] The secret meeting was referred to in the *New York Times* on May 3rd, 1931, commenting on the death of George Baker, one of Morgan's closest associates, it said: "One-sixth of the total wealth of the world was represented by members of the Jekyll Island Club." The reference was only to those in the Morgan group, (Members of the Jekyll Island Club). It did not include the Rockefeller group or the European financiers. When all of these are combined, the previous estimate that one-fourth of the world's wealth was represented by these groups is probably conservative.[22]

At the Jekyll Island meeting, above all the conspirators knew they had to maintain absolute secrecy. If any Wall Street name ever became attached to a central banking Federal Reserve bill it would be the kiss of death. Not only were code names adopted but individuals went to great lengths to avoid public knowledge of their meetings and discussions.[23] In the February 9th, 1935, issue of the *Saturday Evening Post*, an article appeared written by Frank Vanderlip, regarding the trip to Jekyll Island, where he stated: "We were told to leave our last names behind us. We were told, further, that we should avoid dining together on the night of our departure. We were instructed to come one at a time and as unobtrusively as possible to the railroad terminal on the New Jersey littoral of the Hudson, where Senator Aldrich's private car would be in readiness, attached to the rear end of a train for the South.... Once aboard the private car we began to observe the taboo that had been fixed on last names. We addressed one another as Ben, 'Paul,' 'Nelson,' 'Abe' as in Abraham Piatt Andrew. Davison and I adopted even deeper disguises, abandoning our first names. On the theory that we were always right, he became Wilbur and I became Orville after those two aviation pioneers, the Wright brothers... The servants and train crew may have known the identities of one or two of us, but they did not know all, and it was the names of all printed together that would have made our mysterious journey significant in Washington, in Wall Street, even in London. Discovery, we knew, simply must not happen, or else all our time and effort would be wasted. If it were to be exposed publicly that our particular group had got together and written a banking bill, that bill would have no chance whatever of passage by Congress.[24]

On arrival at Jekyll Island, this elite group of financiers had to be absolutely certain no-one would discover their identities, which is why at the Island to further insure secrecy, regular servants were given two weeks holiday and new servants brought in. Later, when they would return to New York, the bankers would refer to themselves as the '*First Name Club*'. Any reasonably sane person would have to ask the question, why would some of the wealthiest men in the world at that point in time, sneak off to a remote island in the middle of the night using code names and disguises? Simply because the money-lenders wanted a *legal monopoly of money* to be granted by Congress, the proceedings then were unconstitutional and fraudulent. As Anthony Sutton put it ...The Federal Reserve System originated in a conspiracy. A "conspiracy" is defined legally as a secret meeting for an *illegal* purpose. The meeting was secret, it involved six persons and it was illegal.[25]

Conjuring the Image of a Federal Bank

Senator Aldrich and company knew that resentment was high towards the banking community in creating a new banking system because of the previous series of panics throughout the nation; a plan would never be accepted by any Congressman if the bill was aligned in any way with Wall Street. But the deception had already been worked out of how to fool the people into believing and accepting it wasn't a central bank created by Wall Street, they were going to say that the regional reserve system was an organization of twelve branch reserve banks located in different parts of the country. What the public didn't realize was that these regional banks were dependent upon their money from the one New York Central bank. The cartel of wealthy financiers also knew they had to conceal the fact that the Federal Reserve System they were creating would be controlled by the banking families, so Paul Warburg commented that they would have to avoid the term 'Central Bank' when drafting their plans. They would have to devise a name which would avoid the word *bank* altogether, a name that would conjure up the image of a Federal Government, and was owned by the government, not by private individuals, especially from Wall Street. Warburg assured the members of the group, even thou it wasn't to be called a central bank; it would certainly operate as one.

Edward Griffin informs us in *the Creature from Jekyll Island* that to convince Congress and the public that the establishment of a banking cartel was, somehow, a measure to protect the public, the Jekyll Island strategists laid down the following plan of action:

1. Do not call it a cartel or even a central bank...
2. Make it look like a government agency...
3. Establish regional branches to create the appearance of decentralization, not dominated by Wall Street banks...
4. Begin with a conservative structure including many sound banking

principles knowing that the provisions can be quietly altered or removed in subsequent years...

5. Use the anger caused by recent panics and bank failures to create popular demand for monetary reform...

6. Offer the Jekyll Island plan as though it were in response to that need...

7. Employ university professors to give the plan the appearance of academic approval...

8. Speak out against the plan to convince the public that Wall Street bankers do not want it.[26]

When the group of financiers returned from Jekyll Island to New York to present the Federal Reserve System to the public, it was known as the 'The Aldrich Bill,' Paul Warburg protested at Jekyll Island against calling it 'The Aldrich Bill,' and he was right, as the press were against Senator Nelson Aldrich, and commented that he was not for the common people or anyone else who had less than a million dollars. His illegal activities were being pointed out in a series of articles at the time by Ida Tarbell, in which she described the poverty in which the workers in Aldrich's factories lived, while he grew orchids in green houses within sight of the slums. The Aldrich plan written by Vanderlip and Strong did not get through Congress. It was shot down. An ailing Senator Aldrich retired and the 'Money Trust' was forced to look elsewhere to get its plans through Congress.[27]

Their task was now to sponsor a nationwide propaganda movement to sell the people on 'The Aldrich Plan', Eustace Mullins notes that all national banks were forced to contribute to a slush fund of five million dollars, and the great universities were used as strong holds of propaganda, abetted by the university presidents and the professors of economics. Woodrow Wilson, president of Princeton University was the first prominent educator to speak in favour of the Aldrich Plan, a gesture which immediately brought him the Governorship of New Jersey and later the Presidency of the United States. During the panic of 1907, Wilson had declared that: "All this trouble could be averted if we appointed a committee of six or seven public spirited men like J. P. Morgan to handle the affairs of our country." This plea for a financial dictatorship had brought him favourable notice to the bankers, and he had been invited by Frank Vanderlip to a luncheon... Eustace then informs us that the support of the National City Bank gave Wilson the Presidency of The United States after

Wilson promised to enact the Federal Reserve Act.[28] And as Antony Sutton observed…What this group proposed to do - and actually did do in 1913 – was replace gold and silver with a paper factory which they controlled. How this could be presented as a public-spirited act is probably beyond most readers.[29]

The Strangest Friendship in History

President Woodrow Wilson had been put into office by the biggest Wall Street banking house of them all, Paul Warburg's firm of Kuhn, Loeb Co. His campaign had been entirely financed by Cleveland H. Dodge, of Kuhn, Loeb's National City Bank, Jacob Schiff, senior partner in Kuhn, Loeb Co, Henry Morgenthau, Sr., Bernard Baruch, and Samuel Untermyer. With such a background, as well as his earlier speeches in favour of the Aldrich Plan and his outspoken reverence for J. P. Morgan, the new, 'Everyman's' Woodrow Wilson smacked of ineffectuality, if not downright hypocrisy.[30] Eustace Mullins describes in *A Study of the Federal Reserve*, that when President Wilson signed the Federal Reserve Act on December 23rd, 1913, he fulfilled the pledge he made to the men who had financed his campaign… The money and credit resources of the United States were now in the complete control of the banker's alliance between J. P. Morgan's First National Bank group and Kuhn, Loeb's National City Bank interests, whose principle loyalties were to the international banking interests then quartered in London, and which moved to New York during the First World War.[31]

President Woodrow Wilson signed the Federal Reserve Bill into effect and was able to push it through because Congress had no idea of its contents. The reason Congress had no idea of the contents of the bill was because it was the Christmas holidays and most Congressmen had left to celebrate the festive season, there was literally no-one present in the house to oppose the bill when it was presented, this again makes the proceedings unconstitutional and fraudulent. Representative Charles A. Lindbergh from Minnesota, father of the world famous flier, was an ardent critic of the Morgan group during his ten years in the House of Representatives. He is said to be the only man in Congress who read the entire 20 volumes of the Aldrich Monetary Commission. He stated: "The financial system has been turned over to the Federal Reserve Board. That board administers the finance system by authority of a purely profiteering group. The system is private, conducted for the sole purpose of obtaining the greatest possible profits from the use of other people's money." After the Federal Reserve Act was passed… six New York banks controlled by the Morgan-Standard Oil group immediately bought control-ling interest of the Federal Reserve Bank of New York, which they have held ever since.[32]

In the same year the Federal Reserve Act was introduced, the internation-al money-lenders also financed the campaign for the introduction of income tax. This Act was also not designed as advertised; to make the wealthy pay for the running of the country. Its specific purpose, as Ferdinand Lundberg points out in *The Rich and the Super Rich*, was to become a siphon... inserted in the pocketbooks of the general public. Karl Marx was the visible author of the plan of using the graduated income tax and the central bank together to destroy the wage earning middle class, and it was Senator Aldrich who was the indi-vidual to introduce the legislation into the Congress of the United States, giving America both the graduated income tax and the central bank.[33]

As can be seen, the whole central bank concept was engineered by the very group it was supposed to strip of power... Paul Warburg was appointed to the first Federal Reserve Board - a board that was hand-picked by "Colonel" House. Paul Warburg relinquished his $500, 000 a year job as a Kuhn, Loeb partner to take a $12,000 a year job with the Federal Reserve.[34] He held that position until 1919.

In 1914, one year after the Federal Reserve Act was passed into law; Senator Aldrich could afford to be less guarded in his remarks. In an article published in July of that year in a magazine called *The Independent*, he boast-ed: "Before the passage of this Act, the New York bankers could only domi-nate the reserves of New York. Now we are able to dominate the bank reserves of the entire country."[35] President Wilson later lamented about his mistake in putting the Federal Reserve System through: "We have come to be one of the worst ruled, one of the most completely controlled and dominated Govern-ments in the World - no longer a Government of free opinion, no longer a Government by conviction and vote of the majority, but a Government by the opinion and duress of small groups of dominant men."

For years the educators of modern history denied that the events at Jekyll Island ever happened, however, a financial writer named Bertie Charles Forbes (who later founded the *Forbes Magazine*), confirmed: "Picture a party of the nation's greatest bankers stealing out of New York on a private railroad car under cover of darkness, stealthily hiking hundreds of miles South, embarking on a mysterious launch, sneaking onto an island deserted by all but a few servants, living there a full week under such rigid secrecy that the names of not one of them was once mentioned lest the servants learn the identity and disclose to the world this strangest, most secret expedition in the history of American finance.

I am not romancing; I am giving to the world, for the first time, the real story of how the famous Aldrich currency report, the foundation of our new currency system, was written . . . . The utmost secrecy was enjoined upon all. The public must not glean a hint of what was to be done. Senator Aldrich notified each one to go quietly into a private car of which the railroad had received orders to draw up on an unfrequented platform. New York's ubiquitous reporters had been foiled . . . Nelson (Aldrich) had confided to Henry, Frank, Paul and Piatt that he was to keep them locked up at Jekyll Island, out of the rest of the world, until they had evolved and compiled a scientific currency system for the United States, the real birth of the present Federal Reserve System, the plan done on Jekyll Island in the conference with Paul, Frank and Henry . . . . Warburg is the link that binds the Aldrich system and the present system together, he more than any one man has made the system possible as a working reality."[36]

Colonel Edward Mandell House

During Wilson's time in the Whitehouse, he was guided by one of the most influential men of the time, British Rothschild's frontman Colonel Edward Mandell House *(The title was honorary, House never served in the military)*; Colonel House was the 'behind the scenes' personal adviser *(manipulator)* to President Woodrow Wilson. House had close contacts with both J.P. Morgan and the old banking families of Europe. House created Wilson's domestic and foreign policies, selected most of Wilson's cabinet and other major appointees, and ran Wilson's state department.[37] His father, Thomas William House, had acted as the confidential American agent of unknown banking interests in London. It was commonly believed he represented the Rothschild's.[38] Mandell House once told biographer Charles Seymour: "During the last fifteen years I have been close to the center of things, although few people suspect it.[39] House believed the Constitution, product of eighteenth-century minds and the quasi-classical, medieval conception of republics, was thoroughly out-dated; that the country would be better off if the Constitution could be scrapped and rewritten. But as a realist he knew that this was impossible in the existing state of political education.[40]

To understand Colonel House's objectives, he had written an anonymous fictional novel, *Philip Dru: Administrator*, in which his fictitious hero, making himself a benign dictator, abolished protective tariffs, set up a system for social security, and arranged for the representation of labour on corporate boards and for a sharing of profits among the workers. Moreover, he imposed a graduated income tax, and developed a banking system that presaged the Federal Reserve; and he united the Great Powers of the world in a league for collective security.[41] Mandell House's book *Philip Dru* was the blueprint for what House was really up to. Colonel House's political views were quite clear in his book, he wanted to conquer America and establish "Socialism as dreamed by Karl Marx." House also described a "conspiracy," which succeeds in electing a U.S. President by means of 'deception regarding his real opinions and intentions.' Among other things, House wrote... 'in order that no candidate might be nominated whose views were not in accord with theirs. Elections were to become mere charades conducted for the bedazzlement of the booboise [the public]. The idea was to use both the Democrat and Republican parties as instruments to promote World Government.'[42] As James Perloff noted; the Wilson administration transferred the Colonel's ideas from the pages of fiction to the pages of history.[43]

In 1911, Colonel House needed a candidate for the presidential election of 1912; House needed someone whom he could depend upon to work for the causes in which he and his masters believed. It was Mandell house who had selected Woodrow Wilson as a Presidential candidate and later became the principle advisor to the Wilson administration. Colonel House had enormous influence in shaping Woodrow Wilson's foreign policies to support the economic collectivist and political internationalist ideas of the international bankers. It is well known today that Colonel House was the real power on which Wilson was totally dependent for all political decisions. Many of Wilson's important appointive posts in government were hand selected by House. He and Wilson even went so far as to develop a private code so they could communicate freely over the telephone.[44]

In *The Intimate Papers of Colonel House*; Professor Charles Seymour refers to the "Colonel" as the "unseen guardian angel" of the Federal Reserve Act. House and Wilson were known as 'The strangest friendship in history', President Wilson was quoted by Charles Seymour: "Mr House is my second personality. He is my independent self. His thoughts and mine are one."[45] Seymour's work contains numerous documents and records showing constant contact between House and Paul Warburg while the Federal Reserve Act was being prepared and steered through Congress. Biographer George Viereck assures us that "The Schiff's, the Warburg's, the Kuhn's, the Rockefeller's, and the Morgan's put their faith in House..." Their faith was amply rewarded.[46]

Secret Un-American Activities

The Rothschild's have manipulated the world into most of the wars that have occurred for nearly the last two and a half centuries. The Rothschild's secret wielding of power was responsible for the total devastation and loss that was caused by World War I. Even thou the German's had been financed by the German Rothschild's, the British Rothschild's had loaned money to the British, and the French Rothschild's had loaned money to the French, the Rothschild's believe the accumulation of compound interest is entirely too slow for them. The robbery of the common people through their manipulation of money and credit, as effective as it is for the money-lenders, is also too slow. War, with all of its attendant human misery, is their surest and best route—and so we have wars and will continue to have them so long as this power dominates the world.[1]

To understand how America was duped into the First World War, we need to look at the influencing of events behind the scenes of history, which can clearly be seen in the outcome of the investigation conducted by the Congressional Special Committee, appointed by the US Congress in 1953 to investigate the American tax-exempt foundations. The Committee was to look for what could be described as '*un-American activities*' by the foundations, to find out what the foundation's effects upon American society had produced over the past half century. '*Un-American activities*' were defined as the determination to effect changes in the country by un-constitutional means, procedures that are not authorised by the constitution. Mr Norman Dodd was appointed Staff Director of the Congressional Special Committee, sometimes referred to as the Reece Committee, in recognition of its Chairman, Congressman Carroll Reece.

In 1982, G. Edward Griffin interviewed Norman Dodd (*The Hidden Agenda for World Government*) shortly before he passed away, regarding what the Reece Committee had uncovered from the Carnegie Endowment. Mr

Dodd related how in the presence of Dr Joseph Johnson, the successor to Alger Hiss, was asked if he (Mr Dodd) could spare a member of his staff for two weeks, a room in the New York branch library would be provided, and the minute books of the foundation since its inception would be provided, everything Congress wanted to know would be obtained from these minutes. Mr Dodd knew that Dr Joseph Johnson and his staff were relatively new to their positions they held within the foundation, had they known what was contained within the minutes of those early meetings of the foundation, they would never have made the offer for American Congress to inspect their records.

Staff member Kathryn Casey was a bright intelligent woman who was appointed to go to New York, to go through the minutes of the early meetings of the foundations. She didn't understand why any person would want to investigate these charitable organisations; as she had the mind-set of "*What could possibly be wrong with foundations, they do so much good.*" Mr Dodd blocked out certain periods of time for Kathryn to focus on, she was to spot read various sections of minutes from the previous fifty years of notes in two weeks. Kathryn came back after two weeks with a Dictaphone full of insightful entries.

It was revealed that in 1908, the Carnegie Endowment began their operations, the trustees, in meeting for the first time, had raised and focused on one specific question, which they had discussed at length throughout the year. The question was: "*Is there any means known more effective than war, assuming you wished to alter the entire life of a people?*" The trustees were to conclude that there was no more effective means than war to alter the life of a people that is known to humanity. In 1909, they raised the second question: "*How do we involve the United States in a war?*" They answer that question as follows: "*We must control the State department; and we must take over and control the diplomatic machinery of this country* [America]." That was what they resolved to aim for as an objective for the Carnegie foundation. As can be seen, the Carnegie Foundation for peace was funded by the money-lenders for the very opposite purpose of peace; they wanted to know the best way of bringing down a whole country, which is a common strategy of the Illuminati. The very same families involved in setting up the Federal Reserve System and initiating the income tax laws, the Morgan's, the Rockefeller's, Colonel House, Jacob Schiff and Paul Warburg were all now busy involving the American nation into the first of the World Wars. But it was Colonel House who was making all the behind-the-scenes arrangements with England, committing the American people to enter the war.

It was reported that a conversation took place between Colonel House and Sir Edward Grey, the British Foreign Minister:

Grey: What will America do if the Germans sink an ocean liner with American passengers on-board?

House: I believe that a flame of indignation would sweep the United States and that by itself would be sufficient to carry us into the war.[2]

As soon as Wilson's re-election had been engineered... a complete reversal of propaganda was instituted. In those days before radio and television, public opinion was controlled almost exclusively by newspapers. Many of the major newspapers were controlled by the International Bankers. Now they began beating the drums over the "inevitability of war."[3]

Churchill's Deadly Secret

The Elite didn't have to wait long for the answer to Sir Edward Grey's question regarding what would the American people do if an ocean liner with American passengers on-board were to be sunk, and the answer to the Carnegie Endowments second question, how do we involve the United States in a war? They found the excuse they needed for the US to declare war in 1915 with the German sinking of the American 'passenger' ship, the *Lusitania*. The Cunard Lines, owner of the *Lusitania* turned the ship over to the First Lord of the Admiralty, Winston Churchill. It now became a ship of the English Navy and was under the control of the English Government... The ship was sent to New York City where it was loaded with six million rounds of ammunition, owned by J. P. Morgan and Co., to be sold to England and France to aid in their war against Germany.[4] German representatives in the U. S. went to great lengths to warn potential passengers that their lives were in danger if they made the trip. As they boarded the ship, the warnings were repeated verbally.[5]

On May 7th, 1915, the *Lusitania* was sunk in the English Channel by a U-boat after it had slowed to await the arrival of the English escort vessel, the *Juno*, which was intended to escort it into the English port. The First Lord of the Admiralty, Winston Churchill, issued orders that the *Juno* was to return to port, and the *Lusitania* sat alone in the channel. Because Churchill knew of the presence of three U-boats in the vicinity, it is reasonable to presume that he had planned for the *Lusitania* to be sunk, and it was. 1201 people lost their lives in the sinking.[6] To cover up this fact, President Wilson ordered the cargo records listing the munitions sealed up in the national archives.[7] It was re-vealed on National Public Radio that the British 'Navy had dispatched a cruiser from nearby Queenstown to undertake a rescue – but the ship was mysteri-ously recalled just as it steamed into view of the survivors. The stricken masses were left frantically waving in disbelief.' The Illuminati used the incident to create a war fever, portraying the Germans as barbaric. Because of President Wilson's handling of the *Lusitani*a affair, William Jennings Bryan, his secretary of State, resigned... The Illuminati-controlled newspapers also publicized and played-up the sinking.[8]

The sinking of the *Lusitania* was the perfect excuse needed to enter the war; Colonel House persuaded Wilson that America had an evangelistic mis-sion to save the world for "democracy". The first major twentieth century trag-edy for the United States resulted: Wilson's war message to Congress and the declaration of war against Germany on April 6th, 1917. By entering World War I, America merely converted it into total war, prolonged it, and made it more savage.[9] It is also worth noting that the Carnegie Endowment for International Peace had also recorded in their minutes during the First World War that they telegraphed President Wilson requesting that he '*see that the war did not end too quickly.*' The foundations surface appearance has nothing to do with charity and good works or philanthropy; their objective has been set by the elite ruling class through the Rockefellers to produce a one world collectivist state. This sinking has been described by Colin Simpson, the author of a book entitled *The Lusitania*, as "the foulest act of wilful murder ever committed on the seas."[10]

The war brought nothing really new into the world; rather it sped up pro-cesses of change which had been going on for a considerable period and would have continued anyway, with the result that changes which would have taken place over a period of thirty or even fifty years in peacetime were brought about in five years during war.[11] The Illuminati Rothschild's – Morgan – Rock-efeller - Warburg – Schiff - Federal Reserve International bankers got what they all wanted, America into the war and a society that was psychologically changed, there was no going back. It is estimated by war historian Alan Brugar that the international bankers made a profit of $10,000 from every soldier who fell in battle.[12] After the First World War, power was now consolidated into fewer hands than before.

How to Justify a New World Order

The First World War was such a catastrophe of such magnitude that, even today, the imagination has some difficulty grasping it... On all fronts in the whole war almost 13,000,000 men in the various forces died from wounds and disease. It has been estimated by the Carnegie Endowment for International Peace that the war destroyed over $400,000,000,000 of property at a time when the value of every object in France and Belgium was not worth over $75,000,000,000.[13]

World War I was so devastating that many statesmen began to look for new solutions on how to settle international disputes between warring nations without having to resort to violence and bloodshed on such a massive scale. But the true reality of why the First World War had been implemented was slowly starting to emerge, the real reason for what had transpired became clear; World War I was organized by the money-lenders as an excuse to usher in a new era, a new 'system' with a 'One World Government.' The American Internationalists expected the frustration and disruption generated by World War I to condition the American people, so the United States could be enticed into the League of Nations as an alleged means of avoiding future wars.[14]

The ruling International bankers at the top of the human food chain understand that war enables a government to divert popular attention from difficulties and problems at home to a war effort abroad... war also conditions populations to accept government intrusions (such as wage and price controls, rationing, wild deficit spending and its accompanying inflation)... war psychology also conditions people to exchange liberty for security.[15] As one prominent Internationalist put it: "*When there is no crisis, no one gives a damn.*"[16] In order to get the general public to move in a desired direction, to 'give a damn', a 'crisis' has to be created. In today's scientific world the 'crisis' doesn't even have to be real, anything could be hyped to 'critical mass' through the media, rising CO_2 levels, global warming, ozone depletion, global cooling, aliens, anthrax, ADD, over-population, swine flu, etc., anything can be used to speed up and implement policy, and as the Carnegie Foundation had already pointed out, there is no other means more effective than war if you want to alter the entire life of a people, the same reasoning used for the 'War on Terror' 'crisis', an imaginary threat that will loom in the air for decades to come.

To further profit from the suffering of humanity, the Rockefeller's being 'insiders' knew well in advance what was coming down the line, in spite of fierce opposition from the American people to war with Germany. In 1914 Percy Rockefeller's National City Bank began its move to take over the U.S. arms industry. This was done by buying into the Remington Arms Company associated with Vickers-Armstrong (a British Arms company) and placing Samuel B. Pryor (a frontman for Percy Rockefeller) at the head of the company. The father of Prescott Bush, Samuel Bush, was given national charge of procuring assistance for Remington and coordinating its relations with the army. Here is demonstrated, that while it is the political leaders who make war, it is always the money-lenders who make obscene profits from such wars. Particularly guilty of this great sin are the arms manufacturers, the suppliers of uniforms, boots and helmets, and the merchants of death, the international bankers on both sides of the conflict.[17]

Another mover and shaker in elite circles was Bernard Baruch who was appointed Chairman of the War Industries Board by Woodrow Wilson where he had control of all domestic contracts for Allied war materials. Baruch made lots of friends while placing tens of billions in government contracts, and it was widely rumoured in Wall Street that out of the war to make the world safe for the international bankers he netted $200 million for himself.[18]

Seeds of World Government

The persistent battle cry heard after WWI was that war is terrible, it should never have to happen again. The international money-lenders always being prepared, were one step ahead, they already had their plans in waiting; Mandell House had persuaded Wilson that the way to avoid all future wars was to create a world federation of nations. On May 27th, 1916, in a speech to the League to Enforce Peace, Wilson first publicly endorsed Colonel House's world-government idea,[19] but without identifying Colonel House as the originator of the plan. House's one world idea was to be brought about by uniting all the nations together through a League of Nations, which sole purpose was supposedly dedicated to peace. Just as the 1907 panic was forced on the American people and used to justify the Federal Reserve System, the First World War precipitated by this elite group was now being used to justify a New World Order.

In September 1916 Wilson (at the urging of House) appointed a committee of intellectuals (the first Presidents 'Brain Trust') to formulate peace terms and draw up a charter for World Government. This committee, with House in charge, consisted of about 150 college professors, graduate students, lawyers, economists, writers and others. Among them were men still familiar to Americans in the 1960's: Walter Lippmann (columnist); Norman Thomas (head of the American Socialist Party); Allen Dulles (former head of CIA.); John Foster Dulles (late secretary of state); Christian A. Herter (former Secretary of State).[20] This group later became known as the 'Inquiry,' who were to come up with and negotiate solutions and topics (Propaganda) likely to arise in the Paris Peace Conference after the war.

The November Criminals

At the closing of the war, the Rothschild's wasted no time getting their New World underway; the Paris Peace Conference was to be the meeting ground of all Allied victors at the end of the First World War, it was held at the luxurious private mansion of Edmond Rothschild. They then set about dividing the map of Europe and the world as if it was a piece of cake. For six months Paris was the center of a world government.

Woodrow Wilson, Colonel House and his US global task force were appointed to the Versailles Peace Conference on January 18th, 1919; to decide the outcome of the war that their team had manufactured. Members of the delegation included Thomas Lamont, a partner of J. P. Morgan; Paul Warburg... Allen Dulles, later the Secretary of State in President Eisenhower's cabinet; Walter Lippmann... and Christian Herter, later the Secretary of State who replaced John Foster Dulles.[21] John Foster Dulles and Allen Welsh Dulles were original members of Colonel House's 'Inquiry.' It's interesting to note that during the Peace Conference, Paul Warburg was Woodrow Wilson's financial advisor representing U.S. interests, while his brother Max Warburg was representing the German interests on the other side of the room. Representing France was Finance Minister Klotz, who, according to Nowell-Baker, had for years been usefully employed by the Rothschild's to distribute bribes to the press.[22]

The Treaty of Versailles forced Germany to accept guilt for the war, and as punishment, Germany was to lose nearly all its military force. The Treaty imposed heavy reparations on Germany, which were even to include the pensions of Allied soldiers. The bankers had deliberately designed the Treaty to be crippling and unworkable. The conditions set for the reparations payments by the bankers were so severe that Germany had no chance of ever repaying the debt. The ministers who signed the terms of the Treaty were known as the November criminals. Lord Curzon of England, the British Foreign Secretary, saw through the Treaty and declared: "This is no peace; this is only a truce for twenty years." Lord Curzon felt that the terms of the Treaty were setting the stage for a second world war, and he correctly predicted the year it would start: 1939.[23] Philip Snowden of the Liberal British Cabinet said of the peace treaty: "It is a death-blow to the hopes of those who expected the end of the war to bring peace. It is not a peace treaty, but a declaration of another war."[24] John Maynard Keynes who was a member of the British delegation stated: "The peace treaty is outrageous and impossible and can bring nothing but misfortune behind it." E. C. Knuth in *Empire of the City* wrote that the financial clauses of the Versailles Treaty were perhaps the most fantastically unreal part of a most perfidious instrument ever devised and from a practical standpoint comprises merely so much gibberish.[25] The injustice perpetrated upon the German people by the terms of the Peace Treaty made another war inevitable.[26]

Working out the peace terms was only one part of the agenda, they also used the conference as a means to discuss the foundation for a League of Nations; the forerunner to the United Nations. Wilson brought with him his famous 'Fourteen Points,' which was the peace program designed for the warring nations. Wilson's Fourteen Points seem to offer a new moral order in international affairs, a League of Nations to protect all countries from aggression. They were based on the research of Colonel House's 'Inquiry,' Wilson was to draw heavily from the work... it reflected his idealism; but in its final form it was simply a fraudulent instrument to give a legal aspect to the control of the affairs of the world by International Finance.[27] In amongst Wilson's plans for peace was the 14th point, which was the one that revealed the true story; it called for a proposal for a 'general association of nations,' this was the hidden seedling for a One World Government. It was also later revealed that Colonel House had actually written Wilson's 'Fourteen Points' at Versailles. Ray Stannard Baker, Wilson's official biographer, said that "practically nothing – not a single idea – in the Covenant of the League was original with the President." It was Rothschild's frontman Colonel House who had written the Covenant.[28]

Wilson returned to the United States on July 8th, 1919, and spent time criss-crossing America trying to 'sell' the idea of the League of Nations to the people, but the Senate, remembering George Washington's advice to avoid entangling themselves in foreign affairs, wanted nothing to do with the League of Nations and refused to ratify the treaty. President Wilson was not a happy man, he saw himself, as Senator Henry Cabot Lodge pointed out "... a *future President of the world*'" Although the League was formed, to the humiliation of President Wilson, Colonel House, and the international money-lenders, the US Congress wanted nothing to do with the ridiculous scheme; the US was out of the League. Although the League carried on, it was a bitter blow to the bankers as the whole plan of war was to get the United States into the League in the first place; this is why we had to have a Second World War to bring in the United Nations in 1945.

On September 26th 1919, Wilson became ill and collapsed; it has been said he became conscious of the fact that he was used as a pawn in the beginning of the destruction of the United States; he was devastated by the deceit and deception of international power politics. Wilson had an idea of something occurring behind the scenes before the war in 1913, when he published *The New Freedom*, in which he stated: "Since I entered politics, I have chiefly had men's views confided to me privately. Some of the biggest men in the U.S., in the field of commerce and manufacturing. They know that there is a power somewhere so organized, so subtle, so watchful, so interlocked, so complete, so pervasive, that they had better not speak above their breath when they speak in condemnation of it."

It was not until later that he finally realized the full impact of what had passed and that he was responsible for putting the US nation on the road to a dictatorship; it was he who had opened wide the doors for International Communism, and at the same time planted the seeds for a Second World War. Wilson stated: "I am a most unhappy man. I have unwittingly ruined my country. A great industrial nation is controlled by its system of credit. Our system of credit is concentrated. The growth of the nation therefore, and all our activities, are in the hands of a few men. We have come to be one of the worst ruled, one of the most completely controlled and dominated Governments in the civilized World — no longer a Government by free opinion, no longer a Government by conviction and the vote of the majority, but a Government by the opinion and duress of a small group of dominant men." Wilson of course, was of no more use to the International Bankers; his collapse ended his political career.

A few months after Wilson's second inauguration the British Ambassador, Sir Horace Plunkett, wrote to Colonel House: "I paid my respects to the President, and was shocked to see him looking so worn; the change since January is terribly marked." At the time of the Versailles conference in 1919, a British government official, Sir William Wiseman, told House that he was "shocked by his appearance... His face was drawn and of a grey color and frequently twitching in a pitiful effort to control nerves which had broken down."[29] Wilson was an invalid for the rest of his life until he died a broken man in in 1924.

THE BRITISH
SECRET SOCIETY

Following the discovery of the secret documents discovered by the Bavarian Government in 1784, the Illuminati were forced underground. Even thou the Illuminati had been exposed; Adam Weishaupt had developed powerful Masonic networks that had spread throughout Europe and America. These Illuminati plans found their way to Britain in the mid to late 1800's, namely at All Soul's College, Oxford, where one John Ruskin (1819-1900) taught socialist policies. Ruskin held the belief that the State should control the means of production and distribution for the people.

Ruskin's philosophies were heavily influenced by the writings of Plato; he considered Plato his God and read him religiously. Cleon Skousen writes in *The Naked Capitalist* that 'Plato wanted a ruling class with a powerful army to keep it in power and a society completely subordinate to the monolithic authority of the rulers. He also advocated using whatever force was necessary for the wiping out of all existing government and social structure so the new rulers could begin with a "clean canvas" on which to develop the portrait of their great new society... The upper dimensions of Plato's "ideal" society included the elimination of marriage and the family so that all women would belong to all men and all the men would belong to all the women. Children resulting from these promiscuous unions would be taken over by the government as soon as they were weaned and raised anonymously by the state.

Plato wanted women to be required to be equal with men to fight wars with the men and perform labour like men. There was to be selective breeding of men and women under control of the government and children considered inferior or crippled were to be destroyed. There was to be a three-level structure of society into fixed classes: the ruling class, the military class and the worker class. Plato said the people would be induced to believe a government-indoctrinated falsehood that people were born with gold, silver or copper in their souls and the rulers would determine which metal was present in the soul of each person and assign him to the appropriate class. Plato admitted all this was a falsehood but said it would facilitate the administration of affairs by the rulers because it would be taught to the people as a religious principle. Plato reserved the full blessings of communism for his ruling class. It would be there that he felt private property could be eliminated, family relations communalized, and intellectual energy devoted to determining what was good for the masses in the lower classes. All this was part of what John Ruskin read "almost every day."[1]

Ruskin's socialist ideas earned him much respect and admiration at Oxford, in which he soon acquired a devoted following. His disciples included Cecil Rhodes whom would later with financial support from Lord Rothschild and Alfred Beit monopolize the diamond mines of South Africa as De Beers Consolidated Mines, and Lord Alfred Milner who was responsible for starting the Boer War of 1899. There was also Arnold Toynbee, whose ideas would later contribute to Rhodes and Milner's plan for the domination of the British Empire across the planet. These men were so moved by Ruskin's philosophy at Oxford that they devoted the rest of their lives to carrying out Ruskin's socialist ideas. Cecil Rhodes was particularly influenced by Ruskin's message, so much so that his inaugural lecture at Oxford was said to have been copied out in longhand, in full, and kept with him for the next thirty years.

To understand what kind of men Cecil Rhodes and Lord Alfred Milner were; the late Eustace Mullins, in *World Order*, informs us that in 1889, because of the discovery of vast wealth in gold and diamonds in South Africa, the Rothschild's came back to loot the nation with 400,000 British soldiers pitted against 30,000 "irregulars", that is, farmers with rifles, whom the Boers could put into the field... The British fought a "no prisoners" scorched earth war, destroying farms and mercilessly shooting down Boers who tried to surrender. It was in this war that the institution of "concentration camps" was brought to the world, as the British rounded up and imprisoned in unsanitary, fever-ridden camps anyone thought to be sympathetic to the Boers, including many women and children, who died by the thousands. This genocidal policy would next be used by the Rothschild-financed Bolsheviks in Russia, who adopted the Boer War concept to murder 66 million Russians between 1917 and 1967. There was never any popular reaction to either of these atrocities, because of the control of media which makes discussion of these calamities a taboo subject... The Boer War was started by Rothschild's agent, Lord Alfred Milner against the wishes of a majority of the British people. His plans were aided by another Rothschild agent, Cecil Rhodes, who later left his entire fortune to the furtherance of the Rothschild program, through the Rhodes Trust, a by no means infrequent denouncement among Rothschild agents, and the basis of the entire "foundation" empire today.[2]

Rhodes rose to be Prime Minister of the Cape Colony, named Rhode-sia, now called Zimbabwe, which was an indication of his influence in that part of the world. Rhodes eventually controlled the production of all diamonds throughout the world. This is how Rhodes was able to later form and finance his own secret society by looting the South African mines with the help of the Rothschild's money. Dennis Cuddy reveals that in the autumn of 1890; Rhodes sent a letter to William T. Stead regarding his idea of a secret society... 'The key of my idea discussed with you is a society, copied from the Jesuits as to organization... an idea which ultimately [leads] to the cessation of all wars and one language throughout the world... The only thing feasible to carry this idea out is a secret one [society] 'gradually absorbing the wealth of the world' to be devoted to such an object... Fancy the charm to young America... to share in a scheme to take the government of the whole world!'[3]

Rhodes Secret Society

The 'Secret Society' was to be a group of imperial federalists, formed in the period after 1889. The use of the economic resources of South Africa was to extend and perpetuate the British Empire throughout the world. The 'Group' was and still is devoted to the one common purpose, to work on plans for the centralization of Government in the New World Order. Carroll Quigley, a historian writes in the *Anglo American Establishment* that this organization has been able to conceal its existence quite successfully, and many of its most in-fluential members, satisfied to possess the reality rather than the appearance of power, are unknown even to close students of British history. This is the more surprising when we learn this is one of the chief methods by which this 'Group' works has been through propaganda.[4] The 'Group' form study groups which prepare opinions on various themes, designed to influence and persuade the decision makers of Government and the general public into accepting ideas they don't like, need or want.

The original instigators who drew up the plans for the secret society were Cecil Rhodes, William T. Stead and Lord Esher, who was the friend and confi-dent of Queen Victoria. The plan of organization provided for an inner circle, to be known as 'The Society of the Elect,' and an outer circle to be known as 'The Association of Helpers.'[5]

This secret society has been one of the most important dominant and important forces in the formulation and execution of British and foreign policy. The Group founded the periodical *The Round Table* in 1910... the mouthpiece of the Group; it has been the most powerful single influence in All Souls, Balliol, and New Colleges at Oxford for more than a generation; it has controlled *The Times* [British Newspaper] for more than fifty years... dominated the British delegation to the Versailles Peace Conference in 1919; it had a great deal to do with the formation and the management of the League of Nations; it founded the Royal Institute of International Affairs in 1919 and still controls it... and to a very considerable extent, the sources and the writing of the history of British Imperial and foreign policy since the Boer War.[6] Students of history have never discussed these affairs of British history because of the secret policy in which the Group conducted its affairs, and also because the Group deliberately concealed itself, hiding behind formally organized groups which on the surface have no obvious political significance.

Rhodes Scholars

Professor Carroll Quigley tells us that before Cecil Rhodes died in 1902, he set up a series of wills; a secret society is mentioned in the first five of his seven wills. In the fifth it was supplemented by the idea of an educational institution with scholarships, whose alumni would be bound together by common ideals – Rhodes ideals. In the sixth and seventh wills the secret society was not mentioned, and the scholarships monopolized the estate. But Rhodes still had the same ideals and still believed that they could be carried out best by a secret society of men devoted to a common cause. The scholarships were merely a facade to conceal the secret society, or, more accurately, they were to be one of the instruments by which the members of the secret society could carry out his purpose. This purpose is expressed in the first will (1877), which was... *The extension of British rule throughout the world.*[7] [Emphasis Added]

Rhodes understood the importance of education, and today those who share the vision of Rhodes are known as 'Rhodes Scholars.' He set up the Rhodes Scholarship Fund in Oxford to "educate" those men and women from around the world who might not be the smartest, but who were made of the right material to inculcate them with his vision so that they might become leaders in their respective countries and carry on his dream. In America, Bill Clinton is the first Rhodes Scholar to become President, and numerous appointees in his cabinet are also Rhodes Scholars.[8] According to Rhodes biogra-

pher Sarah Millin, Rhodes told Stead that the scholars should have the following characteristics: 'smugness, brutality, unctuous rectitude, and tact.' In the
future, President Clinton will be described as smug and brutal. Also, concerning 'unctuos rectitude,' *Webster's Dictionary* defines 'unctuos' as oily in speech
or manner; plastic; moldable; characterized by a smug, smooth pretence of
spiritual feeling, fervour, or earnestness, as in seeking to persuade. This will fit
the nickname 'Slick Willie' given to Bill Clinton.[9]

The Rhodes fortune, through the Rhodes Scholarship Fund, has been
used to promote the concept of globalism and one-world government. Up
to 1953, out of 1,372 American Rhode Scholars, 431 had positions in teaching and educational administration, 31 were college presidents, 113 had
government positions, 70 held positions in the media, and 14 were executives in foundations.[10]

Secret Methods of the Society

Arnold Toynbee was the friend of Rhodes and Milner at Oxford. Toynbee
had stated: "We are at present working discreetly with all our might to wrest
this mysterious force called sovereignty out of the clutches of the local nation
states of the world. All the time we are denying with our lips what we are doing
with our hands."[11] It was Toynbee's ideas that became dominant principles of
the secret society, which later became known as the Round Table or the Milner
Group after Rhodes's death in 1902. Arnold Toynbee held the conviction that
every man should have a sense of duty and obligation to serve the state and
perform educational work among the working classes, his ideas played an
important role in shaping how the Milner Group would operate after Rhodes's
death and were the method by which the Milner Group would bring about
these socialist ideas to the public. The method to be used was '...to gather his
friends around him; they would form an organization; they would work quietly
for a time, some at Oxford, some in London; they would prepare themselves in
different parts of the subject until they were ready to strike in public.'[12] Milner
also revealed later after Rhodes's death, how the Secret Society would operate:
"We also discussed together various projects for propaganda, the formation of
libraries, the creation of lectureships, the dispatch of emissaries on missions of
propaganda throughout the Empire, and the steps to be taken to pave the way
for the foundation and the acquisition of a newspaper which was to be devoted
to the service of the cause." This is an exact description of the way in which the
society, that is the Milner Group, has functioned.[13]

Lord Alfred Milner, although a very wealthy man, had no real political power or influence of his own; the power that the Milner Group utilized was really the power of the Cecil Families power, privilege, influence and control. In the period between 1897-1905 while Lord Alfred Milner was governor-general in South Africa, he recruited young men from Oxford and Toynbee Hall to assist him in the organization of his administration. These ambitious young men were known as Milner's 'Kindergarten.' All these men through Lord Milner's influence later won influential posts within government and International finance. These men became the dominant influence in British Imperial and foreign affairs up to 1939.

It was from between 1909-1913 that they started to organize their semi-secret groups known as the Round Table/Milner Group... they kept in touch with each other through an influential quarterly magazine called *The Round table*, founded in 1910 and largely supported by Sir Abe Bailey's money.[14] *The Round Table* groups claim they are 'think tanks' that meet to discuss world affairs, but it is all a front, they are discussing how to bring about The World State through their propaganda, with their vision of what they think the world should be and look like. The Group are creating discussions that condition the people to accept ideas and changes that they deem necessary. All of the members belong to various organisations with the same gradual global agenda; we are being developed to accept these gradual changes within society as normal, a new normal. It is not possible to describe here the ramifications of the Cecil influence. It has been all-pervasive in British life since 1886.[15]

How the Secret Society Expanded Its Operation

In 1919 [Colonel] House met in Paris with members of the British "secret society" called *The Round Table* in order to form an organization whose job it would be to propagandize the citizens of America, England and Western Europe on the glories of World Government. The big selling point, of course, was "peace." The part about the International Bankers establishing a world dictatorship quite naturally was left out.[16]

After the United States had decided to not enter into the League of Nations following WWI, the bankers were not amused, as stated previously the whole point of the war had been to get the League established with the idea of most, if not all nations joining, but especially the United States, so Colonel

House quickly put together another meeting in Paris on May 30th, 1919. This formal meeting was hosted by Baron Edmond de Rothschild. It was their at the Majestic Hotel Paris, that Colonel House's 'Inquiry' and Lord Milner's Round-table Group met to discuss a merger between the two groups. This meeting saw the birth of the Royal Institute of International Affairs (RIIA), also known as 'Chatham House,' the front organisation for the 'English Establishment.'

During its early years the RIIA was principally funded by the Rothschild's through donations funnelled through Sir Abe Bailey and Sir Alfred Beit... since then, it has been funded with many millions of dollars by the Rockefeller Foundation and the Carnegie Corporation... In 1936 the RIIA $400,000 budget was also funded by the following corporate subscribers: N.M. Rothschild & Sons; British South Africa Co.; Bank of England; Reuters News Agency; Prudential Assurance Co.; Sun Insurance Office Ltd; and Vickers-Armstrong Ltd.; all of which were known as Rothschild enterprises.[17] The public pays no attention to these formally organized groups of no obvious political significance, but they are the underlying forces behind world events. As Professor Carroll Quigley stated: 'The Royal Institute of International Affairs (RIIA) is nothing but the Milner Group "writ large." It was founded by the Group, has been consistently controlled by the Group, and to this day is the Milner Group in its widest aspect. It is the legitimate child of the Round Table organization... [They] used the same methods for working out and propagating their ideas (the so-called Round Table method of discussion groups plus a journal). This similarity is not an accident. The new organization was intended to be a wider aspect of the Milner Group, the plan being to influence the leaders of thought through *The Round Table* [their journal] and to influence a wider group through the RIIA.[18]

The Royal Institute of International Affairs became the blueprint for the American counterpart, the Council on Foreign Relations (CFR) and the Trilateral Commission, to be based in the United States. The League of Nations failed because the American people were not ready for such a radical alteration to their way of living; they needed more conditioning if a One World Government was to be established after the First World War. So it will be the job of the Council on Foreign Relations to convince the American public through unrelenting propaganda, to accept the proposed globalist plans from the United Nations - the money-lenders second attempt at a One World Government in 1945. Before the US will accept this New World Order, their will have to be another 'crisis' for the American people to cry for peace, the international money-lenders through the Council on Foreign Relations will do what they do best and foment the 'War To End All Wars.'

THE COUNCIL ON FOREIGN RELATIONS

The Council on Foreign Relations (CFR), the American branch of the British Royal Institute of International Affairs (RIIA) was formed in 1921; Founding President John W. Davis was a personal attorney of J. P. Morgan; Vice President Paul Cravath also represented Morgan properties. Apart from J. P. Morgan money, CFR funding also came from bankers and financiers - the Rockefeller's, Jacob Schiff, Bernard Baruch, Averell Harriman, Frank Vanderlip, Otto Kahn, and Paul Warburg, practically the whole Federal Reserve crowd. David Rockefeller was director from 1949 to 1985 and chairman from 1970 until 1985. Today (2010), funding comes from such notables as J. P. Morgan Chase, Rockefeller Group International, Shell Oil Company, Standard Chartered Bank, DeBeers, Google, Sony, Microsoft, Wal-Mart, Nike, IBM Corporation, American Express, GlaxoSmithKline, Verizon, Time Warner Inc.,[1] to name a few.

The Council on Foreign Relations (CFR) is referred to by many as '*The American Establishment,*' or the '*Invisible Government.*' Columnist Edith Kermit Roosevelt, the granddaughter of President Theodore Roosevelt described the 'Establishment' as... a general term for the power elite in international finance, business, the professions and government... who wield most of the power regardless of who is in the White House... Most people are unaware of the existence of this "legitimate Mafia." Yet the power of the Establishment makes itself felt from the professor who seeks a foundation grant, to the candidate for a cabinet post or State Department job. It affects the nation's policies in almost every area.[2] President Roosevelt himself once stated "The real truth of the matter is, as you and I know, that a financial element in the large centres has owned the government ever since the days of Andrew Jackson."

How can you join this elitist club? Membership to the CFR is by recommendation and invite only, you will be fully vetted before you get anywhere near this elitist institution. Only after you have proven your world view and beliefs are in line with their view of a One World Government that doors can open to key positions throughout American industry and manufacturing, service, media, foundations, education, and the military etc., including the government. You could be tapped for a prestigious job in the White House, as few people are aware of how a President chooses his administrators and advisors. Pulitzer Prize winner Theodore White said that the Council's roster of members has for a generation... been the chief recruiting ground for cabinet-level officials in Washington.[3] CFR members occupy the major policy-making positions, especially in the field of foreign relations under Roosevelt, Truman, Eisenhower, Kennedy, Johnson, Nixon and Gerald Ford.[4]

Harper's magazine columnist Joseph Kraft, a CFR member wrote the article '*School for Statesmen*,' an admission that the members of the Council learn a "line" of strategy to be pursued in Washington, he said: It has been the seat of... basic government decisions, and sets the context for many more, and has repeatedly served as a recruiting ground for ranking officials.[5] Nixon was said to have had at least 115 CFR members in key positions. Kraft also stated that it makes little difference which administration is in office: "The Council plays a special part in helping to bridge the gap between the two parties, affording unofficially a measure of continuity when the guard changes in Washington."[6] It's not a secret amongst the Establishment media that no matter who is in office, government follows the policies of the Council on Foreign Relations.

It is important to note that through compartmentalization, most of the employees of the outer circles of these organizations are completely unaware of the true *modus operandi* of what they are working towards, and believe in what the institution stands for. It is only the elite money-lenders at the top that fully understand what the role of the organisation is working towards, since they created it. One person who saw through the conspiracy of the American branch of the Royal Institute of International Affairs was Mayor John Hylan of the *New York Times*, when he stated in 1922: "The real menace of our republic is this invisible government which like a giant octopus sprawls its slimy length over city, state and nation. Like the octopus of real life, it operates under cover of a self-created screen. It seizes in its long and power (full) tentacles our executive officers, our legislative bodies, our schools, our courts, our newspapers, and every agency created for the public protection."

Think Tanks

The Royal Institute of International Affairs and the Council on Foreign Relations both promote themselves as '*Think Tanks*,' as vehicles for debate. What they really are, if their past is anything to go by, are highly financed propaganda machines designed to manipulate people and events into accepting plans for a global society, to condition the people to accept the idea that the centralisation of power into a One World Government or a New World Order is somehow better for everyone.

Most of the well-known elite personalities on the world stage espousing one world ideologies, politicians, academics, scientists, media celebrities, etc., are members, or affiliated or connected with these groups in one way shape or form, using their positions within society to disseminate CFR One World philosophies into public life. Most have no idea what they are promoting or talking about; Angelina Jolie was a recent spokesperson at CFR conferences.

Just like Milner's Group of propagandists, the so-called 'experts' at the CFR all write their scholarly pieces to influence decision making in government; the academics all go to work expounding on the wisdom of a better world through more taxes, wars, and a One World Government, etc., and the media outlets disseminate the message. Of course the CFR all deny this and denounce anyone who dare oppose their views as a 'nut-case,' but Naval Officer Admiral Chester Ward, an ex-member of the CFR exposed the *modus operandi* of the Council on Foreign Relations when stating: "Once the ruling members of CFR have decided the U. S. Government should adopt a particular policy, the very substantial research facilities of CFR are put to work to develop arguments, intellectual and emotional, to support the new policy, and to confound and discredit, intellectually and politically, any opposition. The most articulate theoreticians and ideologists prepare related articles, aided by the research, to sell the new policy and to make it appear inevitable and irresistible. By following the evolution of this propaganda in the most prestigious scholarly journal in the world, *Foreign Affairs*, anyone can determine years in advance what the future defence and foreign policies of the United States will be. If a certain proposition is repeated often enough in that journal, then the U. S. Administration in power – be it Republican or Democrat, begins to act as if that proposition or assumption were an established fact."[7] Carl Jensen's Censored 1996 magazine pointed out similar propaganda tactics of Adolph Hitler's philosophy of information control, when he stated: "The masses take a long time to understand and remember, thus it is necessary to repeat the message time and time and time again. The public must be conditioned to accept the claims that are made...no matter how outrageous or false those claims might be." Admiral Chester Ward later stated the Council on Foreign Relations wants "To bring about the surrender of the sovereignty and the national independence of the United States... Primarily, they want the world banking monopoly from whatever power ends up in the control of global government."[8] The CFR also undertakes other activities, such as its "Corporate Program" that indoctrinates businessmen in international matters.[9]

Machines of Mass Misinformation

Council on Foreign Relations propaganda has conditioned and played a heavy role in the influence and shaping of modern society. The Establishment has built and developed a multi-billion dollar media mind machine, which can reinforce any opinion (nonsense) they care to dream up, and through repetition, lodge a bunch of lies, half-truths and deceptions in your brain as 'known' facts. Author and expert on propaganda Jacques Ellul wrote in his 1965 book *Propaganda: The Formation of Men's Attitudes*, that propaganda must be continuous and lasting – continuous in that it must not leave any gaps, but must fill the citizen's whole day and all his days; lasting in that it must function over a very long period of time. Propaganda tends to make the individual live in a separate world; he must not have outside points of reference. He must not be allowed a moment of meditation or reflection in which to see himself... as happens when the propaganda is not continuous. At that moment the individual emerges from the grip of propaganda. Instead, successful propaganda will occupy every moment of the individuals life: through posters and loudspeakers when he is out walking, through radio and newspapers at home, through meetings and movies in the evening. The individual must not be allowed to recover, to collect himself, to remain untouched by propaganda during any relatively long period... [Propaganda] is based on slow, constant impregnation. It creates convictions and compliance through imperceptible influences that are effective only by continuous repetition. It must create a complete environment for the individual, one from which he never emerges. And to prevent him from finding external points of reference, it protects him [from] everything that might come in from the outside. The slow building up of reflexes and myths, of psychological environment and prejudices, requires propaganda of very long duration.[10] He goes on to say... he will hear the truth reassessed a hundred times, he will find it explained and proved, and he does not have the strength to fight against it each day... Propaganda continues its assault without an instant's respite; his resistance is fragmentary and sporadic. He is caught up in professional tasks and personal pre-occupations... The steadiness of the propaganda prevails over his sporadic attention and makes him follow all the turns from the time he has begun to eat of this bread.[11]

You can see and hear the evidence for yourself in today's incessant, repeated 'messages of long duration' throughout the media. Until recently, the 'party line' was war on terror, weapons of mass destruction, weapons of mass destruction, war on terror, global warming, weapons of mass destruction, terrorist, terrorist, global warming, terrorist, weapons of mass destruction, war on terror, terrorist, global warming, weapons of mass destruction, global warming, global warming, terrorist, global warming, war on terror, weapons of mass destruction, war on terror, weapons of mass destruction, global warming, global warming, global warming, terrorist, weapons of mass destruction, war on terror, war on terror, Bingo the Clowno.[12] The public must be conditioned to accept the claims that are made...no matter how outrageous or false those claims might be, 'he must not be allowed to recover.'

Secret Societies Control the Press

Thomas Jefferson (1743-1826) once said "the man who reads nothing at all is better educated than the man who reads nothing but newspapers," which is why the Rothschild's sought to control the press, purchasing the Reuters news service in the 1800's. Reuters has since bought the Associated Press, they now own two of the largest news wire services in the world, where most newspapers get their news. Professor Carroll Quigley stated that the Milner Group followed suit in gaining control of the British press... the Rhodes-Milner group dominating *The Times* [British Newspaper] from 1890 to 1912 and has controlled it completely since... Numerous other papers and journals have been under the control or influence of this group since 1889.[13] Similarly, the American branch of the 'English Establishment' exerted much of its influence through five American newspapers (*The New York Times,* New York, *Herald Tribune, Christian Science Monitor, The Washington Post,* and the *Boston Evening Transcript*).[14] The Rothschild's also gained control of the entire major U.S. Network, plus other aspects of the recording and mass media industry. The Establishments control of the press is verified by Congressman Oscar Callaway, who inserted the following statement in the Congressional Record: In March, 1915, the J. P. Morgan interests, the steel, shipbuilding, and powder interests, and their subsidiary organizations, got together 12 men high up in the newspaper world and employed them to select the most influential newspapers in the United States and sufficient number of them to control generally the policy of the daily press of the United States.

These 12 men worked the problem out by selecting 179 newspapers, and then began, by an elimination process, to retain only those necessary for the purpose of controlling the general policy of the daily press throughout the country. They found it was necessary to purchase the control of 25 of the greatest papers. The 25 papers were agreed upon; emissaries were sent to purchase the policy, national and international, of these papers; an agreement was reached; the policy of the papers was brought, to be paid for by the month; an editor was furnished for each paper to properly supervise and edit information regarding the questions of preparedness, militarism, financial policies, and other things of national and international nature considered vital to the interest of the purchasers [the International Money-Lenders]... This policy also included the suppression of everything in opposition to the wishes of the interest's served.[15]

On June 5th, 1991, David Rockefeller, at a Bilderberger meeting in Baden Baden, Germany, a meeting that was also attended by then-Governor Bill Clinton said in a speech: "We are grateful to *The Washington Post, The New York Times, Time Magazine*, and other great publications whose directors have attended our meetings and respected their promises of discretion for almost forty years. It would have been impossible for us to develop our plan for the world if we had been subject to the lights of publicity during those years. But, the world is now more sophisticated and prepared to march towards a '*world government*.' The supranational sovereignty of an intellectual elite and '*world bankers*' is surely preferable to the national auto-determination practiced in past centuries." [Emphasis Added].

Conspiracy Brainwashing System

The Council on Foreign Relations are at the forefront of America's globalist activity, and yet stories concerning the CFR in the media could be counted on one hand. During its first fifty years of existence, the CFR was almost never mentioned by the mass media. And when you realize the membership of the CFR includes top executives from the *New York Times, the Washington Post, the Los Angeles Times*, the Knight Newspaper chain, NBC, CBS, *Time, Life, Fortune, Business Week, U.S. News & World Report*, and many others, you can be sure that such anonymity is not accidental; it is deliberate.[16]

Gary Allen in his book *The Rockefeller File*, gives us a clear picture of how far CFR influence had penetrated after fifty years of existence into all four corners of the media establishment up to the mid 1970's.... Out of its 1,551 members, 60 were listed in official CFR reports as engaged in "journalism." An additional 61 were listed in "communications management," a highly descriptive title, because CFR members do indeed "manage" mass communications media, especially the *influential segments*. They control or own major newspapers, magazines, radio and television networks, and they control the most powerful companies in the book publishing business.[17] The most influential newspaper is *The New York Times*, Timesman James Reston has written, "...What appears in the *Times* automatically appears later in other places."[18] Alice Widener columnist for *Barron's* notes: It is a fact that most editors and newsmen on the staffs of *Life, Look, Time, Newsweek*, etc., and most editors, reporters, and commentators at NBC, CBS, and ABC take their news, and editorial cues from the *New York Times*. Technically, it is a great newspaper; but it reports much of the news in conformity with its editorial policies.[19] It is also famous for its support of socialist-fascist legislation and portraying support for Communism, treating Stalin and Castro as heroes. The only time you see them waving the flag of the Constitution, or verbalising 'freedom of speech,' which they suppress, was when it opposed the Rockefeller's. When running for President in the late 60's, Nelson Rockefeller always received total support from *The Times*.

Running second to the *New York Times* was the *Washington Post*, then owned by Katherine Graham, a CFR member, as were all the personnel. The *Washington Post* is read by people who run the country, i.e. Senators and Congressmen. The only time the *Post* ever opposed "big government" was when it was used to investigate Communism.

The *Los Angeles Times* was the West Coast's most important newspaper and had become an organ of Establishment socialism. Newspapers such as the *Arkansas Gazette, Des Moines Register & Tribune, the Houston Post, Minneapolis Star & Tribune, The Denver Post* and *Louisville Courier* all had interlocks with the Council on Foreign Relations.

The Rockefeller-CFR-Rothschild consortium had control over the Big Three TV Networks. William S. Paley, chairman of the board of CBS, was a CFR member as well as a trustee of the Ford Foundation. CBS had over 200 TV and 255 radio affiliates nationwide. CBS's president, Arthur Taylor, and Michael O'Neill of CBS publications were both members of the CFR.[20] CBS is sometimes referred to as the Conspiracy Brainwashing System.

NBC was a subsidiary of Radio Corporation of America; RCA was a major financial contributor to the Council on Foreign Relations. Head of RCA was Robert Sarnoff, who was a director of the Advertising Council, a spinoff of the CFR; NBC newsmen were all CFR members as were all the directors. Chase, through its trust department, controlled 14 percent of CBS and 4.5 percent of RCA. Instead of three competing television networks called NBC, CBS, and ABC, what we really had was the Rockefeller Broadcasting Company, the Rockefeller Broadcasting System, and the Rockefeller Broadcasting Consortium.[21]

ABC had 153 TV stations and specialised in escapist entertainment. It generally left the 'documentary' propaganda to the other Big Two. Chase Manhattan Bank then had a controlling interest in ABC.

Look magazine was headed by CFR members John and Garner Cowles of Cowles Communications. The Cowles publishing empire owned *Harper's*, a list of trade journals, newspapers and TV stations. Cass Canfield who managed the Cowles operation was a CFR member. John Cowles was married to Cass Canfield's daughter. Cowles once stated that the traditional American concept of national sovereignty was obsolete. John Cowles ran the *Minneapolis Tribune* and *Des Moines Register*. He was a trustee of the Rockefeller-Carnegie Endowment for International Peace and of the Ford Foundation... He was on the Advisory Council of the U.S. Committee for the U.N. and the ultra-Leftist National Committee for an Effective Congress, which operated a "be kind to the Communists" lobby in Washington.[22] Cowles was one of twenty three others who signed telegrams to U.S. Senators asking for measures that would stifle a Congressional investigation of Communism.

American thinking was formed by Henry Luce of the *Time* Empire. The mammoth conglomerate had a voice in every form of mass media, newspapers, magazines, movies, television, book publishing, and even teaching machines. Theodore White (CFR) had noted: "He [Luce] ...revolutionized the thinking of American readers."[23] Luce was a strong supporter of the United Nations and world government. Luce received funding from Thomas Lamont, a partner of J.P. Morgan, the Harriman's and the Harkness family of the Rockefeller Standard Oil. Jeanne Harmon, a former *Life* staff writer, tells in *Such Is Life* how tolerant Luce was of the Communist cell openly working at *Time-Life*. Mrs Harmon relates how headlines were suddenly altered to convey meanings never intended, and how she and her fellow reporters were subjected to pressures to ignore some stories and push others. She also reveals that Whittaker Chambers was not welcomed back to *Time-Life* after he had testified against Alger Hiss (CFR).[24]

In the late fifties, Henry Luce switched from the "World Government to oppose Communism" line to the "peaceful co-existence and World Government with Communism" line, and *Life* went back to glorifying the Soviet Union as it had done during World War II. In 1966, Luce took a group of 43 U.S. businessmen behind the Iron Curtain to promote aid and trade with the enemy.[25] The chairman at *Time Inc.* was Andrew Heiskell (CFR), who was married to a *New York Times* heiress. Editor-In-Chief of Time Inc. Hedley Donavan was a Rhodes Scholar and CFR member. *Newsweek* was owned by the *Washington Post*. Chairman of the board Frederick Beebe was also a CFR member. Other magazines in the 70's CFR orbit were *Business Week, Atlantic Monthly, McCalls, World Review* and *Scientific American.*

Book publishers with representatives on the CFR included MacMillan, Random House, Simon & Schuster, McGraw-Hill, Harper Brothers, IBM Publishing and Printing, Xerox Corp., Yale University Press and Harper & Row. Many of these specialized in publishing textbooks. The book of the Month Club's chairman Axel Rosin was also a member of the CFR.[26]

It is not an exaggeration to say public opinion was, and still is manufactured by the CFR for distribution through their media. It is one big interlocking CFR web throughout the whole of the media entertainment network, numerous media are interlocked through the CFR. This media establishment decides what issues will be discussed throughout the country and the world, they have the power to turn any subject on or off, as suits the global agenda at any one moment in time.

As expert author Jacques Ellul explains in *Propaganda: The formation of men's attitudes* what the Council on Foreign Relations know very well... that the propagandist must utilize all of the technical means at his disposal - press, radio, TV, movies, posters, meetings, door-to-door canvassing. Modern propaganda must utilize all of these media. There is no propaganda as long as one makes use, in sporadic fashion and at random, of a newspaper article here, a poster or a radio program there, organizes a few meetings and lectures, writes a few slogans on the walls; that is not propaganda. Each usable medium has its own particular way of penetration-specific, but at the same time localized and limited; by itself it cannot attack the individual, break down his resistance, and make his decisions for him. A movie does not play on the same motives, does not produce the same feelings, does not provoke the same reactions a as a newspaper. The very fact that the effectiveness of each medium is limited to one particular area clearly shows the necessity of complimenting it with other media.[27] All the media may be different but it is all heading in the same direction. He continues... one leaves no part of the intellectual or emotional life alone, *man is surrounded on all sides.* [Emphasis Added] ... we must also bear in mind that these media do not reach the same public in the same way. Those who go to movies three times a week are not the same people who read the newspapers with care. The tools of propaganda are thus oriented in terms of their public and must be used in a concerted fashion to reach the greatest possible number of individuals... The propagandist uses a keyboard and composes a symphony.[28]

Propaganda is total; it reaches, encircles and assaults the whole man on all fronts. Propaganda tries to surround man by all possible routes, in the realm of feelings as well as ideas, by playing on his will or on his needs, through his conscious and his unconscious, assailing him in both his private and his public life. It furnishes him with a complete system for explaining the world... the organized myth tries to take over the entire person. Through the myth it creates, propaganda imposes a complete range of intuitive knowledge, susceptible of only one interpretation, unique and one-sided, and precluding any divergence. This myth becomes so powerful that it invades every area of consciousness, leaving no faculty or motivation intact. It stimulates in the individual a feeling of exclusiveness, and produces a biased attitude. The myth has such motive force that, once accepted, it controls the whole of the individual, who becomes immune to any other influence. This explains the totalitarian attitude that the individual adopts-wherever '*a myth has been successfully created*'- and that simply reflects the totalitarian action of propaganda on him.[29] [Emphasis Added] The Mediacracy has the power to paint the image of any person as a hero or a fool, mad or sane, and has the power to promote a 'nobody' to the highest office in the land.

How to Condition Public Opinion

The Advertising Council is a tax-exempt non-governmental agency created during 1942 as a contribution to help the war effort. The Advertising Council was in fact a spinoff of the CFR. The Ad Council was designed to address 'critical' issues for generations of Americans, to serve as a public relations operation to promote selected projects supported by the Council on Foreign Relations. It is a disguised tool to condition and manipulate public opinion to accept ideas the CFR want to promote. Once the Ad Council has an idea to 'sell,' a government project, like rationing for example, they swing into action. Dan Smoot noted that.... The Adverting Council continued after the war to perform this same service – selecting, for free promotion, projects that are "importantly in the public interest." ...they arbitrarily decide what is, and what is not in the public interest. When the Advertising Council "accepts" a project, the most proficient experts in the world – leading Madison Avenue people-go to work, without charge, to create (and saturate the media of mass communications with) the skilful propaganda that "sells" the project to the public... Officials of the Advertising Council are aware of their power as moulders of public opinion.[30] Your thoughts are not your own.

Although the Ad Council has made some contributions to society over the years... there have been many Advertising Council projects which were vehicles for the propaganda of International Socialism.[31] One such example was the "World Peace through World Law" propaganda, designed to prepare the people for giving the World Court jurisdiction over American affairs as a major step toward world government... The new "mental health laws, which the Advertising Council is helping to persuade people in all states to accept, eliminate the constitutional safeguards of a person accused of being mentally ill, this making it easier for bureaucrats, political enemies, or selfish relatives to commit him and get him out of the way.[32]

In reality propaganda cannot exist without using mass media. One hundred years ago, the newspaper was the vehicle for propaganda. The present day structure of society is a dictator's dream; The dissemination of entertainment – "popular culture" – and useless factoids has channelled public attention away from far more important issues such as poverty, human rights abuses, the equitable distribution of wealth of the world, true political representation for the vast majority of humans – and media control by the elite.[33]

He Who Controls The Past

Nations can be easily persuaded when they are deprived of their heritage, history is the means of falsifying the record of past events. George Orwell, in his fictional novel 1984 states: *'He who controls the present controls the past. He, who controls the past, controls the future.'* The central character Winston Smith is employed as a clerk in the Records Department of the Ministry of Truth. His job is to rewrite historical documents so they match the constantly changing current party line. Winston also knows that the 'Party' rewrites newspapers... books, periodicals, pamphlets, posters, leaflets, films, sound-tracks, cartoons, photographs – every kind of literature or documentation which might conceivably hold any political or ideological significance. Day by day and almost minute by minute the past was brought up to date. In this way every prediction made by the Party could be shown by documentary evidence to have been correct; nor was any item of news, or any expression of opinion, which conflicted with the needs of the moment, ever allowed to remain on record.[34]

James Perloff's, *the Shadows of Power* notes a non-fiction account of 'authorized' accounts of World War II... the eminent historian Charles Beard, former president of the American Historical Association, stating in the *Saturday Evening Post* editorial in 1947...The Rockefeller Foundation and [the] Council on Foreign Relations... do not want journalists or any other persons to examine too closely and criticize too freely the official propaganda and official statements relative to "our basic aims and activities" during World War II. He goes on to say... Dr Beard noted that the Rockefeller Foundation had granted $139,000 to the CFR, which in turn hired Harvard professor William Langer to author a three-volume chronicle of the war. Historians whose writings concurred with the "authorized" versions of events... were generally guaranteed exclusive interviews, access to government documents and statesmen's diaries, sure publication, and glowing appraisals in the front of the *New York Times* Book Review. Most of these men had served in the administrations they wrote about... On the other hand, historians who dared question foreign policy... found themselves blacklisted by the publishing world that had previously welcomed their works.[35] Any modern day mainstream history is to be read with extreme caution. If all records told the same tale – then the lie passed into history and became truth.'[36]

RED WALL STREET

Establishing a New World Order requires the whole world to be on-board with the planned agenda, which includes their biggest threat to the plan – Russia. Rothschild's had set their sights on the vast land, wealth and resources of the nation in the late 19th Century, they knew the Russian Czar was abusing his power while in government; with the Russian people practically in slavery, the situation was causing civil unrest to germinate throughout Russia, creating near perfect conditions for the money-lenders to foment a revolution. Andrew D. White, a U.S. citizen returning from a tour of duty as attaché in the American Embassy at St. Petersburg in 1885 described the Russian situation as follows: "The whole governmental system is the most atrociously barbarous in the world. There is on earth no parallel example of a polite society so degraded, a people so crushed, an official system so unscrupulous." When White made this statement, the population of Russia was slightly over 70,000,000. Of these, 46,000,000 were in virtual captivity as serfs.[1]

The Russian serfs were not only starved, exploited and pauperized, but they were subjected to an ironclad system of feudal political suppression. Always there was the plague of the secret police, the threat of arrest and sentencing to forced labor camps in Siberia and the cruel indecencies imposed upon them by the Tsar's ever-present military. A Russian serf seemed to enjoy no sacred immunities whatever, neither in his person, his possessions, his children, nor, sometimes, his wife.[2] To make matters worse, Russia was being manipulated into war with Japan by the Rothschild's, who pretended to be Russia's friend. To help them, they said they would help finance the war for Russia, but when the time came, the defeat of Russia was to be made certain by the Rothschild's withdrawing financial aid when it was most needed.[3]

To make sure Russia had no chance of winning, Rothschild front Kuhn-Loeb and Co. of New York secretly financed the Japanese government's war efforts... Kuhn-Loeb and Co. New York extended to Japan all the credit

85

asked for.[4] These international loans were raised by Jacob Schiff (New York), senior partner in Kuhn-Loeb and Co. He co-operated with Sir Ernest Cassels (England) and the Warburg's (Hamburg).[5] According to the *New York Journal-American* of February 3rd, 1949: "Today it is estimated by Jacob's grandson, John Schiff, that the old man sank about 20,000,000 dollars for the final triumph of Bolshevism in Russia."[6] The war eventually crippled the Russian economy, and the people were starving which was further creating the atmosphere for revolution, just what the Rothschild's intended. The War was planned and implemented by the international bankers to create the conditions necessary for the revolution to overthrow the Russian Tzar. With the conditions set, all the International Bankers needed was someone to organise and lead the revolution. They would find their man.

Nikolai Lenin was greatly influenced by his older brother Alexander, who in 1887, while attending the University at St. Petersburg, entered into a plot with several associates to construct a bomb which would be used to kill Tsar Alexander III. The police discovered the assassination plot and arrests were made, and Lenin's brother was sent to the gallows and subsequently hanged. Lenin, like his brother had lost faith in religion and his nation, and was reconciled to the Marxist view of life. The death of his brother Alexander only accelerated and strengthened Lenin's resolve to become an active revolutionist, he made a serious study of the French Revolution (the first of the Illuminati Revolutions), and when he discovered the powers that brought about the French Revolution were still active, he made it known he wanted to join; the International Bankers on seeing his commitment to revolutionary plans, brought him on board. At last, the international money-lenders, through Lenin, realized their opportunity to capture, subdue and control all future competition and to stifle the future development of Russia. The revolution eventually broke out as a result of the 'Bloody Sunday' tragedy in St. Petersburg in January 1905. The massacre of innocent men, women and children was the spark that lit the fuse for revolutionary war.

The Bloody Sunday tragedy was a peaceful march on the Tzars palace. According to the authentic reports the procession was entirely orderly... At the Palace gates, without the slightest warning, the procession was thrown into utter confusion by a withering volley of rifle and machine gun fire. Hundreds of workers and their families were slaughtered. The square in front of the palace was turned into a space of agonised chaos. January 22nd, 1905 has been known as 'Bloody Sunday' ever since. It is a proven fact that he [the Tzar] was not in the Palace, or in the city, at the time. It is known that an officer of the guard ordered the troops to fire. It is quite possible he was a "cell" carrying out the terrorist policy of his superiors.[7] The event was said to be the start of the revolution, however the revolutionary attempts were unsuccessful. The Tzar was forced to establish an elected parliament called the Duma. The Czar instituted a series of reforms which would allow the people to share in the law-making process.

The Czar, possibly the richest man in the world, deposited $400,000,000 in the Chase Bank (the Rockefeller interests), the National City Bank, Guaranty Bank (the Morgan interests), the Hanover Trust Bank, and the Manufacturers Trust Bank, and $80,000,000 in the Rothschild Bank in Paris. It is possible that he realized that his Government was in trouble and he was hoping that his deposits would buy toleration from these interests after their attempt to remove him failed in 1905.[8] This may have brought the Czar some time as the next wave of revolution was not to come for another twelve years.

In March 1917, the citizens were in revolt and Tzar Nicholas II abdicated seven months earlier in favour of a provisional government. The provisional government was then established by Prince Lvov, but eventually taken over by the socialist and Freemason Alexander Kerensky. Kerensky continued the war with Germany, and issued a general amnesty for the 250,000 Communists and revolutionaries to enter back into the country after being exiled from the country previously. This was a big mistake, and the cue that allowed for exiled revolutionaries such as Lenin, Trotsky and one Joseph Stalin to enter back into the country after the previous revolutionary plans had failed.

In the United States funding for the next round of revolution was under way with the formation of the American International Corporation in New York on November 22nd, 1915. Its principal goal was the financial assistance to the Bolsheviks which had previously been provided by Jacob Schiff and various other bankers. The American International Corporation (AIC) was initially organized by J. P. Morgan with major participation by Stillman's National City Bank and the Rockefellers. The original capital was $50 million and the board of directors represented the leading lights of the New York financial world.[9]

The central character who was to arrange the loans between the U.S. and Russia was one Olof Aschberg. Aschberg was head of the Nya Banken, founded 1912 in Stockholm; he was to become known as the "Bolshevik Banker," he arranged many loans for the Morgan-Rockefeller consortium. Aschberg also had some interesting business associates, Max May of the Guaranty Trust of

New York, and Lord Earl Grey, a former associate of Cecil Rhodes. Apart from arranging American loans for Russia, Aschberg was also funnelling funds from the German Government to Russian revolutionaries, who would eventually bring down Alexander Kerensky and establish the Bolshevik regime.

With the outbreak of World War I the Red Cross was unable to cope with the demands of the war, they needed to raise money. The Red Cross arranged a fund-raising campaign and raised $2 million. This was only successful because they received donations and support from firms such as the Morgan's, who contributed $100,000, and seven other contributors in New York City who amassed $300,000.[10] The Red Cross became heavily dependent on the financial support of Wall Street, but the funding was to come with strings attached. In exchange for raising the necessary funds for the Red Cross, Wall Street had asked for a Red Cross War Council to be formed, of which Henry P. Davison, a partner with the J. P. Morgan Company, and also part of the New York Fund-Raising Committee became the War Council's chairman. The Elite then brought in more of their own business associates to staff the Council. The list of administrators for the Red Cross then began to take on the appearance of the New York Directory of Directors: John D. Ryan, president of Anaconda Copper Company; George W. Hill, president of the American Tobacco Company; Grayson M. P. Murphy, vice president of the Guaranty Trust Company; and Ivy Lee, public relations expert for the Rockefellers. Harry Hopkins, later to achieve fame under President Roosevelt, became assistant to the general manager of the Red Cross in Washington D. C.[11]

On Friday, May 29th, a meeting was held at the Red Cross Building in Washington, D. C. Where upon a Red Cross Mission to Russia was put forward for the Council. At a later meeting it was made known that William Boyce Thompson (founding CFR member), director of the Federal Reserve Bank had "offered to pay the entire expense of the commission."[12]

William Boyce Thompson was a prominent Wall Street financial operator of substantial means with access to political and financial power, who had a flair for promotion and implementation of capitalist projects. The mission was approved and a delegation of twenty four was sent to Russia in 1917. The Mission consisted of only five doctors; the rest of the group was made up of lawyers, financiers and their assistants, more than half the total of the Russian Medical Mission came from the New York financial district. The medical staff in disgust, later quit in August 1917, [they] protested the political activities of Colonel Thompson and returned to the United States.[13] The medical staff realized it was not a humanitarian mission.

What was the purpose of the Wall Street American Red Cross Mission? The truth was the 'Establishment' didn't want another United States in the world; the big boys didn't want another free enterprise system to rival their own; having another competitor to the United States was out of the question. The Wall Street cartel had long since set their sights upon Russia and used the Red Cross 'Humanitarian Mission' as a cover to sneak in the back door of the vast un-tapped resources of Russia. The Big Boys plan was to exploit the Russian nation and its people under the guise of well-meaning aid. Wall Street wanted a captive market, they wanted the Russian market all to themselves and their American business associates. They had foreseen the opportunity to retain Russia as a market for post-war American enterprise, and they knew if they didn't act quickly, the German war machine was going to beat them to the commercial and industrial exploitation of Russia. The Bolsheviks then, who were to start the revolution weren't the enemy; the real enemy, according to the International Bankers was German industry and German banking.

The American bankers knew that if they didn't stop the German's from getting into Russia, they would lose untold profits in post-war business, so the only way to keep Germany out of Russia was to keep Russia in the war. William Thompson, while in Russia invested $1 million of his own money to establish newspapers, news bureaus, printing plants, and speakers' bureaus to promote propaganda to keep the war going with the message – *"Fight the Kaiser and save the revolution."* The bankers just needed to keep Russia in the war, to continue the war against Germany until they could secure a means of controlling the Russian economy. The financiers didn't care about the Russian people, or their ideology, Kerensky or any of the Bolshevik Revolutionaries, all the money-lenders sought was to monopolize the political process in Russia for their own personal financial ends.

Trotsky had a Fridge!

Leon Trotsky (1879-1940), was in exile from Russia because of his involvement with the revolution of 1905, he ended up in France, and was later expelled from that country for writing inflammatory articles, Trotsky, whose real name was Lev Davidovich Bronstein, arrived in New York on January 13th 1917.

Trotsky's only income at the time was writing a few articles for a New York Russian socialist journal, and although he had no visible means of support, the Trotsky family had travelled across Europe to the United States, acquiring an excellent apartment in New York - paying rent three months in advance - and they had use of a chauffeured limousine.[14] Trotsky also had a refrigerator which was very rare in those days. Where was all this money coming from to pay for all these luxuries? It wasn't hard to work out when he was often seen coming to and from the Jacob Schiff mansion in New York. Trotsky had discovered that wealthy Wall Street bankers were willing to fund revolutionary activities in Russia.

After a few months stay in New York, on March 27th, 1917, Trotsky was notified to leave immediately for Petrograd, Russia. The Rockefellers gave him $10,000 in cash for his journey.[15] He boarded the S. S. Christiania, with an entourage of 275 revolutionary men; their first port of call was Halifax, Nova Scotia, but they soon ran into trouble. The Trotsky party was removed from the S. S. *Kristianiafjord* under official instructions received by cablegram of March 29th, 1917. The reason given to the naval control officer at Halifax was that "these are Russian Socialists leaving for purposes of starting revolution against present Russian government for which Trotsky is reported to have 10,000 dollars subscribed by Socialists and Germans."[16] The British Government (through intelligence officer Sir William Wiseman, who later became a partner with Kuhn, Loeb and Co.) and the American government (through Col. House) urged them to let Trotsky go. Wilson said that if they didn't comply, the U. S. wouldn't enter the war.[17] President Wilson was the fairy godmother who provided Trotsky with a passport to return to Russia to "carry forward" the revolution.... Wilson, despite the efforts of the British Police, made it possible for Leon Trotsky to enter Russia with an American Passport.[18]

The Famous 'Sealed Train'

When the revolution broke in October 1917; Lenin was in Geneva consulting with the money-lenders, he was instructed to get across the border to organize the revolution. In April 1917 Lenin and a party of 32 Russian Revolutionaries, mostly Bolsheviks, journeyed by train from Switzerland across Germany through Sweden to Petrograd Russia.[19] With him Lenin took some five to $6 million in gold. The whole thing was arranged by the German high command and Max Warburg, through another very wealthy and life-long socialist by the name of Alexander Helphand alias "Parvus."[20] Max Warburg was Paul Warburg's brother who helped establish the Federal Reserve System. When news leaked out in American papers about brother Max running the German finances, Paul Warburg resigned from his Federal Reserve post without a whimper.[21] German High Command helped support Lenin's journey because once Lenin was in control of Russia, he had agreed he would help the Germans by withdrawing Russia from the war.

Trotsky met up with Lenin, and by November, through bribery, cunning, brutality and deception, they were able to hire enough thugs and make enough deals to impose out of the gun barrel what Lenin called "all power to the Soviets"... the whole Bolshevik Revolution took place in one city – Petrograd.[22]

Leading the revolution, Lenin seized power from Alexander Kerensky on November 7th, 1917; he replaced the democratic republic with the communist soviet state, but the revolution for the people would turn out to be just another prison by any other name. While most members of the provisional government were killed, Kerensky was allowed to live, possibly because of the general amnesty he extended to the communists exiled in 1905. Kerensky later admitted to receiving private support from American industry, which led some historians to believe that the Kerensky government was a temporary front for the Bolsheviks.[23] The preparations for the Bolshevik Revolution itself were well known at least six weeks before it erupted... The British Government warned British residents in Russia to leave at least six weeks before the Bolshevik phase of the revolution.[24] When Woodrow Wilson received word about the Bolshevik Revolution on November 28th, 1917; he ordered no interference because he had received a cable from Colonel House from Paris that it was... "Exceedingly important" that U.S. newspaper comments advocating that "Russia should be treated as an enemy" be "supressed."[25]

With Lenin installed, the bankers were in position to take control of the Russian economy. On November 8th, the day after he took over the Russian government, Lenin declared: "The right of private property in land is forever abolished. All land owned by the church, private persons, by peasants, is taken away without compensation."[26] So what then was Wall Street supporting? Lenin had answered that question by writing: "Our power does not know liberty or justice. It is entirely established on the destruction of the individual will. We are the masters. Complete indifference to suffering is our duty. In the fulfilment of our calling, the greatest cruelty is a merit." And: "Through a systematic terror, during which every breach of contract, every treason, every lie will be lawful, we will find the way to abase humanity down to the lowest level of existence. That is indispensible to the establishment of our dominance."[27] Concepts of Religion, morality and the family were to have no place in this Communist society.

Without the support of Wall Street, the Bolsheviks could never have succeeded, because they weren't even much liked by the Russian people. Since the Bolsheviks had earlier called for elections, Lenin was forced to hold them on November 25th. More than seventy five per cent of the population voted against him. On January 18th, 1918, when the People's Congress met, it was filled with anti-Bolshevik representatives. Lenin demanded that the Congress dissolve. They refused. The next day, Lenin sent armed guards to the legislative body and dissolved it for them. The Communists summarily eliminated the nearest thing to a representative government Russia had ever known.[28]

Even thou Lenin was in power, he had only taken control of a tiny part of Russia, they had to expand their operations throughout the rest of Russia if they were too have absolute control, they did this with a forced starvation plan of the Russian people. The Bolsheviks, in keeping with Lenin's dictum to utilize terror in their quest for political power, would move into an area, grab all of the food supplies and the livestock, and then inform the peasants who previously owned these items that they were to be placed on a 'collective farm' where the property would be owned by the state in the name of the people. Those who resisted the imposition of the collective were either starved or murdered, or placed into concentration camps so that they could learn about the merits of collectivism through the teachings of the Bolsheviks.[29]

From 1916-21, famine swept through Russia and close to five million died of starvation because industry was shut down. On September 21st, 1921, American relief services began in Russia, after President Herbert Hoover received a plea from famous Russian writer Maxim Gorky. The United States appropriated $10 million for the country, with $8 million spent for medical supplies. Over 700, 000 tons of goods were sent to feed 18,000,000 people. As it turned out, the U.S. was actually supporting the Communist Civil War, which ended in 1922.[30] In his book *Herbert Hoover and Famine Relief to Soviet Russia*, Professor Benjamin Weissman of Rutgers University revealed that Hoover continued to send public foodstuffs to Russia long after it was obvious the Bolsheviks were shipping their own food abroad in order to purchase machinery.[31] Although Lenin was at the forefront of all the activity, he knew he wasn't running the show and stated: "The state does not function as we desired. How does it function? The car does not obey? A man is at the wheel and seems to lead it, but the car does not drive in the desired direction. It moves as another force wishes." Obviously he was referring to the whims of the international money-lenders.

Sell, Sell, Sell!

With the Bolsheviks successfully installed, William Thompson, the propaganda financier, left Petrograd to sell the Bolshevik regime to the governments of Europe and the United States. Colonel Raymond Robins was left in charge of the humanitarian 'mission.' It was Robins who was left to help organize the Russian revolutionaries with the newly organized 'William Thompson Plan' for spreading Bolshevik propaganda. Before Thompson left Petrograd, he cabled Thomas W. Lamont, a partner of the J. P. Morgan firm, who was in Paris with Colonel Mandell House at the time, to meet him in London to sell the idea to David Lloyd George, the British Prime Minister.

The most important achievement of Thompson and Lamont in London was to convince the British War Cabinet-then decidedly anti-Bolshevik-that the Bolshevik regime had come to stay, and that British policy should cease to be anti-Bolshevik, should accept this new reality, and support Lenin and Trotsky. Thompson and Lamont left London on December 18th and arrived in New York on December 25th, 1917. They attempted the same process of conversion in the United States.[32]

When William Thompson and Lamont met David Lloyd George in London, Lloyd George was not a free man; he was beholden to Sir Basil Zaharoff, an international arms dealer, whose fortune was made by selling arms to both sides in several wars. Remind you of anyone? Zaharoff wielded enormous behind the scenes power and was consulted on war policies by the Allied leaders. Lloyd George as well as Woodrow Wilson was known to have met at Zaharoff's home in Paris. Zaharoff was an important man and "Allied statesmen and leaders were obliged to consult him before planning any great attack."[33] Zaharoff had links to the Bolsheviks and diverted munitions away from anti-Bolsheviks. It was also revealed that Lord Milner was pulling the strings behind the scenes, not the British Prime Minister.

After hearing Thompson and Lamont arguments for the Bolshevik Regime, the British War cabinet decided to go along with their plans. [Lord] Milner had a former British consul in Russia-Bruce Lockhart-ready and waiting in the wings. Lockhart was briefed and sent to Russia with instructions to work informally with the Soviets.[34] Bruce Lockhart was Lord Milner's personal representative who controlled Lenin and Trotsky.[35] This was the beginnings of the infiltration and installation of the British and American Establishment within Russia, the takeover and control of the Soviet's vast economy and resources.

OCCULT NAZI BEGINNINGS

Germany's already devastated economic situation after World War I and the signing of the Treaty of Versailles led to chronic hyper-inflation throughout Germany. By 1921, 4 Billion Marks could just about buy one dollar, the German people were literally wheeling trolleys and suitcases full of money to buy a loaf of bread. The extent of this inflation was so great that a pound of butter that cost 3 German marks in 1918 cost six-trillion marks by 1923.[1] Under these conditions, only the super-rich could profit, the middle class lost all wealth and the working class starved, this was the despair of the German people. In *Descent into Slavery*, Des Griffin tells us that the value of the German paper money evaporated at such an alarming rate that, towards the end, the treasury was only printing bills on one side. To prevent the paper on which the bank notes were printed becoming more valuable than the amount specified on its face, the Reich bank only issued notes representing astronomical amounts... Many workers were paid twice a day, at lunchtime and in the late afternoon. Wives met their husbands outside their places of employment, collected the bundles of money, and rushed to the nearest store to purchase food and other necessities ahead of the next increase in prices.[2] This state of affairs for the German people was all courtesy of the international money-lenders. Germany was descending into anarchy, food supplies dwindled; the stage was set for a leader who could end the inflation and struggles of the country. The people would be attracted to a leader who could provide the solutions to end the appalling conditions. That man was Hitler.

In 1923, Hitler landed himself in prison when he led a private army of storm-troopers in an attempt to over-throw the Bavarian Government. This so called 'prison' was Landsberg Castle, a very comfortable, privileged, pastoral setting where Hitler was groomed for the job of Fuhrer. While in 'prison,' Nazi politicians Rudolph Hess and Herman Goering helped Hitler write his book '*Mein Kampf*. With the support of the Rothschild's and Warburg money, it would become the springboard for Hitler's political career.

From the very beginning there were two driving forces behind Hitler's Nazi Party, one was based in the United States in Wall Street, and the other was based in 19th century occult practices from the East. The early Nazi high chain of command, Himmler, Rudolph Hess, and Alfred Rosenberg were dedicated to reviving the Aryan Master race and worshipped all the occult sciences; their ideology was closely related to the ideas of the Bavarian Illuminati.

Alfred Rosenberg (1893-1946) was a Moscow student who fled to Germany when the Russian Revolution broke; he was an early influential member of the Nazi Party, he later held several important posts in Nazi government, considered one of the main authors of Nazi ideology, including racial theory and the persecution of the Jews. He is also known for his rejection of Christianity. In Germany he met Dietrich Eckart, who would later introduce him to Adolf Hitler.

Rosenberg was also introduced to the Thule Society, a discussion group founded by Baron Rudolf von Sebottendorff, named after the mythic German homeland of icebound Ultima Thule. They were known as a harmless study group made up of members from wealthy Munich society that researched early German history, but the Thule Society was much more than just an innocent study group: the Thule Society was a secret brotherhood with secret meetings behind closed doors away from public gaze. The society proved to be a front for a more secret society, the German Order. The Thule society based its foundation on the superiority of the Aryan race believing the lost civilisation of the Teutons possessed psychic abilities that were far beyond the technical achievements of the twentieth century. They hoped to rediscover the secrets of this legendary civilisation through occult practises. They sought to use the power of the past to deliberately manufacture a mystical image of Germany's past in order to control its people.

During the 1930's, the grand design of the Aryan race ideology had already been in development for the past two decades by Austrian born mystic Guido Von List, born in Vienna in 1848, a respected author of the time who claimed to have had psychic visions of the past in which he was initiated into the secrets of the ancient Teutonic tribes. Von List believed in the superiority of the racist philosophy of the Aryan race and the worship of the Germanic Religion of the God Wotan. Von List believed the Runes were a primitive system of writing, and magical symbols which contained deep meanings, and were to become the language of German National Socialism. Study of the Runes later became required learning for all SS officers.

The main influence of Nazi ideology was realized through occultist Madame Helena Petrovna Blavatsky (1831-1891); she not only influenced the Third Reich, but has had a profound effect upon all occult 19th, 20th and 21st century religions. Blavatsky had made the pilgrimage to Tibet where she was led into a secret room underneath a Tibetan monastery where ancient occult texts and mystical secrets of the universe were revealed. These mystical secrets of the Universe were said to reveal the future course of human history. Within these writings, Blavatsky discovered several powerful symbols, but there was one she believed to be more powerful than all the others, this was the symbol of the swastika. She wrote there were 7 stages of evolution – she named them *'route races'*, the race which should rise again to the true spirit she called Aryan. The Swastika was known as the *'son of fire and creation'*, in Blavatsky's teachings; the Swastika was to be the symbol for the Aryan race, the race of upward spiritual evolution.

Blavatsky later founded the Theosophical Society in New York with Henry Steel Olcott and others in 1875; a German branch of the Theosophical Society was formed in 1884. Blavatsky used the swastika extensively, incorporating it into the seal of The Theosophy Society. Hitler would later believe that the swastika was the sign for the mission for the struggle of the victory of Aryan man, he had stated: "Anyone who interprets National Socialism merely as a political movement knows almost nothing about it. It is more than religion; it is the determination to create a new man."[3] The same idea Karl Marx was dreaming of.

It was Madame Blavatsky's followers who first introduced the occult doctrines to the German people. Writing in 1924, Webster warned: "The Theosophical Society is not a study group, but essentially a propagandist society which aims at substituting for the pure and simple teaching of Christianity the amazing compound of Eastern superstition, Cabalism and 18th century charlatanism."[4]

Blavatsky had a lot of admirers at the time, one of them being freemason Albert Pike. Blavatsky published *The Secret Doctrine*, published as two volumes in 1888 in which she stated: "Satan is the God of our planet and the only God." The whole of the Theosophy movement is based on the teachings of Lucifer, racial superiority, mysticism, and humanism, which set the tone for the Third Reich and what we know today as the modern day New Age agenda.

In 1916, Baron Rudolf von Sebottendorff assumed leadership of the Thule Society along with Guido von List, Alfred Rosenberg and other members of the Thule Society; together they influenced the National Socialist German Workers' Party with Blavatsky's ideas. "The inner core within the Thule Group were all Satanists who practiced Black Magic... And the Master-Adept of this circle was Dietrich Eckart."[5]

Master-Adept Dietrich Eckart who founded the German Workers Party was on the lookout for a new leader, stating: "We need a fellow at the head who can stand the sound of a machine gun. The rabble needs to get fear into their pants. We can't use an officer because the people don't respect them anymore. The best would be a worker who knows how to talk... He doesn't need much brains... He must be a bachelor, then we'll get the women." Eckart found his leader in the form of an Army intelligence agent sent to infiltrate the party - a failed Austrian born painter named Adolf Hitler, once described as a "child of Illuminism."[6] Eckart on his deathbed had remarked: "Follow Hitler. He will dance, but it is I who have called the tune! I have initiated him into the '*Secret Doctrine*,' opened his centres of vision and given him the means to communicate with the powers. Do not mourn for me: I shall have influenced history more than any other German."[7] *The Secret Doctrine* imparted to Hitler by Eckart were the philosophies of Madame Blavatsky and the Theosophical Society.

Hitler quickly gained control of the German Workers Party which he renamed the National Socialist German Workers Party in April 1920, abbreviated to Nazi, which soon had three thousand members. Jim Marrs in *Rule by Secrecy* notes that a study of the Twenty-five points formulated in 1920 by Hitler, Drexler, and Eckart as the basis of the Nazi Party, reveals many which are nearly identical with the stated ideals of Marxism, indicating a common origin.[8] It is also worth noting at the Nuremburg Trials after the Second World War, the occult aspect of the Nazi Party was ruled as inadmissible at the trials as they feared it could be used as a defence to plead insanity. Jim Marrs further tells us "Sir Winston Churchill himself... was insistent that the occultism of the Nazi Party should not under any circumstances be revealed to the general public... The failure of the Nuremberg Trial to identify the nature of the evil work behind the outer facade of National Socialism convinced him that another three decades must pass before a large enough readership would be present to comprehend the initiation rites and black magic practices of the inner core of Nazi leadership."[9]

While Hitler and the Nazi party were acquainting themselves with the deeper secrets of the 'Dark Arts,' he was also building Germany for World War II, with the assistance from some well-known families from Wall Street; the Morgan and Rockefeller International Bankers.

Wall Street Rides Again

Germany couldn't afford to pay back reparations agreed upon at the Treaty of Versailles, which led to France and Belgium occupying the Ruhr, the main manufacturing part of Germany. A series of loans had to be arranged by the Morgan Bankers, designed to scale down the reparations so that Germany could afford to pay her bills, this was known as the Dawes Plan, arranged in 1924 as a series of loans totalling $800 million over a four year period. In charge of the Plan in the United Stated was Charles Dawes and Owen Young, a Morgan representative and president of the General Electric Company (Owen Young was a Council on Foreign Relations director from 1927 to 1940). The organizer on the German side was Hjalmar Schacht, president of the German Reichsbank. As Antony Sutton tells us in *Wall Street and the Rise of Hitler*... This interplay of ideas and cooperation between Hjalmar Schacht in Germany and, through Owen Young, the J. P. Morgan interests in New York, was only one facet of a vast and ambitious system of cooperation and international alliance for world control.[10]

These huge loans led to the creation of two monolithic industry cartels in Germany, the first being chemical giant I. G. Farben, created by Hermann Schmitz with Max Warburg as director. In addition to Max Warburg and Hermann Schmitz, the guiding hand in the creation of the Farben Empire... included Carl Bosch, Fritz ter Meer, Kurt Oppenheim, and George von Schnitzler. All except Max Warburg were charged as "war criminals" after World War II.[11]

The director of the American branch of I. G Farben was Max Warburg's brother Paul Warburg, the creator of the Federal Reserve System. From 1929 to the start of World War II, I.G. Farben was to double in size, and receive further loans totalling $30 million from the Rockefeller's National City Bank.[12] As Antony Sutton informs us: "These loans for reconstruction became a vehicle for arrangements that did more to promote World War II than to establish peace after World War I.[13]

The money-lenders also created steel giant United Steelworks; a German industrial conglomerate producing coal, iron, and steel, Fritz Thyssen was chairman of the board and also a board member of the German Reichsbank. These two inter-dependent cartels would later go on to produce 95 per cent of German explosives for World War II; they dominated the chemical and steel industry, aiding the production of the bulk of key German war materials used during World War II. Without the Rockefeller owned Standard Oil assistance, Nazi Germany could not have even considered entering the war. Another important factor of Germany entering WWII was they had a lot of coal, but no oil, with Rockefeller Standard Oil technical assistance, Nazi Germany was able to manufacture their own synthetic gasoline. Sutton again tells us that this hydrogenation process was developed and financed by the Standard Oil Laboratories in the United States in partnership with I.G. Farben.[14] Without the backing of the money-lenders, there would have been no German industry, without the money-lenders, there would have been no Hitler, and without the money-lenders there would have been no World War II. As Antony Sutton put it... The contribution made by American capitalism to German war preparations before 1940 can only be described as phenomenal.[15] Professor Carroll Quigley also writes that Germany paid reparations for five years under the Dawes Plan (1924-1929) and owed more at the end than it had owed at the beginning.[16]

In 1930, to help facilitate German reparation payments, Hjalmar Schacht proposed the idea to facilitate the flow of money between countries, which saw the birth of the Bank for International Settlements (BIS) in Basle, Switzerland. The BIS would be the Central Bank for Europe's National Banks, such as the Bank of England and Germany's Reichsbank. Each nation's money could then be controlled from one central place (it is also a means to control a national money supply in disguise).

The Bank for International Settlements is the 'central banks, bank,' often referred to as the Rothschild's first World Bank. Professor Carroll Quigley described it another way... The powers of financial capitalism had another far-reaching aim, nothing less than to create a world system of financial control in private hands able to dominate the political system of each country and the economy of the world as a whole. This system was to be controlled in a feudalist fashion by the central banks of the world acting in concert, by secret agreements arrived at in frequent meetings and conferences. The apex of the system was to be the Bank for International Settlements in Basle, Switzerland; a private bank owned and controlled by the world's central banks which were themselves private corporations.[17] The Bank for International Settlements became the meeting place for bankers to meet once a month to discuss 'common interests.'

It then became Schacht's job to arrange finance for the building of Hitler's Third Reich; Allied powers would channel funds through the BIS for the expansion of Germany's economy. By 1939, 294 million gold Swiss francs had been channelled into the German economy; Germany was being built up for war, the National and Commercial Banks had created a system which can now fund the Nazis to power. The BIS apex continued its work during World War II as the medium through which the bankers – who apparently were not at war with each other – continued a mutually beneficial exchange of ideas, information, and planning for the post-war-world.[18]

Financing Hitler

In 1930 Owen D. Young, after whom the Young Plan for German reparations was named, became chairman of the Board of General Electric Company in New York City.[19] As a member of the U.S. delegation at the reparation meetings, Young used the U.S. Government to further the plans of the General Electric Company, of which he was the director. The German companies that were not affiliated with Wall Street during World War II were heavily bombed; the A.E.G plants in Germany with Wall Street connections somehow avoided all bombing raids.

I.G. Farben contributed 30 percent of the 1933 Hitler National Trusteeship (or takeover) fund.[20] Young, the director of International General Electric supplied funding for Hitler's rise to power.

Henry Ford was an early (1922) Hitler backer and Edsel Ford continued the family tradition in 1942 by encouraging French Ford to profit from arming the German Wehrmacht. Subsequently, these Ford-produced vehicles were used against American soldiers as they landed in France in 1944, and for his early recognition of, and timely assistance to the Nazis, Henry Ford received a Nazi medal in 1938.[21]

Through Adolf Hitler's rise to fame, it is known that he went to great lengths to cover up his family history. A Chancellor Dollfuss had ordered the Austrian police to conduct a thorough investigation into Hitler's family background, Dollfuss was promptly assassinated. Registration cards which were compulsory at the time revealed a secret document of a housemaid named Maria Anna Schicklgruber, a servant at the home of the Rothschild's in Vienna. Salomon Rothschild had a reputation as a womanizer; Maria was to become one of his conquests. As soon as the family discovered Maria was pregnant, she was dismissed and sent back to her home in Spital where Alois, Hitler's father was born; Hitler had Jewish blood running through his veins.

Reichstag 911

Hitler was sworn in as the Chancellor of Germany on January 30th, 1933... thirty-nine business leaders, with familiar names like Krupp, Siemens, Thyssen, and Bosch, signed a petition to Hindenburg urging that Hitler be appointed Chancellor of Germany.[22] On February 27th, a week before the German elections, just four weeks after Hitler was made Chancellor, the Reichstag (parliament) building in Berlin was burnt to the ground. A Dutch communist brick-layer named Marinus van der Lubbe was blamed for the attack; Hitler proclaimed it as a Communist plot against the German government and used the incident to push the Nazi Party to power. Hitler consolidated his power by arresting one hundred communist politicians, with their parliament seats empty; one week later the Nazis became the majority. The Nazi's then pushed through parliament a set of laws known as the emergency decrees, which dispensed with all constitutional protection of political, personal and property rights, there was little resistance from the German people who wanted to be 'protected' from the Communist [war on] terror. The swastika flag was flying high one day after the Reichstag fire. The burning of the Reichstag building was the planned key event in the establishment of Hitler's Nazi dictatorship.

The Dutch brick layer van der Lubbe who was blamed for the crime, when under German Police interrogation also confessed to many other crimes, even thou at his trial, van der Lubbe could give no details of how or why he started the fire. The Nazis claimed that van der Lubbe climbed through a second story window to commit his crime; this however seemed unlikely as it was revealed later in the trial that van der Lubbe was over seventy five per cent blind. Van der Lubbe didn't have the mind or the body to invent such a scheme, let alone carry it out. Even thou it was also established that it would have been impossible for a single person to start the fire, and with no evidence, van der Lubbe was found guilty and later beheaded. It is later known that a detective warned other detectives not to pursue other suspects; they were to confine their investigations to only look for Communist suspects.

Fifty six years later with the fall of the Berlin wall in 1989, new evidence regarding the burning of the Reichstag was revealed, which show a carefully planned act of terrorism which was blamed on the communists to establish a Nazi dictatorship. As revealed in the British *Telegraph* newspaper, 2001, journalist Tony Paterson reveals... After pouring over 50,000 pages of hitherto unexamined documents from former East German and Soviet archives, four leading German historians concluded that the fire was a Nazi plot... They base their case on remarks by Adolf Rall, a thief and Nazi storm trooper, whose body was found in woods near Berlin in November 1933. Rall is said to have told prosecutors of a meeting of the SA storm troopers during which the SA leader, Karl Ernst, ordered them to enter the Reichstag through a tunnel and sprinkle flammable liquid inside. Ernst is said to have told his men that an excuse was needed to begin attacking Communists. Hitler used the fire to justify the arrest and torture of 25,000 Left-wing activists and to pass an emergency decree establishing absolute Nazi authority. According to the historians, a former storm trooper working in the jail where Rall was serving a sentence, heard of his statement and tipped off the SA. Its leaders are then said to have arranged for the statements to be destroyed by accomplices in the prosecutors' office and for him to be murdered.[23]

One of the darker aspects of the German legacy was also that the industrial giant I.G Farben supplied the gas Zyklon B used in the Nazi concentration camps in World War II to exterminate the Jews.... Antony Sutton wrote... enough gas to kill 200 million humans was produced and sold by I. G. Farben... The Kilgore Committee report of 1942 makes it clear that the I.

G. Farben directors had precise knowledge of the Nazi concentration camps and the use of I. G. Chemicals.[24] The money-lenders were well aware of how their money was being spent.

WORLD WAR II

World War I was instigated by the International Money-Lenders with the intention of establishing a One World Government under the League of Nations ratified on January 10th, 1920, and signed by President Wilson on behalf of the American Government. Unfortunately for Wilson when he brought the treaty back to the States and asked the Senate to ratify it, the Senate remembering George Washington's advice to avoid foreign entanglements and reflecting the views of the American people, had no intention of joining the League and refused to ratify the treaty. President Wilson was not pleased, possibly because he saw himself, as Senator Henry Cabot Lodge was quick to point out, as: "...a future President of the world."[1] The International Bankers were also not pleased; this was not in line with their plans, the League of Nations was completely useless without the United States involvement, which was the whole point of World War One in the first place. So the International Bankers did what they do best and began manipulating international affairs in Europe and the US in preparation for the next World War in 1939, with the intent of setting up their second attempt at World Government.

In Britain, many well-educated people including members of parliament and high ranking military personnel began to suspect what the bankers were up to. In 1938, two such high ranking officers from the military were Captain Ramsay and Admiral Sir Barry Domvile, who, through their own investigations had established that the International Bankers were the hidden 'Secret Power,' manipulating events behind the scenes, and convinced they were using their wealth and power to influence international affairs to bring nations into conflict with each other. They also had their suspicions that the Bolshevik revolution in Russia had been planned, financed and directed by the same men, of which their suspicions were spot on.

Captain Ramsay had been a member of British Parliament for years and warned his fellow countrymen of the forces at work in his country [Great Britain], for his effort in trying to inform the public "...he was put in prison without trial for 4+ years, for 'reasons' so preposterous that those who framed them dared not submit them to a court of law."[2]

Both Ramsay and Domvile tried from 1936 to 1939 to prevent Britain becoming engaged in war, they knew the international bankers intended to arrange the war in such a way that the German and British Empires would destroy each other, and the people who survived could be easily subjugated by Communism afterwards in exactly the same way Russia had been communized.[4]

In the late 30's, Neville Chamberlain took over as Prime Minister from Stanley Baldwin. Neither of these men was ever fully under the control of the 'Money Monopolists.'[5] Captain Ramsay and Sir Barry Domvile knew that the bankers were trying to start a Second World War and warned Prime Minister Chamberlain that it wasn't within the interests of the British Empire. Chamberlain was interested but wanted proof of a conspiracy which prompted Captain Ramsay to produce documentary evidence. Ramsay's evidence consisted of secret coded cables which had passed between Winston Churchill and President Roosevelt... Tyler Kent was the coding officer who had decoded these secret documents in the American Embassy in London.[5]

Chamberlain kept this in mind when he travelled to Munich, where upon he negotiated a compromise with Hitler, returning to England he waved exuberantly his famous umbrella and a paper which he said was the agreement which guaranteed 'Peace in Our Time.' Ramsey remarked on the very evening of Chamberlain's return that every newspaper in the country and the war mongers in the British Parliament would attack Chamberlain for having secured peace... regardless of the fact that in so doing they were flouting the real wishes of the people. This remark was only too true, as events proved.[6]

Immediately the announcement was made, the press, controlled by the International Bankers, started an anti-Fascist campaign of hate. The controlled press damned Chamberlain as "An old woman willing to buy Peace at any price." They lampooned him with his umbrella. They accused him of being Pro-Fascist. Their agents in Moscow burned Chamberlain in effigy in the public squares.[7]

Versailles Revisited

In 1919, the Treaty of Versailles had awarded Poland the Polish Corridor, a strip of German territory. The arrangement had always caused chronic friction between Poland and Germany. Hitler wanted to take back the Polish Corridor which rightfully belonged to Germany, and sent a note to Poland looking for a peaceful solution to the long running problem between the two nations. However, the press made it appear that the German note to Poland suggesting a peaceful solution was 'another demand.'

William Guy Carr writes in *Pawns in the Game*, that the bankers had tricked Chamberlain into signing a guarantee to protect Poland from German aggression by presenting him with a false report to the effect that a 48-hour ultimatum had been delivered by Germany to the Poles. The facts are that German government did not issue any 48-hour ultimatum. The German note set forth reasonable suggestions for a 'peaceful' solution of the problems created by the Treaty of Versailles in regard to the Polish Corridor and Danzig.[8] History shows that the Polish government ignored the German note because agents of the International Bankers advised its leading statesmen that a British guarantee assured them against German aggression.

Poland ignored Hitler's peaceful solution to the conflict, which led to Germany launching an attack on Poland at dawn on September 1st, 1939; the attack guaranteed another World War would be underway very soon. Under the terms of the Versailles Treaty signed twenty years earlier, both England and France were obligated to enter the war on the side of Poland. As Lord Curzon, the British Foreign Secretary had predicted twenty years previously that the treaty was not peace, but "...only a truce for twenty years," and Philip Snowden of the Liberal British Cabinet had said the treaty was "...a death-blow... not a peace treaty, but a declaration of another war," and John Maynard Keynes stated the treaty could bring nothing but "...misfortune behind it," were all now proving prophetic. History records now reveal that none of the 'reasons' used by the Big Powers for entering the struggle were valid.[9]

Though a state of war was declared to exist between Britain and Germany in September of 1939, it very soon became apparent that no war was being conducted by Germany against this country [Great Britain].[10] ... Hitler did not bomb Britain, and while Neville Chamberlain remained Prime Minister,

Britain did not bomb Germany. Chamberlain would not initiate the offensive because he was almost convinced that he had been the victim of international intrigue. The controlled press called it 'A Phony War.'[11]

It is quite obvious that two great empires cannot destroy each other if they will not fight. This was no surprise to those who knew the facts of the case. Hitler had again and again made it clear, that he never intended to attack or harm Great Britain or the British Empire, and in the absence of bombing of civilian populations ultimately the war must peter out altogether. No one was quicker to perceive this than the International Bankers; and they and their friends inside and outside the House of Commons very soon began exerting pressure for... the bombing of Germany to be started.[12]

Winston Churchill had been given powers and responsibilities regarding all naval, military, and air operations and decided he would take the initiative, in which he conceived the idea of 'The Norway Gamble,' a poorly planned and executed operation involving the British army, navy and air force. The fact that the operation could not possibly succeed was pointed out to Churchill.

The 'The Norway Gamble' was a fiasco, but was not blamed on Churchill. Instead, the International Bankers used their controlled press to release their full powers of hatred, criticism, invective, censure, sarcasm, and satire against Chamberlain for the failure. They wanted Chamberlain out of the way so they could put Winston Churchill in his place and turn the "Phony War" into a "Shooting War." This propaganda campaign eventually forced Chamberlain to resign,[13] giving Winston Churchill control - who immediately started bombing raids in Germany. J. M. Spaight, in his book *Bombing Vindicated*, published in 1944, reveals that the ruthless bombing of German cities started on May 11th, 1940, the *evening of the day Winston Churchill became Prime Minister*. Britain *started* the bombing and, as was to be expected, Germany retaliated. Thus the war was now placed on a destructive basis.[14] [Emphasis in original]

On May 23rd, 1940, during the first two weeks of Churchill's Premiership, he used an obsolete regulation known as regulation '18-B' to arrest all the prominent people who had tried to prevent and resist Britain from being dragged into a war with Germany, and those who had opposed his policy to turn the 'Phony War' into a Fighting war. Many hundreds of British subjects were arrested without any charge being made against them. They were thrown into prison without trial under regulation 18-B *which deprived them of the rights and privileges of the Habeas Corpus Act.* Magna Carta was ignored and ridiculed. [Emphasis in original] Captain Ramsay, Admiral Sir Barry Domvile, their wives and friends, and hundreds of other citizens were thrown into Brixton prison. Some of them were detained until September 1944. They were treated like criminals, and far worse than prisoners on remand.[15]

Lusitania Revisited

In the US in 1940, Franklin D. Roosevelt made the same promise's to the public Woodrow Wilson made in 1916 to keep America out of the affairs of Europe, but unfortunately, behind the scenes he was busy implementing a similar performance to the *Lusitania*, the ocean liner sunk to bring the US into the First World War. James Perloff points out in *The Shadows of Power* that when the *Lusitania* went down, Winston Churchill was head of the British admiralty, and FDR was an Assistant Secretary of the U.S. Navy, now some twenty five years later in 1940, a similar problem exists for them both of how to get the US into a Second World War. It was also the same year the code clerk Tyler Kent discovered the secret dispatches between Churchill and FDR, revealing their true intentions to bring the U.S. into the war with Britain and Germany. Tyler Kent tried to smuggle some of the documents out of the embassy, hoping to alert the American people, but he was caught and confined to a British prison for the duration of the war.[16]

The Japanese brought the US into World War II earlier than they otherwise would have. Just like the *Lusitania*, Pearl Harbour was the excuse needed. Over the years, a number of books have documented that FDR had foreknowledge of the attack on Pearl Harbor, the most authoritative is *Infamy: Pearl Harbor and Its Aftermath* (1982) by Pulitzer-Prize winner John Toland, summarized in *The Shadows of Power:* American military intelligence had cracked the radio code Tokyo used to communicate with its embassies. As a result, Japanese diplomatic messages in 1941 were known to Washington, often on a same day basis. The decoded intercepts revealed that spies in Hawaii were informing Tokyo of the precise locations of the U.S. warships docked in Pearl Harbor; collectively, the messages suggested an assault would come on or about December 7th.[17]

Even as late as the day before the Japanese attack on Pearl Harbor in December 1941, the American people were still overwhelmingly 'isolationist' – a word which internationalists use as a term of contempt but which means merely that the American people were still devoted to their nations traditional foreign policy. With the invasion of Pearl Harbor... any American, who continued to advocate a traditional foreign policy of benign neutrality would be an object of public hatred, would be investigated and condemned by officialdom as a "pro-Nazi," and possibly prosecuted for sedition.[18] Robert Sherwood, the President's friendly biographer, once said: "If the 'isolationists' had known the full extent of the secret alliance between the United States and Britain, their demands for the Presidents impeachment would have rumbled like thunder through the land."[19]

After five years of another World War, the most costly war in the history of mankind, over fifty million people lost their lives because of the scheming of the International Money-Lenders. The emerging world from the horrors of the war were designed to exhaust the nations of the world, to demoralize the people so far that they would be willing to accept any offer of peace that would be presented. The world was now primed for their next trick, the League of Nations-Mark II, to be known as the United Nations. The new World Government was to be promoted with its own vast array of propaganda as 'The last hope of mankind... the only means to 'protect' the world from the horrors of war.'

TOWER OF BABEL

Edward Griffin's *The Fearful Master* tells us of Senator William Jenner who spoke before the US Senate on February 23rd, 1954, who told the story of a young married man who worked in a baby-carriage factory in Germany during the early days of the Nazi regime. Since his wife was soon expecting their first child, the young man began to save his money to purchase one of the baby carriages he was helping to build. But for some reason the Nazi government refused to let anybody buy them. So he decided to collect secretly the parts-one from each department-and do the assembly himself at home. Finally, when all the parts had been gathered, he and his wife began to put them together. To their utter astonishment, they wound up with, not a baby carriage at all, but a *machine gun!* And, as Senator Jenner observed: The pattern ... was divided into separate parts, each of them as innocent, safe and familiar looking as possible. The leaders did not intend to assemble the parts until they needed machine guns. But let's keep in mind that when the parts of a design are carefully cut to exact size to fit other parts with a perfect fit in final assembly, the parts must be made according to a blueprint drawn up in exact detail. This does not happen by chance. The men who make the blueprints know exactly what the final product is to be. They have planned the final assembly years ahead. They do not think they are making baby carriages.[1] The innocent looking baby carriage disguised as a machine gun is what the International Money-Lenders have laboured for since 1776, the United Nations, the new Tower of Babel which houses the embryo of a One World Government to bring about the New World Order.

The potential for evil in building the original tower of Babel was not to 'reach unto heaven,' nor was it to build a city. The potential danger of the tower was in the concentration of power it could wield and the elimination of the division of nations. A division of nations is of paramount importance because it has served to control the spread of evil throughout the earth.[2]

The new Tower of Babel's 17 acre headquarters stands at the East River of New York, of which the Rockefellers donated $8,500,000 for the land the tower now sits on. The United Nations tower came in at a cost of $65,000,000, courtesy of an interest free loan from American taxpayers.

Of all the clichés that have played a role in the historical development of the United Nations, none has been used more extensively than the claim that the UN is 'man's last and best hope for peace.' Even today it is difficult to locate a pro-UN article, speech, or book that does not emphasize this central theme, despite the fact that not a single provision in the United Nations Charter contemplates an end to war.[3] Under the banner of 'peace,' with its roots firmly based in communism, the United Nations has slowly established itself as a structure to unite all nations into a One World Government. Though the United Nations was not initially set up as a world government, the intent was that it would develop into one over time. John Foster Dulles (CFR), an American delegate to the UN founding meeting who later became Secretary of State under Eisenhower, acknowledged as much in his book *War or Peace*: "The United Nations represents not a final stage in the development of world order, but only a primitive stage. Therefore its primary task is to create the conditions which will make possible a more highly developed organization."

In 1942, the International Free World Association, organized in 1941, stated in their periodical *Free World* that their objective was to create the "machinery for a world government in which the United Nations will serve as a nucleus... in order to prepare in time the foundations for a future world order."[4]

Deja Vu

After World War One Rothschild agent Mandell House persuaded President Wilson that the only way to avoid all future wars was to put forward the League of Nations, peace terms were formulated and 'the inquiry' group was formed to draw up plans for the charter for the secret world government. The same procedures were used during the Second World War, designed to force the new and improved version, the United Nations upon an unsuspecting world. When Britain and France declared war on Germany in September 1939 after Hitler invaded Poland, the Council on Foreign Relations in the US promptly formed a committee to plan Post War Foreign Policy.

The Council on Foreign Relations with the intention of influencing the State Department, sent Fish Armstrong and Walter H. Mallory to offer the services of the CFR to the government. It was agreed that the Council would do research and make recommendations for the State Department, without formal assignment or responsibility... The Rockefeller Foundation agreed to finance, through grants, the operation of this plan.[5]

In January 1943, Secretary of State Cordell Hull formed a steering committee composed of himself, Leo Pasvolsky, Isaiah Bowman, Sumner Welles, Norman Davis, and Myron Taylor. All of these men – with the exception of Hull – were in the CFR. Later known as the Informal Agenda Group, they drafted the original proposal for the United Nations. It was Bowman – a founder of the CFR and a member of Colonel House's old "Inquiry" – who first put forward the concept. They called in three attorneys, all CFR men, who ruled that it was constitutional. They then discussed it with FDR on June 15th, 1944. The President approved the plan, and announced it to the public the same day.[6]

United Nations Charter

World War II ended and a meeting was scheduled in San Francisco on June 26th, 1945 for the signing of the United Nations Charter – which would be accepted by representatives of fifty countries. Dr John Coleman's *Diplomacy by Deception* tells us that the senators were given only three days to discuss the implications of the treaty, which could not have been fully examined in under at least a full 18 months of discussion. Had the senators properly understood what they were discussing, which, apart from a few exceptions, they did not; there would have been a demand for a proper period for discussion. The fact is that the Senate did not understand the document and therefore should not have voted on it. Had the senators who debated the United Nations treaty properly understood the document it surely would have been rejected. Apart from any other considerations, the document was so poorly written and, in many instances, so vague, deceptive and contradictory, that it could have been rejected on these grounds alone.[7]

At the signing of the United Nations Charter, forty-seven members of the Council on Foreign Relations were members of the United States delegation, including Edward Stettinius, the Secretary of State; John Foster Dulles; Nelson Rockefeller; Adlai Stevenson; and the first Chairman of the United

Nations, Alger Hiss. It was Hiss and Joseph E. Johnson (who later became Secretary of the Bilderbergers) who wrote much of the UN Charter, patterning it after the Constitution of Russia, and the *Communist Manifesto*. An Associated Press dispatch from April 7th, 1970 which appeared in the *Los Angeles Times* said: "Secretary-General U Thant praised Vladimir I. Lenin, founder of the Soviet Union, as a political leader, whose ideals were reflected in the UN Charter." It contained self-granted powers for a one-world government.[8]

Dr John Coleman writes that Rep. Jessie Sumner, of Illinois knew the United Nations fine words in the Charter were not designed for peace when stating: "Mr Chairman, of course you know that our government peace program is no peace. The movement is led by the same old warmongers, still masquerading as the princes of peace, who involved us in war while pretending their purpose was to keep us out of war... while promising to keep us out of war, this measure (the U.N. Treaty) will involve us in every war hereafter."[9] He is joined by Rep. Lawrence H. Smith who stated: "To vote for this proposal is to give approval to world communism."[10] J. B. Mathews, former chief investigator for the House Committee on Un-American Activities said: "I challenge the illusion that the UN is an instrument of peace... It could not be less of a cruel hoax if it had been organized in Hell for the sole purpose of aiding and abetting the destruction of the United States."[11] The Charter was also left intentionally vague to allow for future updates and amendments. As Senator Bricker said, referring to these statements and proposals: "The doctrine that the UN Charter can be amended without the consent of the President and the Senate is a blueprint for tyranny."[12] It is, in fact, the Fabian way of communist world revolution. It is powered by faith that coercive collectivism is the highway to peace and human progress. That was the faith of those who founded the United Nations. To that faith the UN Charter pledges every clerk, official and Member Government of the organization. That faith is the theme of resolutions, covenants and reports which UN agencies pour out, day after day, in a never-ending torrent. That fervent faith of Karl Marx and his communist disciples is the guiding light of hosts of "experts," "observers," "advisors," whom the UN sends to the far corners of the earth to promote measures for collectivizing the wealth and work and lives of all human beings. This dedication to the Marxian world-reactionary fallacy is inherent in the very nature of the United Nations and in all its affiliated agencies.[13]

With all the talk of peace, within weeks of the signing of the Charter on June 26th, 1945... the atomic bomb exploded on Hiroshima and Nagasaki. In 1965, Luis Quintanilla (a former representative of Mexico in the UN General Assembly) "suggested that the atom bomb deserves the Nobel peace prize for having spurred mankind's efforts toward realization of a warless world."[14] Those are the rationales of United Nations delegates. As Lenin had stated: "We are the masters. Complete indifference to suffering is our duty. In the fulfilment of our calling, the greatest cruelty is a merit."

Communists in the House

It was soon discovered that Alger Hiss, the first UN Secretary General was a Soviet agent; he later served time in prison for lying about his connections to a Soviet spy ring. Hiss had been invited by Woodrow Wilson's son-in-law, Francis B. Sayre, to work for the State Department. He was denounced by Soviet defector Igor Gouzensky, who worked in the office of the GRU (Soviet military intelligence) in Ottawa, Canada.[15] The FBI knew who Hiss was and had kept files on him. Hiss had been the Rockefeller's first choice to do their bidding, as he was already deeply involved in espionage for the USSR, the Royal Institute of International Affairs (RIIA) and the Council on Foreign Relations (CFR), and they also knew that Hiss would do what he was told. When Hiss was exposed as a Soviet agent, CFR-Rockefeller puppet Roosevelt ignored the information and decided to promote him instead. Hiss received a special staff appointment to the Carnegie Endowment Fund for International Peace at a salary of $20,000 per annum... The idea was to place Hiss above the law... Rockefeller also paid his legal expenses to the tune of $100,000.[16] According to an "informed estimate" quoted by the carefully edited *U.S. News & World Report*, as many as one-half of the 1,350 administrative executives of the United Nations were either communists or persons who willingly did the communist bidding.[17]

Eustace Mullin's in his book *World Order* notes that many people that were associated with Alger Hiss had become a liability to the New World Order plans, and were subsequently eliminated without mercy. When Hiss, White and others faced Congressional investigation, many of their acquaintances who were asked to testify didn't quite make it to the hearings. A lawyer named Marvin Smith, a close friend of Hiss, fell out of a window.

Laurence Duggan, an intimate of both Hiss and White, was slated to testify when he fell out of a twelfth story window. Duggan was an official of the Institute of International Education, of which his father was founder and president, but these family ties offered him no protection. In his haste to get to the window, he tore off one shoe, and left his office in a shambles as he fought his way across it. The verdict was "suicide". The Canadian diplomat, Herbert Norman, and the Harvard Professor F.O. Matthiesen, also went out the window before they could be made to testify about their associations. The phenomena became so common that it gave rise to a new term "defenestration", meaning the avoidance of testimony, and a suitable warning to others who might think of talking.[18]

United Nations Propaganda

G. Edward Griffin's, *The Fearful Master* explains the bias of the media towards the United Nations... Mr George Todt, a well-known columnist, outlined some cold hard facts about the United Nations on his Hollywood NBC program on September 5th, 1954. Todt stated he was in favor of the American Constitution, not the United Nations Charter; he was immediately notified by NBC he was off the air without any word of warning. Everything had been fine up until the time he spoke about the UN.[19] Griffin further explains the process of squelching opposition to the United Nations is far from limited to just mass media. In 1955, Ramsey, a sixteen-year-old high school student in Compton, California, wrote well written, factual, but strongly critical letters of the United Nations to magazines and newspapers. As a result, he became the target of a vicious smear campaign. A Communist front calling themselves the "anti-Nazi League," sent out thousands of postcards calling Ramsey a 'Hitlerite' and rallied neighbours and fellow students against him. Ramsey was subsequently committed to a county institution as a 'mental case' with no formal charges ever being brought against him... he was eventually released on the condition he stop writing letters to the newspapers.[20]

From the very beginning, there has been an avalanche of pro –United Nation's propaganda and how they can do no wrong. The Communist *Daily Worker* reported on the UN's tenth anniversary: Radio and TV coverage of the UN's tenth anniversary was the best in that world organizations history. The UN concert with Soviet pianist Emil Gilels, the New York Philharmonic and Schola Cantorum was televised by WOR and heard on radio stations

WQXR and WNYC. One report said that a movie of the concert was being sent to Latin America and that a tape recording of same would be aired by Voice of America. In addition, station WINS in New York and 55 other U.S. stations carried Norman Corwin's play *The Charter and the Saucer,* a British Broadcasting drama on the UN with Sir Lawrence Olivier. A quarter hour film titled *Your Seat at the Table* with Clifton Fadiman was heard on WABC and many other stations across the country. *The Family Tree* was broadcast by ABC. Throughout the weekend of the anniversary, NBC's *Monitor* featured spot salutes to the UN from delegates and celebrities. The popular children's TV show *Let's Take a Trip* visited UN headquarters last Sunday. *Ding Dong School* also had its enormous following watching a movie on the UN. The Carousel's weekend show was devoted to the UN. CBS's *Morning Show* did a series of live pick-ups from the UN, and Dave Garroway's NBC show featured UN posters.[21]

Equal Rights Con

The universal appeal of high sounding noble phraseology to gain support of the people has been used since the beginning of history. With high-minded aspirations, the United Nations created their own version of the Declaration of Human Rights. Des Griffin points out the United Nations many references to 'equal rights' stating that... merely to guarantee equal rights to everyone is no guarantee of rights at all. If the rights of all people were reduced to zero,[22] we would all have an equal share of no rights. People have natural rights; they belong to them as a condition of being human. The western world had rights long before government, money-lenders and the United Nations came along, the government and the UN have no business interfering with the God given rights of citizens; the United Nations is slowly changing these silly 'out-dated' ideas and beliefs about which human rights you should have.

Government can give the people nothing that it has not first taken away. When your rights come from the State, citizenship means total allegiance to government, not God. God alone has the power to grant privileges, benefits and rights to human beings, when and where has government gained the right to interfere with citizens private affairs? Rights are gradually becoming a government entitlement; the law is what the State says it is. This was exactly the Nazi definition of citizenship.

The United Nations Declaration states human beings are born free and equal in dignity and rights... everyone is entitled to all the rights and freedoms set forth in this Declaration, which sounds noble and just, but Article 6 of the Charter states... Everyone has the right to recognition everywhere as a person *'before the law'* [Emphasis added]. Article 7 states... all are *'equal before the law'* [Emphasis added] and are entitled without any discrimination to *'equal protection of the law'* [Emphasis added]. The United Nations will happily grant us all the rights *'equal to the law.'* The Declaration further emotes everyone has the right to life, no one shall be held in slavery or servitude, subjected to torture or to cruel, inhuman or degrading treatment or punishment, etc., etc., all designed to appeal to the highest of the emotions. All these lofty ideals and expressions sound great, until we reach the bottom of the Declaration, where in Article 29, section (2), it states... In the exercise of his rights and freedoms, *everyone shall be subject only to such limitations as are determined by law...* [Emphasis added]. The Council on Foreign Relations through the United Nations are slowly defining what 'law' is, given their history; I wouldn't put too much faith in their humanitarian motives.

Article 29 Section (3) goes on to say... These rights and freedoms may in no case be exercised *contrary to the purposes and principles of the United Nations.* [Emphasis added]. What are the purposes and principles of the United Nations? The purpose of the United Nations and its principles is to establish a One World collective society; every human right is slowly being superseded by the many laws that are continually passed under the name of national security, terrorism, public safety, etc. The two clauses stated in Article 29 of the Declaration will deny the existence of everything that was stated before it. Rights are yours simply by the fact that you are human, they do not have to be 'earned' from the United Nations or government – but that is where it's going.

War Is Peace

World Government needs a world army to keep world 'peace.' The UN's unchallengeable military power has steadily increased to bring 'peace' to the world. Evidence is proving that the definition of peace which the United Nations operates under means 'no opposition to the agenda.' The UN is responsible for some of the most violent war atrocities since its birth. Terrorist regimes have received support in the form of military troops to 'enforce' their particular brand of peace through military takeover. Never has the world seen so much hate, violence and terrorism perpetrated by such a small group of elitists in the name of peace. The hands of the United Nations are caked in the blood of millions of innocent victims, through the legalized political plundering of nations.

The United Nations has been called nothing short of a war-making outfit. "*We the peoples of the United Nations, determined to save succeeding genera-tions from the scourge of war...*" High sounding phrases appeal to the universal longing for peace, the reality is that up until 1991... there were 157 wars. In his August, 1945, analysis of the UN Charter, J. Reuben Clark, Jr., Ambassador to Mexico and Under-Secretary of State wrote: "The Charter is built for war, not to promote peace... The Charter is a war document, not a peace document..." He is quoted in the book *The United Nations Today* as saying: "Not only does the Charter Organization (UN) not prevent wars, but it makes it practically certain that we shall have future wars; and as to such wars, it takes from us (U.S.) the power to declare them, to choose the side on which we shall fight, and to determine what forces and military equipment we shall use in the war, and to control and command our sons who do the fighting."[23]

It was never the intention of the Founding Fathers of America to interfere with the affairs of other nations, to bully and pick fights with those who don't conform to their particular brand of 'peace.' George Washington especially warned against interfering in foreign affairs. There is no place in the US Constitution that gives anyone but Congress the authority to declare war against any nation. There is certainly no legal authority for a group of power-mad megalomaniacs to make the U.S. an international aggressor in order to create a New World Order.[24] An article about the UN in the March 2nd, 1964 edition of the *Santa Ana Register* made this comment: "The whole purpose and, indeed, the method of the UN is to use armed might against any nation presumed to be an aggressor. Its function is to make war..."[25]

The United Nations began flexing their military muscle between 1951-1952; these military manoeuvres were first practiced on the American people. "Military Government Reserve Units" *simulated an invasion and seizure of nine California cities!*: As V. Orval Watts describes in *The United Nations: Planned Tyranny...* on July 31st, 1951, the UN's... invading forces did not fly the American flag, they came in under the flag of the United Nations, and their officers stated that they represented the United Nations. These forces arrested the mayors and police chiefs, and pictures later appeared in the newspapers showing these men in jail. The officers issued manifestoes reading "by virtue of the authority vested in me by the United Nations Security Council." On April 3rd, 1952, other units did the same thing at Lampasas, Texas. They took over the town; closed churches, strutted their authority over the teachers and posted guards in classrooms, set up concentration camps, and interned businessmen after holding brief one-sided trials without habeas corpus[26] (Protection against illegal imprisonment). He goes on to say... A Texas newspaper reported the invasion: "But the staged action almost became actual drama when one student and two troopers forgot it was only make-believe. "Aint nobody going to make me get up," cried seventeen year old John Snell. One of the paratroopers shoved the butt of his rifle within inches of Snell's face and snarled: "You want this butt placed in your teeth? Get up." The invaders put up posters listing many offenses for which citizens would be punished. One of them read: "25: Publishing and circulating or having in his possession with intent to publish or circulate, any printed or written matter... hostile, detrimental, or disrespectful... to the Government of any other of the United Nations.[27] Is this a fore-taste of the United Nations World Government?

Surrender by Conquest

The road towards a New World Order with the United Nations having the only "peace keeping Force" in the world began with the Strategic Arms Limitation Talks (SALT). The media began their propaganda with the story that leftist scientists and academics feared America's superior nuclear capacity would frighten a worried Soviet Union into launching a major war against the West.

By 1955, the parliamentary Association for World Government issued a call for a series of "Conferences on Science and World Affairs." These were to be held between Russian and American scientists and intellectuals. The first conference in 1957 was hosted by Cyrus Eaton in Pugwash, Nova Scotia. Cyrus Eaton began his career as secretary to John D. Rockefeller, now Rockefeller business partner promoting Red Trade. He later won the Lenin Peace Prize for fronting the Pugwash conferences. Some twenty conferences were financed by the tax-exempt Rockefeller-CFR foundations.

As a result of the Pugwash conferences, three years later on September 23rd, 1960, the Soviets presented the United Nations with a plan for "total and complete disarmament," a call for the systematic reduction in powers of the world. This 'Soviet Plan' received an instant endorsement from the Council on Foreign Relations. Coincidentally, one year previous to the Soviets presenting their plan to the UN, the CFR had created a secret disarmament program entitled "Study No. 7," which wanted to "...maintain and gradually increase the authority of the UN..." It was identical to the Soviet plan.

In September 1961, the Department of State released Publication 7277, entitled *Freedom from War: The United States Program for General and Complete Disarmament in a Peaceful World*. It was a three-stage program, where stage III called for a progressive control of disarmament, then proceeding to a point where no state would have the military power to challenge the progressively strengthened United Nations 'Peace Force.' Within the same month, Congress created the United States Arms Control and Disarmament Agency, 48 hours later, the new Agency presented its disarmament scheme to the United Nations. It was a carbon copy of the CFR-Soviet-Pugwash proposal presented to the UN by Communists the year before. While all the talk of the disarmament of the United States was front page news, no-one was pointing out the systematic arming of the United Nations.

The first Secretary of Defence to implement these strategies was CFR member Robert McNamara; he destroyed more operational U.S. strategic weapons than the Soviets could have in an actual war. Through the Strategic Arms Limitation Talks (SALT), American production was frozen and technology was exported to the Kremlin, allowing the Soviets to 'catch up' and overtake U.S. military power. America's military industrial complex had been destroyed to make the Soviet threat more plausible.

The Establishment want their World Government, whether by conquest or by consent, that's why the Soviets had to be built up to deliver the New World Order by force, should the United States citizens decide to not to give up their national sovereignty. The propaganda from the very outset was that the United Nations should run the show because the 'Russians' might blow us all up, but the reality was that the Strategic Arms Limitation Talks (SALT) hadn't limited the Soviets in any way.

The United Nations military police force is able to take over lesser governments, suppress local opposition, and enforce decrees of its world rulers, as can be clearly seen in the African Congo in 1961. Much has been written on the Korean War and the Vietnam War, but little is known of the war fought in the State of Katanga in the African Congo in 1961, under the guise of protecting the citizens from Communism.

KATANGA:
THE UNTOLD STORY

Forty six civilian doctors of Elisabethville lodged a complaint against the United Nations for grave and repeated violations of the International Conventions of the Red Cross in Geneva. Katanga's untold story is the tragic experience of the courageous Katangese, anti-communist Christian people to govern themselves and run their own affairs with a sense of peace, order and justice. The United Nations had other plans. The UN carried out one of the most brutal military campaigns of the century, sending in their military force and annihilating the Katangese people. Belgian Foreign Minister, M. Spaak was able to say that it had been in certain respects carried out under conditions that were truly inhuman.[1] What they [Katanga] stood for could not be tolerated by the forces of "anti-colonialism" in the Kremlin, the U.S. State Department, the Western news media, and especially the United Nations.[2] United Nations troops were sent to the Congo to keep the peace. The truth was the exact opposite; the United Nations were sent to the Congo to unleash a vicious bloody war against the people of Katanga, to take away their freedom and independence and force the Katangese people back into a coalition government with the Central Congo.

On June 30th, 1960, the Belgium King arrived in Léopoldville, the capital of the Central Congo to grant independence from Belgium to the newly created Central Congolese government. With political independence from Belgium, control of the entire Congo was turned over to the Central Congo Government in Léopoldville. The Congo received a premature independence because the Belgians were forced to evacuate the country early by strong United Nations pressure, plus the threat of Communist guerrilla warfare, in which all the whites in the Congo would be massacred. Belgian troops left the Congo, taking with them the rule of law; the new leaders of the Congo immediately aligned themselves with Communism.

Congressman Donald L. Jackson, a Member House Foreign Affairs Committee 1947-1960, tells us the Communist conquest is always the same, first a front man or a group create confusion, insight racial hatred, foment internal strife, then move in and take over. This is exactly what happened. With the Belgian army gone, the new leaders of the Congo began a campaign of terror and destruction in order to eradicate all traces of opposition to themselves. Who was the new front man to take over the Central Congolese Government? G. Edward Griffin in *The Fearful Master*, tells us that the new communist leader was Patrice Lumumba... a deranged and degenerate dope addict; he was a willing agent of the Communists; he worked tirelessly to bring chaos, anarchy and bloodshed to the Congo as the necessary first stage toward his ultimate goal of complete and unlimited dictatorship with himself nominally at the top and with Communist power to back him up.[3] It is well known that for at least two years the Soviets had been supplying Lumumba with arms, ammunition, military vehicles and other necessary supplies to insure an appropriate "spontaneous" uprising of the people against their "colonial imperialist masters." In addition to the hardware, they provided $400,000 a month with which to buy followers and provide them with the little extras that insure loyalty, such as cars, extravagant parties, and women. Lumumba's Communist backing was widely acknowledged and had been described in detail in both the House of Representatives and the Senate.[4]

Like all Red agitators following the pattern of ultimate chaos, Lumumba was laying the groundwork for Communist takeover, promising unattainable economic and political gains to the people. Like all communist dictators, he lied and later sent the leaderless Congo-troops on a rampage, terrorizing, murdering and raping the civilian population. Lumumba, in his own words, sent the troops to "exterminate the white race in the Congo." European residents fled in terror by the thousands leaving behind their homes, their possessions, their businesses, and everything they had worked for.[5] The Reverend Mark Poole of the Luluabourg Presbyterian Mission and other missionaries in the Congo confirmed that the outbreaks of violence were undoubtedly Communist inspired and that they were too widespread and well-coordinated to have just happened by chance.[6]

The Lumumba Plan

To understand what kind of a man Lumumba was G. Edward Griffin further reveals a statement issued by Lumumba on September 15th to the heads of all provinces throughout the Congo:

SUBJECT:

Measures To Be Applied During the First Stages of the Dictatorship.

Sir,

I have the honour and the pleasure to inform you that with a view to the rapid restoration of order in the country, the House of Representatives and the Senate [of the central government], meeting in special session on 13th September of this year, decided to grant the government full powers.

Full powers should be understood to mean that the government is free to act as it thinks fit in all respects, for the purpose of suppressing abuses, disorders and any action which is contrary to the will of the government over which I have presided legally since the attainment of independence by the Congo...

The most effective and direct means of succeeding rapidly in our task may be summarized as follows:

1. Establish an absolute dictatorship and apply it in all its forms.
2. Terrorism, essential to subdue the population.
3. Proceed systematically, using the army, to arrest all members of the opposition. I will be personally responsible for those at Leopoldville including the Head of State and his close supporters. A few weeks ago, in view of the present situation in Katanga and Sud-Kasai, I sent the National Army to arrest Tshombe and Kalonji and even to kill them if possible...
4. Imprison the ministers, deputies and senators, who sometimes abuse their parliamentary immunity. In such case I should be glad if you would not spare them but arrest them all without pity and treat them with ten times more severity than ordinary individuals.
5. Revive the system of flogging and give the rebels 10 lashes, morning, and evening, for a maximum of 7 consecutive days. N. B. Double the number in the case of ministers, senators, and deputies, reducing the number gradually according to the condition of each individual.
6. Inflict profound humiliations on the people thus arrested, in addition to the obligatory treatment described above. For example, strip them in public, if possible in the presence of their wives and children. Make them carry heavy loads and force them to walk about in that state. In case of such a walk, however, drawers may be worn.

7. In view of the seriousness of the situation of the country, which is in danger of sinking into anarchy, it would be well to imprison repeated offenders in underground cells or prisons for at least six months, never allowing them out to breathe fresh air.

    N.B. If some of them succumb as a result of certain atrocity, which is possible and desirable, the truth should not be divulged but it should be announced, for instance that Mr X has escaped and cannot be found.

8. Those who do not succumb in prison should not be released for at least a year. In this case they shall be exiled to a country to be determined by me in agreement with certain foreign countries which have already signified their agreement in principle.

Some of the provincial presidents will say that the measures described are severe. In reply I would point out to them that certain politicians have attained power by means of dictatorship. Moreover, the measures of execution that I have indicated above constitute only the first stage of the basic regime that we hope will succeed in the Congo. The second stage will be to destroy anyone who criticizes us...

In conclusion, I would point out that this letter should be communicated only to those authorities under your orders in whom you have entire confidence.

(Signed) P. Lumumba, Prime Minister.[7]

Moise Tshombe

The Congo descended into chaos, except for the peaceful independent province of Katanga, which decided it wanted no part of the Red revolution in the Congo. President Moise Tshombe, the people's courageous leader declared a pro-western philosophy, stating his independence and aligned himself with the west. He was anti-Communist and stood for political freedoms cherished by the western world. He advocated limited government and the free enterprise system, which gained him the hearts of his people, but political hatred of the communists. Congressman Donald L. Jackson stated that Katanga saw no reason to accept the jurisdiction of the central government, for historically Katanga had always been an independent state, they considered the Congo Government to be Communist infiltrated, and they wanted no part of such a coalition. The people declared Katanga to be an independent Republic; they went on record before the world saying they were militantly anti-communist and pro-western in their sympathies.[8] But the State of Katanga had become a thorn in the Central Congolese government, an embarrassment, they wanted Katanga back under their control because they couldn't exploit or tolerate a free nation. It didn't matter what Tshombe or the people wanted, the American Establishment wanted him out and had already begun to turn public opinion in the west against him.

United Nations Help

Belgian troops were sent back into the Congo to protect the lives and the property of citizens. In a fit of rage Lumumba officially declared war on Belgium. Lumumba couldn't bring the Congo and especially the state of Katanga under communist control with the Belgian troops controlling law and order, so he came to Washington to seek help, where the red carpet was rolled out. The Soviets proclaimed that Lumumba was on a supreme peace mission. When addressing the United Nations, Lumumba blamed the Belgian troops for the massacre of the people in the Congo and demanded intervention from the United Nations to evict the Belgian troops from the Congo. He also attacked the state of Katanga as the obstacle to political unity and demands its capitulation to the central government.

The United Nations embraced Lumumba's murderous campaign against the Congo with open arms. The UN condemned Belgium and demanded the immediate withdrawal of her troops. The United Nations then authorized their troops to the Congo to assist Lumumba with his communist plan. While in the US, Lumumba made use of the western media to muster support for his cause. He was then wined and dined in the President's official guest house. Eisenhower then announced that he had sent the first five million of an expected 100 million dollars to Lumumba to help the Congo meet its most pressing needs.[9] While Lumumba wined and dined with American heads of State, the US State Department refused to even grant a visa for Katanga's President Moise Tshombe to enter the United States to present his case for the Katangese people.

Within four days, the first four thousand United Nations troops were flown into the Congo by U.S. Air Force planes. Many additional thousands were on the way. By July 23rd most of the Belgian troops had withdrawn. The territory was now in the hands of Lumumba's mutinous army and the United Nations "peace-keeping" forces. The plunder and rape continued and spread.[10]

Province of Katanga

The Province of Katanga remained calm, even thou they were surrounded by bloodshed and violence. The streets of Elizabethville were filled with the sound of a healthy economy with all lines of communication operating smoothly. The city was a picture of flourishing prosperity with the transport of planes and trains departing on regular schedules. Industrial and well developed Katanga is the key to Congo control, the primary target for communist takeover. Most other factories throughout the Congo were shut down; due to massacres or deported by Lumumba's gang, Katanga was in full production. While the United Nations troops are keeping the "peace" in the Congo, raped and persecuted nuns and missionaries continue to flee the central Congo. Meanwhile, United Nations troops were preparing to enter Katanga.

The UN unconditionally pledged to President Tshombe, if he permitted the United Nations forces to enter temporarily, it would pledge no interference in Katanga's internal affairs. Dag Hammarskjold, Secretary-General of the United Nations personally conveyed his assurances to Tshombe that the United Nations would "not be used on behalf of the central government to force the provisional government of Mr Tshombe to a specific line of action."[11] Tshombe was suspicious of the whole operation and protested to United Nations Hammarskjold that there was no need for troops to enter the state of Katanga, as they were already peaceful; however, Tshombe, as an act of good faith allowed UN troops to enter Katanga who came by the thousands, who set up headquarters in Elizabethville.

Lumumba Murdered

Lumumba mysteriously disappeared, according to some; he was seized and beaten to death by villagers. Moise Tshombe, showing willingness to solve the problems of a plagued Congo moved quickly to make plans to reunite the Congo; he reached an agreement with the leaders of the central government to work toward Congo unification and block communist advance... they wanted to prevent the establishment of what they referred to as a United Nations "regime of tyranny."[12] It was well known in the Congo that "The UN opens doors to Communism."[13] Tshombe put a conference together to reiterate that Katanga's succession had taken place primarily to resist the communist dictatorship of Lumumba.[14] A second conference was held where they worked out their differences and finalized a workable plan, which was based closely on western ideals. Tshombe then announced to the world: "We have resolved our problems ourselves and now we want both West and East to leave us alone."[15] The United Nations completely ignored Tshombe and the Central Congo Government, and replaced murdered Lumumba with acknowledged Soviet agent Gizenga. Gizenga declared himself the Premier of the Congo, the successor of Lumumba and the United Nations continued to send troops to the Congo as if nothing had happened.

The UN troops disregarding their agreement with Tshombe's government, not to interfere with Katanga's internal affairs, establish tight military security and control. As barbed wire barricades, road blocks and check-points go up, and areas are sealed off limits to all Katangese, it becomes increasingly clear that UN forces have established a military law and rule in Katanga, which is synonymous with a military occupation of enemy territory.[16]

The Congolese leaders started to see the writing on the wall and eventually decided to go along with UN plans. Tshombe didn't find out until a later meeting. The Congolese leaders had betrayed him and so he left the meeting in disgust. While leaving he was arrested without charge, thrown into prison where he stayed in solitary confinement for the next two months. He was later released and showed even more resolve and determination to resist the takeover of Katanga.

Forty Six Angry Men

At four o' clock in the morning on August 28th, 1961, while Elisabethville slept in peace, the United Nations launched a surprise attack. The U.N.O. (referred to back then as the United Nations Organization) waged war on the Katangese people, bringing ruin to a country where peace, order and racial understanding had been maintained. Katanga now found itself involved in a bloody war that lasted for over two years.

Three months after the first attack, November 21st, 1961, the United Nation's, the world's foremost 'peace organization' launched a complete reign of terror of death and destruction on the Katangese people. UN forces were to crush Katanga at any cost. Supported by jet fighters and bombers to clear a path of death and destruction, not only made a mockery of the UN resolution to the world... but also shatters the myth of UN forces sent to the Congo to bring peace.[17] Aerial destruction of houses, schools, social homes, churches, temples, missions, post-offices, offices, factories, fuel tanks, civilian railway material and the bombing of hospitals came without warning. UN troop's later would rape, murder, assassinate unarmed civilians, machine gun civilian houses, and rob murdered victims of jewels, rings, wallets and wristwatches, and steel cars, vans and trucks.

Forty six civilian doctors of Elisabethville in disgust, denounced the U.N.O. for violations in Katanga of its own Charter, the Declaration of Human Rights and the Geneva Conventions. The doctors put together a short book, '*Forty Six Angry Men*', the innocent slaughtering of civilians committed by 'soldiers' from different nations in the name of the United Nations. The forty six doctors were compelled to notify the world of the senseless inhumanity afflicted upon the peaceful state of Katanga. As the civilian doctors had said: "What could we do against an organization having the most powerful means of broadcasting false news, lies, and denials? We had the weak voice of Katanga radio, the official telegraph service, one or two teleprinters, and the small amateur radio stations."

The following references of United Nations atrocities committed in Katanga below are summarized from '*Forty-Six Angry Men*':

Mrs Szeles, and her mother, Mrs Szigethy, hear a convoy of U.N.O. forces approaching their home. As their house has already been machine gunned *four times* by previous passing U.N.O. troops, they are suspicious and the two ladies seek shelter in the corridor. This time hand-grenades are thrown against the house. Mrs Szeles is wounded in the thigh by a piece of exploding hand-grenade. There were 355 bullet holes in the house caused by firing. All the windows and the blinds were broken, the furniture, the wireless, etc.

U.N.O. snipers killed civilians unexpectedly without warning, while going about their daily occupations. Moise Sonda's, a Red Cross worker had his leg amputated after being machined gunned whilst getting out of his ambulance to pick up and help wounded victims. Civilian telephone-operator Emmanuel Kasamba was shot in front of his switchboard at the post office. Mr Kipilipili was shot in front of a police station on his bike. Mr Tenbossche was shot while buying a loaf of bread. Mrs B is dragged into her house by a U.N.O. soldier and raped while four others keep watch in the garden. On Christmas Eve, two U.N.O. soldier's successively rape Mrs N and Mrs A.

Father Michel had gone missing, his vehicle was discovered, completely burnt out with his charred body inside... it had been "bazookaed."

Troop's fired a bullet into a retreating vehicle, assassinating civilian Mrs Servais with a bullet in the back of the head ... as the bullet comes out; it explodes and completely smashes up the lower part of her face from the wings of her nose down to her chin, Mr Servais rushes his wife, with the death-rattle in her throat to a police camp where she dies immediately.

A Red Cross ambulance carrying supplies for the evacuation of families is fired upon... two bazooka rockets are fired at the ambulance... Mr Smeding's skull has been blown away. The U.N.O allows the Red Cross to go and pick up the bodies eleven days later. The bodies are lying in a ditch covered by his personal flag as delegate of the International Red Cross and a Red Cross Helmet.

Two peaceful Katangese civilians obtained written permission from the U.N.O *to stay in their own home*. Mr Tshibamba is shot down in his kitchen: as well as his legitimate wife, Mrs Suzanna Kabeena, with a burst of machine-gun fire which breaks both their legs, they are plundered and their house looted. The gang leaves but comes back to finish off the wounded. All this is related by the second wife, concubine of Mr Tshibamba, who managed to escape the slaughter.

Mr Guy Deken was shot running back to his house... his left arm had been cut to the bone from the shoulder to the elbow by a knife or a sharp machete.

Mr Stutterheim and Mr Beugnies fetched supplies and remained in their home after most people who lived in the street had left. The U.N.O. advanced house by house, when they came across the two men, they made them undergo severe questioning, with blows given with the fist, rifle butts, sticks or truncheons, and also kicks. Mr Stutterheim, who most probably tried to defend himself, had his wrists tied together. They assassinate Mr Stutterheim by shooting two bullets in his mouth and Mr Beugnies with a bullet in his heart. The troop's tried to conceal their crime by digging two shallow graves in the garden to bury the bodies.

Two elderly European civilians who were known for their generosity, sixty year old Mr Guillaume Derriks and his elderly mother aged eighty seven are assassinated. Troops enter their garden; machine gun two cars parked in the garage, a boy Andre Kapenga, is panic stricken and locks himself in the food-store next to the kitchen. With a burst of machine gun fire, they kill Mr Jean Fimbo, a Katangan servant of 30 years who sought refuse under the sink. They enter the drawing room and with a burst of machine gun fire, blow off half of Mr Derrik's face and skull, then proceed to kill Mrs Derrik's with shots to the right breast, coming out the left side and then one in the throat.

Mr Olivet, a delegate of the International Red Cross tells of the mortar shelling on the Red Cross hospital... a total of forty-odd shells were fired on the hospital and on the school and the convent of the nuns which were next to it. Trees were shattered or uprooted in the gardens. An unexploded shell was identified as belonging to the U.N.O. Many of the 700 patients were seeking shelter in the corridors and under their beds.

The U.N.O. went on to bomb other hospitals, including the Shinkolobwe Hospital which was visibly marked with an enormous red cross on the roof.

At about 8 a.m., according to the testimony of several Katangans who were present at Shinkolobwe at the time it happened, two aeroplanes flew over the hospital, twice at very low altitude; at about 9.30 a.m. the aeroplanes started machine-gunning, also at very low altitude... In the maternity ward, roof, ceilings, walls, beds, tables and chairs are riddled with bullets, a bomb exploded in the pavilion; another pavilion also contained thousands of holes of various sizes.

The Lubumbashi hospital is mortar shelled from the air, one hundred and sixty civilians including sisters, pupils and families seek shelter in the cellars. A shell explodes where 50 nuns have sought shelter under the roof-loft. The next day, machine-gunning and shelling continues. The day after, the firing becomes more intense. At midday, everything quietens down. The group of nuns decide to evacuate... an aeroplane sees the group, who is easily recognizable by their white clothes, and machine guns them from the air. Pupils are loaded into a truck, clearly marked with the Red Cross; they are machine gunned from the same aeroplane.[18]

This is only a brief glimpse into the United Nations, the World's Premier Peace keeping force in action. The $200 million operation was financed entirely by the United States, through the co-operation of the State Department,[19] which assured the UN's eventual crushing of the peaceful nation of Katanga. United Nations Secretary General Dag Hammarskjöld had since left the UN and was replaced by U. Thant, who congratulated the UN military for the "mastery" which they displayed!"[20]

In the last days, Moise Tshombe made a dramatic farewell speech to his soldiers. About two thousand of them gathered in the market square. Standing in a drizzling rain, Tshombe told his men: "You have fought bravely against the enemy three times in the past two and one-half years. The odds have become overwhelming against you."[21] The United Nations has never admitted any wrong doing on their part. In fact, the UN regards the whole episode as a resounding success, which it is, if you are looking for Communist control. U Thant sent a telegram to Belgian Foreign Minister after the slaughter of Katanga stating: "Formal orders were given to the U.N.O. troop's so that they would do everything possible to protect and safe-guard the life and properties of the civilian populations and I know they have executed these orders so far as it is possible – Stop – IN TRUTH I HAVE EVERY REASON TO BE PROUD OF THEIR DISCIPLINE AND THEIR CONDUCT." (Telegram from U. Thant to M. Spaak.)[22] [Emphasis in original]

LOOTING THE WORLD

CHAPTER

13

One year before the signing of the United Nations Charter, over seven hundred delegates from forty-four countries met in New Hampshire at the 1944 Bretton Woods Conference, to construct a world monetary system to control the economies of every nation. The ability to dictate the world's credit and money supply became a reality for the Money-Lenders when they established the International Monetary Fund (IMF) and the World Bank, which are the single most important private institutions affecting the economic development of nations across the globe. Under the banner of helping nations in financial trouble with 'development loans,' these CFR created monsters have used billions of dollars of tax payer money to gradually take control of the planet, a final push to dominate what's left of the earth's resources.

The IMF's official job sounds simple and attractive. It is supposedly there to ensure poor countries don't fall into debt, and if they do, to lift them out with loans and economic expertise. It is presented as the poor world's best friend and guardian. But beyond the rhetoric, the IMF was designed to be dominated by a handful of rich countries – and, more specifically, by their bankers and financial speculators. The IMF works in their interests, every step of the way.[1]

They are at the forefront of political and social change worldwide, all designed to bring about World Socialism. Harry Dexter White (CFR), along with Fabian socialist John Maynard Keynes were the architects who drew up plans for the International Bank for Reconstruction and Development which later became the World Bank. Harry Dexter White, just as with Alger Hiss was later identified as a Soviet spy.

As can be seen from the events of Katanga, the United Nations are not interested in 'peace,' the same goes for their World Bank, which is not interested in helping to solve the economic problems of a nation; all they are interested

133

in is the overtaking of a nation with the view to control it. The last half century has seen the World Bank gradually take control of agriculture, forestry, food and now the new blue gold, the water supplies of a nation. When issuing loans to poor nations to 'help' rebuild their broken economies, The Bank will impose conditions exactly the opposite of those required for a country's economic growth and stability, and it should come as no surprise that human rights and property rights are ignored along the way, and the wants and needs of the poor are ignored or deemed irrelevant.

While the United Nations and World Bank trots out empty and meaning-less rhetoric about the predicament of the poor, the Bank has gradually turned a large part of the earth's land surface into a global battlefield, destroying lives and exterminating millions of species in the name of progress. The Bank has financed irresponsible and irrelevant projects that have come to mean danger, untold ecological destruction of environments, social upheaval and terrible loss for some of the world's poorest people. In the name of development they trample vulnerable people underfoot and, frequently do irreparable damage to the environment.

The Poverty Business

The World Bank hold lavish meetings every three years for all the bu-reaucratese to ponder the hopes and the fears of the poor and underprivileged, at the same time pampering themselves with every luxury imaginable, while consuming mountainous piles of beautifully prepared exotic foods. Bruce Rich's *Mortgaging the Earth* tells of the meeting in Bangkok in 1991; how the Thai government spent $100 million on the Queen Sirikit Conference Center, complete with a quarter-of-a-million dollar gold statue at the entrance to the building because the World Bank and the IMF were coming to town for a three day meeting to discuss money and growth. The finance minister of Thailand spent a further $17 million for additional meeting related expenses for his special honoured guests.

Among the many problems preparing for the event were the views from the windows of the prestigious new conference building which would present the delegates with unsightly sprawling neighbourhood clusters of prostitutes and street vendors, mostly rural refugees from Thailand's poorest areas in the northeast, who were living out of makeshift cardboard shacks. These squalid conditions were not something the Thai Prime Minister wanted his guests to witness while relaxing and reflecting in a tranquil setting, munching hors d'oeuvres, sipping Singapore Slings, discussing economics, money and deliberating on how to eradicate poverty.

The problem was easily solved when the finance minister decided to call in the army and just relocate the unsightly disturbing looking poor people somewhere else. The people protested as it would destroy the little access they had to an already precarious livelihood, but with no more than a week's notice the families were evicted - forty three families were sent to the community school after their homes had been bulldozed away, and a few hundred yards from the conference center, seventy evicted families from their shacks huddled in army tents underneath an elevated expressway. The area under the expressway was dark and damp, and the air was noxious, filled with dust and exhaust. The army tents had no insulation from the humid ground. The families were cut off from electricity and water, and lived by candlelight.[2] Children as young as two months old were 'living' in these horrendous conditions, they later developed respiratory problems. [Similar events had happened before with delegates at the Hilton International in Seoul where... in order to make space for a parking lot big enough to accommodate the fleet of limos used by delegates, the Korean government helpfully raised to the ground the poverty-ridden red-light district adjacent to the hotel - demolishing a total of 128 buildings.[3] Another World Bank event was held in Washington estimated at a cost of $10 million; if the delegates of the conference were really so concerned about the plight of the poor and genuinely had their interests at heart, with the $10 million they could have made a gigantic contribution by supplying a year's worth of vitamin A for 47 million children at risk in the developing countries.[4] A meeting held in Berlin in 1988; the demonstrators knew the Big Boys were in town and how the World Bank 'helps' nations in trouble. On the nights they were in town, protesters deliberately banged pots and pans to disturb and harass delegates to stop them from sleeping. The German protesters also deliberately blocked limousines and the local taxi drivers went on strike for an afternoon in solidarity. 80,000 demonstrators marched through the center of Berlin to protest the policies of the World Bank and the IMF. They carried banners alleging the Bank and the Fund were destroying ecological stability through their short-sighted development policies, and "organizing the poverty of the world's peoples."[5] They wanted to call the people together to form a "Permanent People's Tribunal" to try the World Bank and IMF for crimes against humanity."[6]]

Across town from the Bangkok Queen Sirikit Conference Center, there was another meeting being held, a 'People's Forum' at the Chulalongkorn University, attended by the Bangkok street vendors, slum dwellers, numerous students, academics, sympathetic foreigners and spokeswomen for the nations prostitutes. The 'People's Forum' gathered to discuss the ecological cost and neglect of what the government sponsored development was doing to their country. The first speaker, a well-known outspoken middle aged woman affectionately called Auntie Roy told how she had come from the poor northeast twenty eight years earlier in search of a better life, but was still no better off, she said: "I pass it every day; I can see it from my window [the Queen Sirikit Conference Center]. It looks like the dwelling place of the angels. We have tried to imagine these thousands of angels arriving in their flying boats-that's what we call airplanes-and we ordinary people wonder if we will ever be able to sit in that meeting room"[7]

A former artillery officer spoke of how his life was ruined by Thailand's first hydroelectric dam, Bhumibol, financed by the World Bank in 1964, which displaced more than three thousand people from their homes. The government controlled Electrical Generating Authority of Thailand (EGAT) promised electricity, land, houses and water, but delivered nothing. Bhumibol was only one of the first of numerous World Bank loans to EGAT for large-scale dams and power plants: sixteen loans amounting to nearly $700 million were approved by 1991... The Sirindhorn dam also displaced thousands, who were resettled on infertile land and suffered increased poverty. The Sirindhorn refugees have been asking for adequate rehabilitation since 1967, to no avail.[8]

The latest Pak Mun dam project was discussed in which the World Bank was violating the most basic criteria of environmental assessment, in which twelve thousand villagers had protested the project. The dam was the fifth major dam project in three years to be the subject of massive grass-roots protest in Thailand. The dam was to be built in the middle of Kaeng Tana National Park which had spectacular rapids upstream and downstream from the proposed dam. The Bank stated the dam would not destroy the rapids, but EGAT refused any public access to environmental studies that had been made. Eventually a leaked copy of the Environmental study was obtained by University of California biologist Walt Rainboth, one of the world's leading experts on the fish of the Mekong River basin stated: "Based on the importance of the project and the capacity for irreversible damage, the report is *criminal* [emphasis in original], if something like this were submitted to Congress in order to solicit funds, its fraudulent nature would deserve criminal indictment." Rainboth further stated: "The Pak Mun dam would destroy untold identified and unidentified species."[9] The study had also grossly underestimated the risks and magnitude of parasitic diseases. The disease Schistosomiasis spread by snails that typically proliferate in large man-made reservoirs in the tropics, had crippled and killed millions in the Third World was overlooked. The World Bank officials ignored all that and claimed... it was a worthy example of sound environmental planning.[10]

Over the past thirty years the Bank had promoted programs that encouraged the conversion of huge areas of forest into large-scale exploitations for export crops such as sugar cane, palm oil, cassava, rubber, and of course, timber... Ninety five percent of the rubber produced is destined for export.[11] A Moslem farmer stated at the forum...."I am so angry about this fund. It promotes the destruction of all kinds of plants..." They had been promoting rubber for years, but in 1985 a new government regulation actually forbade farmers to have any other species of tree on land being subsidized by the fund. If they find a mango or jack fruit tree, they charge people about [ten dollars] per tree.[12] Fishermen and small-scale rice farmers described the destruction of the coastal ecosystems on which their livelihoods depend, promoted by government tax incentives for export-orientated shrimp farming. The large scale expansion of industrial shrimp farming help destroy nearly half the country's coastal mangrove forests between 1985 and 1990, devastating fish habitats and causing the salinization of water supplies for rice paddies.[13]

Saving the Poor

Bruce Rich reveals in *Mortgaging the Earth* in 1994 that ongoing World Bank projects were forcibly resettling more than one and a half million people worldwide, and projects in preparation would displace at least another million and a half people... In India alone, officially sponsored development projects had evicted more than 20 million poor people from their lands and homes, mostly without compensation... Huge forests had been destroyed, gigantic river basins filled with dams, and vast agricultural expanses consolidated into larger holdings for export production at tremendous ecological cost.[14]

The same story is reported in Graham Hancock's *Lords of Poverty*, that in India, for example, on the borders of the states of Madhya Pradesh and Uttar Pradesh, the Singrauli Power and Coal Mining Complex has received almost a billion dollars in World Bank funding since 1977 – the most recent loan being for $250 million. Here, because of 'development,' 300,000 poor rural people have been subjected to frequent forced relocations as new mines and power-stations have opened. Some families have been obliged to move as many as five times... unable to put roots down anywhere, they are utterly destitute.[15] Hancock also reveals that in all directions around Singrauli, as far as the eye can see: the land has been totally destroyed and resembles scenes out of the lower circles of Dante's inferno. Enormous amounts of dust and air and water pollution of every conceivable sort have created tremendous public health problems. Tuberculosis is rampant, portable water supplies have been destroyed, and Chloroquine-resistant malaria afflicts the area.[16]

A once prosperous village was replaced by 'unspeakable hovels and shacks on the edges of the huge infrastructure projects... some people are living *inside* the open pit mines.' Furthermore, over 700,000 previously self–sufficient peasant farmers – deprived of all other possible sources of income – now have no choice but to accept the indignity of intermittent employment at Singrauli for salaries of around 70 cents a day: below survival level even in India.[17]

John Pilger's 2001 documentary, the *New Rulers of the World* informs us of similar events in Indonesia: "The World Bank said its aim was to help poor people, promoting what it called 'global development.' In Indonesia, the hand-outs to the poor have been extra-ordinary to say the least, internal documents of the World Bank confirm, up to a third of the Banks loans to the Dictatorship of Suharto went into the pockets of his cronies and corrupt officials, that's around $8 Billion." Author and former political prisoner Pramoedata Ananto Toer regarding the IMF and World Bank in Indonesia stated: "For hundreds of years Indonesia was sucked dry by the rich countries of the west. Now we are dictated to by the IMF and The World Bank... A country as rich as Indonesia has been turned into a country of beggars."[18]

The World Bank brought poverty to Africa as Byron Richard's relates a case in Malawi, which was forced to use their stored corn to pay their debt to the International Monetary Fund (IMF) and World Bank... now they are experiencing famine because their food reserves were taken. In order to get seeds, they need to take out a loan from the IMF or World Bank, using their land as collateral. They can't buy seeds they want. Instead, they are being forced to buy genetically modified seeds, which only work for one year. Thus, they will have to take out another loan. If they default on these loans, their land will be taken.[19]

Don't Ask the Poor

Graham Hancock's *Lords of Poverty* tells us to manage World Bank projects, the United Nations Development Programme sends 8,200 experts 'into the field' to guide and manage the poor[20] …and has 'financed the assignment of 193,000 experts of 164 nationalities to work in nearly every sector in 170 countries and territories.'[21] But even with all these 'experts,' no one has bothered or is remotely interested in what the locals have to say regarding their situation. There is no in-depth field investigations amongst the poor who live in and around the project sites, these so called 'experts' don't take the time to talk to the poor or understand their local knowledge, the poor are entirely left out of the decision making process – almost as though they did not exist. As a Senegalese peasant commented after one mission of high powered development experts had made a cursory tour of his village: "They do not know that there are living people here."[22] The only views that matter are United Nations experts... or representatives of large private corporations.[23]

In most cases United Nations and World Bank 'experts' have nothing to do with the locals, United Nations and World Bank officials are no-where to be found in the poorest areas they are supposed to be helping. Graham Hancock further reveals staff residences are always in the best areas, as far away from the poor as it is physically possible to get, and sometimes designed to cut off all contact with them… In Nairobi, Kenya, the Bank has its own exclusive compound with a barbed wire perimeter guarded by furious attack dogs; burglar alarms in every house are connected to all the others and there is a hot-line to a security company that can send in teams of uniformed men armed with cudgels in the event of a break in.[24] Nepal was described as 'over-advised and under-nourished,' there is a widely held view that experts and consultants are dishonest, lazy, unimaginative, insensitive to local priorities and, as a result of all this, unable to come up with useful insights and suggestions.[25] A West

African stated it bluntly: "If you want to know what they think of us, just look at the way they treat their servants... basically they are racialist."[26]

All the heart felt 'philanthropy' and 'development loans' from the United Nations and the World Bank have created a new phenomenon in the Third World, that poor people no longer wished to be 'helped,' the poor now mistrust and reject the poisoned gifts thrust upon them by outsiders.[27] It is with authentic conviction bred for years of sad experience that Chief Raoni of the Brazilian Xingu tribe insists: "We want nothing from the white man. He has brought us only death, illness and murder. He has stolen our forest. He wants to destroy it all."[28]

500,000 inhabitants in Cordillera Mountains in the Philippines rejected the hydroelectric dams, mining and logging projects stating: "We oppose these programs and policies because they threaten our very existence."[29] Mexican activist Gustavo Esteva stated "... development has been recognized as a threat. Most peasants are aware that development has undermined their subsistence on century-old diversified crops..."

Many people have been forcibly removed from their homes to make way for hydroelectric dams, reservoirs, giant roads, etc. In Ethiopia's Awash Valley, Afar nomads whose traditional dry season pasture lands have been sown with cash crops and surrounded by barbed wire are today reduced to absolute penury, their independence gone, their way of life shattered, their dignity destroyed as they queue in rags for food hand-outs. Brazilian Indians whose rainforests have been felled in the name of progress now face genocide: their unique knowledge and skills are about to be lost to mankind forever. In Indonesia's 'thousand islands' paradise, tribal peoples are remorselessly being extinguished and priceless ecological resources turned to ash and mud amidst the folly of the largest resettlement programme in human history.[30]

Highway of Death

The World Bank issued a statement in 1986 asserting their deep concern over the destruction of the Amazonian tropical rain forests, and announced they would intensify their efforts to effectively deal with the problem. What the Bank failed to mention in their statement was that they had sponsored two of the biggest projects in the Amazon, Polonoroeste and

Carajas, which were actually destroying large parts of the rain forest.

Bruce Rich's *Mortgaging the Earth* tells us that Polonoroeste, the highway of death was the first project of destruction in the rain forest. As Jaime da Silva Araujo, a rubber tapper stated: "The Amazon rain forest is being brutally destroyed by large projects, financed by foreign banks, and planned by Brazilian interests that do not take into account the living beings in the forest, projects that take away their right to life."[31] It was well known that more than forty tribal groups lived in the area... parts of the region were so isolated and pristine that there remained several tribes who had no contact with the outside world.[32] But between 1981 and 1983 that didn't stop the UN World Bank lending... $443.4 million to Brazil for the Northwest Region Development Program, known by its Brazilian name as Polonoroeste (northwest pole). More than half these loans financed the paving of Brazilian national highway number 364 (BR-364), a 1,500 kilometre dirt track that connected Brazil's populous south central region with the rainforest wilderness in the northwest... the plan was to support settlers in raising tree crops for export.[33]

The project brought only death and destruction with everything it came into contact with. With the project underway so many colonist migrated, nearly half a million between 1981 and 1986, that the Brazilian land colonization agency, INCRA became extremely overwhelmed. Polonoroeste had transformed the region into one of the highest rates of forest destruction in the Brazilian Amazon, increasing its deforested area from 1.7 percent in 1978 to 16.1 percent in 1991. By the mid 1980's the burning of Rondonia's forest became a major focus of NASA research as the single largest, most rapid human-caused change on earth readily visible from space.[34] ...between 1978 and 1988 an incredible 22,000 square kilometres annually... it was described as an environmental and social tragedy of global dimensions.[35] Life threatening diseases also ravaged the settlers and the indigenous population. The incidence of malaria approached 100 percent in some areas, and more than 250,000 people were infected. Some Indian tribes were menaced with physical extermination from measles and influenza epidemics. And infant mortality rates of 50 and 25 percent were reported in two recently contacted tribes.[36] The colonization scheme had created a public health nightmare that was spreading all over Brazil... the World Bank had to approve a further $99 million loan to support a $200 million emergency project to deal with the malaria epidemic in the Amazon.[37]

Pig Iron

At the other end of the Amazon, the World Bank was an accomplice in an even bigger major international crime... 150,000 square kilometres were deforested in a gigantic region known as the area of influence of the Greater Carajas Program. More than three-quarters of this destruction took place on either side of a 780-kilometer railway financed by the World Bank in 1982. The Bank lent $304.5 million to the Brazilian state mining company Companhia Vale do Rio Doce (CVRD) to build the railroad from the world's largest reserves of high grade iron ore to the sea. The World Bank proclaimed it was a safe project, an environmental model, and stated their "due regard to ecological and environmental factors" with a 'Special Report' to protect the more than 10,000 Indians in twenty-three groups who live in the area of influence of the mine and the railroad. The total cost of the project was over $3 billion.[38] But the clearing of 150,000 square kilometres of prime Amazonian Rain Forest to make way for a railway was just the beginning of the disaster – they financed the licensing and construction of thirty-four private charcoal burning industrial projects all the way along the railway corridor; and as all the factories would need fuel to operate, the local trees would be used as free fuel for the industry.

Many of the indigenous reserves in the project area (which were supposed to have been protected in the Special Project) have large areas of standing forest and are already partially occupied by desperately poor peasants. As the smelters went into operation, they threatened to degrade and destroy these forested Indian lands, as well as other remaining forest reserves, by attracting into them an army of small scale charcoal producers desperate for income.... they used the native tropical forest as a free source of charcoal, and together they would exhaust this fuel source in as few as a dozen years.

In August 1987, twenty-nine environmental and indigenous rights organizations from around the world, including ten Brazilian organizations, sent a letter to World Bank President Barber Conable calling upon the Bank to use its influence to halt the charcoal-fuelled industrial schemes.[39] They insisted they had no leverage in the situation and that the project they were financing was environmentally sound. These two projects alone were an unprecedented ecological and human calamity that continued even after Bank loan disbursements were completed.

Financing Communist Regimes

The United Nations and the World Bank have a humanitarian program that only funds the most brutal tyrannical regimes on the planet. Ethiopia is just one of many countries which has seen some of the worst human rights violations under the rule of a tyrannical dictator. The Marxist regime of Mengistu Haile Mariam with funding from the World Bank planned and implemented the famine of 1984-85, which claimed the lives of millions of Ethiopian people. As G. Edward Griffin explains, the famine was modelled after Stalin's starvation program in the Ukraine in the 1930s and Mao's starvation of the peasants in the '40s. Its purpose was to starve the population into total submission to the government, for it is the government which decides who will eat and who will not. Yet, right up to the time Mengistu was overthrown; the World Bank continued to send him hundreds of millions of dollars, with much of it going specifically to the Ministry of Agriculture, the very agency in charge of the resettlement program.[40] He also tells us that these massive resettlement programs had torn hundreds of thousands of people from their privately owned land in the north and deported them to concentration-camp 'villages' in the south, complete with guard towers. A report by a French voluntary medical-assistance group, Doctors without Borders, reveals that the forced resettlement program may have killed as many people as the famine itself.[41]

Graham Hancock's *The Lords of Poverty* states that during the height of the famine in Ethiopia it was perfectly possible during the course of a single morning to travel by light aircraft from the luxury of the Addis Ababa Hilton to the surreal horror of the relief camp at Korem where tens of thousands of gaunt and ragged people lay strewn like the casualties of some brutish medieval battle across a blasted heath. One could then take pictures, take notes, or otherwise appraise and evaluate the situation, and then fly back to Addis Ababa again in time to catch an hour of sunbathing at the side of one of the finest swimming pools in the world... even the Secretary-General of the United Nations turned up at one point to find out for himself what starving children looked like – and to be photographed doing so. By 8a.m. each day the lobby of the Hilton would thus be crammed with bureaucrats in safari suits, some self-consciously clutching lunch boxes from the coffee shop, waiting for the mini-bus that would take them to the airport to catch the morning shuttle to hell.[42]

G. Edward Griffin gives further examples of Communist Vietnam during the 1970's, where settlement programs, forced collectivization, concentration camps, atrocities, and tens of thousands of dissidents escaping to the sea only to drown in overcrowded, leaky boats. Throughout it all, the regime was generously funded by the World Bank.[43] Syria massacred 20,000 members of its opposition; Indonesia uprooted several million people from their homelands in Java; the Sandinistas in Nicaragua murdered their opposition and terrorized the nation into submission; Poland, while a puppet state of the Soviet Union, brutally suppressed its trade-union movement; China massacred its dissident students and imprisoned its religious leaders; and the former Soviets slaughtered civilians in Afghanistan while conducting a relentless espionage war against the entire free world. Yet, these regimes have been the recipient of literally billions of dollars from the World Bank.[44]

Nowhere is this pattern more blatant than in Africa. Julius Nyerere, the dictator of Tanzania, is notorious for his 'villagization' program in which the army has driven the peasants from their land, burned their huts, and loaded them like cattle into trucks for relocation into government villages. The purpose is to eliminate opposition by bringing everyone into compounds where they can be watched and controlled. Meanwhile the economy staggers, farms have gone to weed, and hunger is commonplace. Yet, Tanzania has received more aid per capita from the World Bank than any other nation.[45] In Uganda, government security forces have engaged in mass detentions, torture, and killing of prisoners. The same is true under the terrorist government in Zimbabwe. Yet, both regimes continue to be the recipients of millions of dollars in World Bank funding.[46]

Blue Gold

Apart from 'development loans' to poor nations and funding Communist regimes, the World Bank looks towards acquiring the most basic element of all civilizations, the most valuable global resource, the new commodity for the 21st century - Blue Gold; the next global monopoly the Money-Lenders are looking to dominate. The world's water, once considered a natural resource protected by government agencies is now up for sale to the highest bidder. When you begin to treat water as a commodity, where the price of the water is dependent on supply and demand, you end up with corporate control of all of our drinking water. When you start commodifying the necessities of life in such a way to make it more difficult for people to gain access to those necessities, you have the basis for serious political instability.[47] Water privatization is big business, according to Ruth Caplan; the World Bank places the value of the world water market at $800 Billion.[48] Even the cost of bottled water today is more expensive than the cost of gasoline.

The World Bank in cooperation with global corporations are rapidly buying up local water supplies, and turning it into a private commodity. 75% of the earth's surface is covered with water, only 1% is drinkable. Communities face losing control of one of their most precious resources. Activists are claiming that water is a basic human right, while corporations declare it as a commodity. The IMF and World Bank when entering some countries call for agreements that bind the people to a collection of economic policies that often violate human rights, one of those being the privatization of public water systems as a requirement for loans. The control of water is being taken out of the hands of the people and into the hands of large multinational corporations; they are slowly defining who owns the water.

In 1999, The Bechtel Corporation took over the public water system of Cochabamba, Bolivia. After taking over the water system, they increased water prices for the poorest people by 40%-50%, and in some cases by more than double. Families were literally forced to choose between feeding their children or paying their water bills... When Bolivians sought to exercise their right to peacefully assemble the government sent armed troops into the streets to break the protests. More than 170 people were injured and one 17 year old boy, Victor Hugo Daza, was shot in the face and killed. Protest leaders were arrested in their homes in the middle of the night and flown to a remote jail in Bolivia's jungle.

In the era of economic globalization, these are the lengths to which poor governments feel compelled to go in order to protect the interests of foreign corporations... The World Bank implicitly violated Cochabambinos' right to affordable water by coercing Bolivia into water privatization to begin with (though the Bank argues that it opposed the ultimate deal because it included a dam project that the Bank did not favor). In 1996 Bank officials told Cochabamba's mayor that privatization of the city's water was a condition of assistance for water development. In 1997 Bank officials told the Bolivian President that privatizing Cochabamba's water was a condition of the country receiving $600 million in international debt relief.[49]

World Bank loans are systematically reducing the poorest of people of the developing nations into extreme poverty and misery and then placing even more impossible debt upon their shoulders. The impact of these policies in many countries is devastating. "The Bank, more than any other international institution is responsible for the Third World's rush to socialism and economic collapse."[50]

EUGENIC
BEGINNINGS

One of the many problems the International Money-Lenders have always encountered throughout history is the problem of actually controlling the people they want to dominate. The ruling elite believe there are too many people on the planet, which was made clear in June 1979, when unknown Mr R. C. Christian paid for a huge granite monument engraved with 10 Guides or commandments in eight different languages, the monument is commonly referred to as The Georgia Guidestones; they sit on a hilltop in Elbert County, Georgia in the US. Christian said he represented a group of men who wanted to offer direction to humanity, to transmit a message to mankind. One of the messages to be transmitted is there are too many people on the planet. The first guide or mandate written in stone - states to maintain humanity under 500,000,000 in perpetual balance with nature. At the time of writing there are currently 6.5 billion on the planet, which is 6 billion too many, this will require a reduction of nine-tenths of the world's people.

The current 'population-crisis' is all propaganda and plays an important role in the New World Order Agenda, as the Money-Lenders only need a certain amount of people on the planet at anyone time to keep them in the lifestyle to which they have become accustomed. Environmental concerns are being used as the pretext to bring the planet down to a more manageable size. International media stars, academics and celebrities all on the CFR world stage, all support the environmental cause with pessimistic predictions of global disaster, to justify ever more increasing governmental controls over the economy, the environment and family life. This is nothing new as the global prophets of doom have repeated the same 'out of control' population 'theories' that have gained momentum for the past two centuries.

In the 1800's, Thomas Malthus (1766–1834) highlighted potential dangers of overpopulation in his *Theory of Population*, believing an increase in population would eventually outgrow the food supply, resulting in the starvation of the weakest in what he termed a 'Malthusian catastrophe.' He made the assumption that food supply increases arithmetically while population grows exponentially, meaning that as humans keep breeding, a point is reached where there is 'not enough resources to go round,' and the quantity of food available becomes insufficient to feed everyone; 'everyone' at the time meant the English population... His conclusion was that the English population could not be allowed to continue to grow on its present path. The poor and the lower members of the social scale were to be discouraged from having children. An end had to be put to their "sexual mania."[1]

Malthus viewed overpopulation as the fountain of all misery and believed in depopulation by any means necessary. In his essay on the *'Principle of Population'* Malthus wrote: 'All the children who are born, beyond what would be required to keep up the population to a desired level, must necessarily perish, unless room be made for them by the death of grown persons... if we dread the too frequent visitation of the horrid form of famine, we should sedulously encourage the other forms of destruction, which we compel nature to use... and court the return of the plague.' Apart from the spread of disease, Malthus believed that using vaccines and zoning programs against the poor was a good idea. These ideas were to herald the beginning of the self-preservation method for the ruling class-by the systematic extermination of the lower classes.

On the heels of Malthus in the 1850's, English sociologist Herbert Spencer published *Social Statistics*, popularizing the phrase "survival of the fittest." He asserted the idea that man and society followed the laws of science and not God, he wrote that through evolution; the "fittest" would naturally survive and continue on to perfect society, while the "unfit" would become impoverished, less educated and ultimately die off. He stated: "The whole effort of nature is to get rid of such and to make room for better... If they are not sufficiently complete to live, they die, and it best they should die... All imperfection must disappear."[2] Spencer also advocated no charity for the poor when stating: "Fostering the good-for-nothing at the expense of the good is an extreme cruelty. It is a deliberate storing up of miseries for future generations. There is no greater curse to posterity than that of bequeathing them an increasing population of imbeciles."[3]

In 1859, Charles Darwin's *Origin of Species* introduced the 'scientific theory' that populations evolve from generation to generation through a process of natural selection. Darwin's attention was caught by Malthus's *Essay on the Principle of Population* (1798); Darwin then confirmed that his own theory "is the doctrine of Malthus applied with manifold force to the whole animal and vegetable kingdoms..." These ideas put forward by Malthus, Spencer and Darwin were the foundations to shape the evolutionary ideology of the next century.

The driving force behind this new ideology was the half cousin to Charles Darwin, Sir Francis Galton Darwin, who wanted to increase the good stock or 'good genes' of mankind, while decreasing the inferior stock. Through scientific breeding, Galton believed he could improve the physical and mental qualities of future generations of the elite society, while discouraging the lower classes, the 'unfit,' from perpetuating their offspring. Poverty or "pauperism" as it was called at the time was scientifically held by many esteemed doctors and universities to be a genetic defect, transmitted from generation to generation.[4]

In 1883, Galton named the new 'science' Eugenics; positive eugenics being the philosophy to improve humanity by encouraging wealthy society to have more children, promoting favourable genetic traits using such governmental programs as marriage counselling, state subsidies of large families with a healthy genotype, and so on. 'Negative eugenics' meant the extermination of all people who had undesirable and unfavourable genetic traits, mainly by eliminating procreation. Since marriage counselling by itself was not enough- the government tried unsuccessfully to convince people with unfavourable genetic traits to voluntarily sterilize themselves - a legal means had to be found that would allow the compulsory sterilization of *genetically damaged* men and women.[5] [Emphasis Added] Negative eugenic policies in the past have ranged from segregation, sterilization and even genocide.

Galton and others believed that the mentally 'unfit' suffered from the mental affliction of *'feeblemindedness,'* although no one was quite sure how 'feebleminded' was defined; *'feeble-mindedness'* was truly in the eye of the beholder and frequently depended upon the dimness or brightness of a particular moment.[6] Often the so-called feebleminded were just shy, too good-natured to be taken seriously, or simply spoke the wrong language or were the wrong color.[7] Anyone who was normal but caused trouble could be labelled as 'feeble-minded.' The eugenics movement was gaining ground and went on to argue that 'defectives' should be prevented from breeding, through custody in asylums or compulsory sterilization.

In the late 19th century, feminist author Victoria Woodhull, in her 1891 pamphlet, *The Rapid Multiplication of the Unfit*, insisted: "The best minds of today have accepted the fact that if superior people are desired, they must be bred; and if imbeciles, criminals, paupers and [the] otherwise unfit are undesirable citizens they must not be bred."[8] Even thou 'the best minds' were deciding who can live and who should die; it was all guesswork, self-indulgence and mathematical acrobatics with no scientific evidence to back up theories of 'feeble-mindedness.' In 1892, in the preface to the second edition of *Heredity Genius,* Galton admitted that his theories and formulae were still completely un-provable: "The great problem of the future betterment of the human race is confessedly at the present time, hardly advanced beyond the state of academic interest."[9] Even thou the eugenics movement had no foundations in scientific evidence; this didn't stop the wealthiest of families from forging ahead with the persecution of the most vulnerable, poor and helpless of society with forcible sterilization, committing to mental institutions, and the prohibiting of the 'defectives' from marriage. Although much of the persecution was simply racism, ethnic hatred and academic elitism, eugenics wore the mantle of respectable science to mask its true character.[10]

In 1910, the eugenic extremist and Fabian Socialist George Bernard Shaw lectured at London's Eugenics Education Society about mass murder of the lower classes with lethal gas chambers. Shaw proclaimed: "A part of eugenic politics would finally land us in an extensive use of the lethal chamber. A great many people would have to be put out of existence, simply because it wastes other people's time to look after them."[11]

Coming to America

The English Eugenics movement migrated to America, finding its leader in Dr Charles Davenport, who was fascinated by Galton's work. Davenport's beliefs were revealed when stating: "We protect the members of a weak strain... and then let them free upon the community, and encourage them to leave a large progeny of 'feeble-minded'...[they] are again set free to reproduce, and so the stupid work goes on of preserving and increasing our socially unfit strains."[12] Davenport, esteemed for his Harvard degrees, gained funding from the Carnegie Institution. Now with the prestigious position of operating from the Station for Experimental Evolution of the Carnegie Institution, he was able to lead the 'wandering faithful out of the wilderness of pure prejudice and into the stately corridors of respectability.'[13] Davenport led the American human breeding program for decades, methodically identifying exactly which families were qualified to breed and which were not, it was Davenport who later turned eugenics into a worldwide movement.

In 1910, Mrs E. H. Harriman of the railway fortune provided the funding for the new Eugenics Records Office (ERO), at Cold Spring Harbor New York, built to register and house the genetic backgrounds of all the people of America. Mrs Harriman donated $15,000 per year for operations and would eventually provide more than half a million dollars in cash and securities.[14] John D. Rockefeller's fortune also contributed to the funding... Initial Rockefeller contributions amounted to just $21, 650 in cash... Rockefeller philanthropic entities donated more than just cash; they provided personnel and organizational support, as well as the visible name of Rockefeller.[15]

Harry Laughlin was hired as the 'superintendent' of the ERO; his first major project was to promote the sterilization of 'defectives.' In 1914, he published a Model Eugenical Sterilization Law that proposed to authorize sterilization of the "socially inadequate" – people supported in institutions or "maintained" wholly or in part by public expense. The law encompassed the "feebleminded, insane, criminalistics, epileptic, inebriate, diseased, blind, deaf; deformed; and dependant" – Including "orphans, ne'er-do-wells, tramps, the homeless and paupers." By the time the Model Law was published in 1914, twelve [US] states had enacted sterilization laws.[16]

First International Eugenics Congress

Eugenicists were looking for international acceptance of their beliefs, towards this end; an international conference in London was scheduled. Organized by the British Eugenics Education Society and dedicated to Galton who had died the year prior, the first International Eugenics Congress, July 24th, 1912, opened for five days at the Hotel Cecil in London. Four-hundred delegates representing twelve countries attended the Congress.

Leonard Darwin, son of the famous evolution theorist Charles Darwin and head of the British Eugenics Education Society, the official sponsor of the Congress, presided. Many famous scientists and other prominent individuals and luminaries attended, including Winston Churchill; First Lord of the British Admiralty and Lord Alverstone, the Chief Justice, Lord Balfour, who said the study of eugenics was one of the most pressing necessities of the age. He based his belief in the future progress of mankind on the application of scientific methods to practical life. *The New York Times* announced Dr. C. B. Davenport, Trustee of the Eugenics Record Office, will read a paper on "Marriage and Eugenics" and Bleeker Van Wagenen will deliver an illustrated lecture which will embody the report to the Congress of the Eugenics Section of the American Breeders' Association. This will consist of a study and report as to the best practicable means of cutting off the defective 'germ-plasm' in the human population.[17]

The first Eugenics Congress with notables like Churchill and Darwin was designed to give eugenics panache; and it had worked, the pseudoscience of eugenics had gained an air of respectability. The Congress succeeded in fulfilling its stated goals, particularly regarding the mission of international organization. The London Congress strengthened existing informal contacts between eugenicists of different countries and led to the creation of the Permanent International Commission of Eugenics.[18] The medical establishment began to take notice, presenting eugenics as a legitimate medical concept.[19] Eugenics rocketed through academia, becoming an institution virtually overnight. By 1914, some forty-four major institutions offered eugenic instruction. Within a decade, that number would swell to hundreds, reaching some 20,000 students annually.[20]

The Black Stork

Eugenics received main stream treatment in 1915 when Harry J. Haiselden (1870-1919), Chief Surgeon at the German-American Hospital in Chicago advocated eugenics. Haiselden had caused controversy when refusing to perform needed surgery for children born with severe birth defects, in a blatant act of eugenics he allowed babies to die; one particular child was Alan Bollinger. Haiselden revealed that it was his regular practice to withhold treatment or intentionally hasten the deaths of infants he described as 'defective.' Never before had a physician who supported the non-treatment of those 'better off dead' taken his campaign to the public. Haiselden displayed dying infants to reporters, wrote a six-week-long series of articles for a prominent Chicago newspaper, and lectured on eugenic euthanasia to public audiences.[21] Even Helen Keller endorsed Haiselden's practice of refusing to treat some babies.[22]

In 1917, Eugenics received Hollywood treatment when the eugenics propaganda movie *The Black Stork* was released which was based around Chief Surgeon Haiselden. The film was given a massive national distribution and promotion campaign. Haiselden actually starred in the film, playing himself in a fictionalized account of a eugenically mismatched couple who are counselled by Haiselden against having children because they are likely to be defective. Eventually the woman does give birth to a defective child, whom she then allows to die. The dead child levitates into the waiting arms of Jesus Christ. It was unbridled cinematic propaganda for the eugenics movement... In 1917, a display advertisement for the film encouraged: "Kill Defectives, Save the Nation and See '*The Black Stork*'"[23]

The Abortion Industry

Eugenics began to make in-roads into various institutions. An article in the Eugenics Review, July, 1912, *The Eugenic Appeal in Moral Education* by John Russell advocated sex-education in schools; he writes: "...that it is always a duty to mate eugenically, and sometimes a duty not to mate at all."[24] Eugenics also found its way into child welfare, prison reform, human hygiene, clinical psychology, medical treatment, world peace and immigrant rights, as well as charities and progressive undertakings of all kinds. The most striking of these movements was also one of the world's most overdue and needed campaigns: the birth control movement. The global effort to help women make independent choices about their own pregnancies was dominated by one woman: Margaret Sanger.[25]

Birth control advocate Margaret Sanger established the Planned Parenthood Federation of America (PPFA) in Brooklyn, New York, 1921. Sanger believed that 'feeble-mindedness' was on the increase and that it had 'leaped the barriers,' and as 'scientific eugenicists' had all pointed out, the feeble-minded posed a peril to future generations-unless the feeble-minded are prevented from reproducing their kind.[26] Sanger joined the choir of eugenicists stating that the great problem of which all authorities agreed... was to prevent the birth of those who would transmit imbecility to their descendants. Feeble-mindedness as investigations and statistics from every country indicate is invariably associated with an abnormally high rate of fertility. Modern conditions of civilization... furnish the most favourable breeding-ground for the mental defective, the moron and the imbecile.[27]

Edwin Black's *War on the Weak*, tells us that Sanger always considered birth control a function of general population control and embraced the Malthusian notion that a world running out of food supplies should halt charitable works and allow the weak to die off... Sanger even considered naming her movement "Neo-Malthusianism." She vigorously opposed charitable efforts to uplift the downtrodden and deprived, and argued extensively that it was better that the cold and hungry be left without help, so that the eugenically superior strains could multiply without competition from "the unfit." She repeatedly referred to the lower classes and the unfit as "human waste" not worthy of assistance, and proudly quoted the extreme eugenic view that human "weeds" should be "exterminated."[28]

Sanger became a member of both the American Eugenics Society and the English Eugenics Society. Through close association with some of America's most fanatical eugenic racists, through her publication, *Birth Control Review*, and her public oratory, Sanger helped legitimize and widen the appeal of eugenic pseudoscience.[29]

In her 1922 book, *Pivot of Civilization*, Sanger wrote: The emergency problem of segregation and sterilization must be faced immediately. Every feeble-minded girl or woman of the hereditary type, especially of the moron class, should be segregated during the reproductive period. Otherwise, she is almost certain to bear imbecile children, who in turn are just as certain to breed other defectives. The male defectives are no less dangerous. Segregation carried out for one or two generations would give us only partial control of the problem. Moreover, when we realize that each feeble-minded person is a potential source of an endless progeny of defectives, we prefer the policy of immediate sterilization, of making sure that parenthood is absolutely prohibited to the feeble-minded.[30]

Sanger saw birth control as the highest form of eugenics. "Birth control, which has been criticized as negative and destructive, is really the greatest and most truly eugenic method, and its adoption as part of the program of eugenics would immediately give a concrete and realistic power to that science... Birth Control has been accepted by the clearest thinking and far seeing of the Eugenists themselves as the most constructive and necessary of the means to racial health."[31]

Sanger also founded the American Birth Control League in 1921, which in 1942 became part of the Planned Parenthood Federation of America, Inc. The American Birth Control League advocated the imperative necessity of a 'world program of Birth Control.'[32] Since then, it has grown to have over 820 clinic locations in the United States, with a total budget of approximately US $1 billion, and provides an array of 'services' to over three million people.

The Second Eugenics Congress

The eugenicists held their Second Congress in New York, on September 25th–27th, 1921. The Congress was held at the American Museum of Natural History, who sponsored the meeting; the museum gave the event a Darwinian evolutionary theme. The trustee for the American Museum was Madison Grant, author of *The Passing of the Great Race*, which would later have a big influence on Hitler.

Edwin Black tells us that to give the Congress the appearance of elegance and prestige, money played a major role, with Mrs Harriman donating an extra $2,500 to fund the more than 120 exhibits erected throughout the museum.

These included a prominent exhibit on sterilization statues in the United States. The Carnegie Institution extended a special grant of $2,000 to defray travel expenses for several of the key European speakers.

The *New York Times*, Sept 25th, 1921, reported on the conference that Major Leonard Darwin; son of Charles Darwin attended the Eugenics Congress, stating that the feeble-minded in the United States numbered between 300,000 and 400,000... And all who had studied the problem agreed they should all be segregated and prevented from becoming parents. He called attention to the experiments of the American Stock Breeders' Association in using X-ray for sterilization and preventing criminals from taking up family life.[33]

Major Darwin also proposed that persons of good character and good endowment should be awakened to the danger threatening their race, and that the elite members of society should have more children, stating: "What is necessary is to make it deeply and widely felt that it is both immoral and unpatriotic for couples sound in mind and body to unduly limit the size of their families." He went on to say: "There ought to be a great moral campaign against the selfish regard for personal comfort and social advancement, for these aims must be in a measure sacrificed on the altar of family life, if racial progress is to be insured."[34]

During the Congress Davenport orchestrated the renaming and broadening of the International Eugenics Committee into a permanent International Commission on Eugenics. This renamed entity would sanction all eugenic organizations in "cooperating" member countries, which now included Belgium, Czechoslovakia, Denmark, France, Great Britain, Italy, the Netherlands, Norway, Sweden, Argentina, Brazil, Canada, Colombia, Cuba, Mexico, Venezuela, Australia, New Zealand and the United States.[35]

A decade later, on August 22–23, 1932, the third meeting was also arranged at the American Museum of Natural History in New York City, dedicated to Mary Williamson Averell and presided by Davenport. The *New York Times*, 23rd Aug, 1932, writes that Major Darwin now 88 years old, was unable to attend but sent a report predicting the doom of civilization unless eugenic measures were implemented immediately.[36] It was here at the third Eugenic conference that one Ernst Rüdin was unanimously electexd as the new president of the International Federation of Eugenics Societies. Rudin was the director of the Kaiser Wilhelm Institute for Psychiatry in Munich, which was funded by Rockefeller money. In 1931, Rockefeller approved a ten-year grant totalling $89,000 to Rudin's Institute for Psychiatry.[37] Rudin was the man appointed by Hitler to shape Germany's 'Racial Hygiene' program; the Nazi holocaust was built from American eugenics.

The Passing of the Great Race

Hitler had studied and admired American eugenics, especially *The Passing of the Great Race*, by Madison Grant, Director of the American Museum of Natural History. Hitler claimed *the Passing of the Great Race* was 'his Bible,' and had sent private telegrams of appreciation to Grant for such fine work.

Otto Wagener, head of the Nazi Party's Economic Policy Office from 1931 to 1933, claimed that Hitler had said: "Now that we know the laws of heredity, it is possible to a large extent to prevent unhealthy and severely handicapped beings from coming into the world. I have studied with great interest the laws of several American states concerning prevention of reproduction by people whose progeny would, in all possibility, be of no value or be injurious to the racial stock. I'm sure that occasionally mistakes occur as a result. But the possibility of excess and error is still no proof of the incorrectness of these laws."[38]

The Nazi government proceeded to implement eugenics according to the recommendations as made by Harry Laughlin of the American Eugenics Records Office and modified by Ernst Rüdin. In 1930, Ernst Rudin wrote: "...we have to do something about the positive and negative eugenics before it is too late. For the negative, the sterilization of the genetically sick has to be closely looked at... It would be a blessing to know that genetically incompetent, unhappy people would not be produced anymore. Much more national expansion would be created through positive eugenics than we can imagine.

The fertility rate of the genetically undesirables is so great today that we have every reason in the interest of humanity to address ourselves to the prevention of the genetically weak. The increase of the hereditarily healthy that is so necessary to us as a nation today will cause us less of a headache in the future."[39]

On July 14th, 1933, the Law for the Prevention of Genetically Diseased Children was passed, to go into effect on January 1st, 1934. The main proponent of this legislation was Ernst Rudin. (Translation of the German Law has slight variations; sometimes referred to as the Law for the Prevention of Hereditarily Diseased Offspring, or the Law on Preventing ill Progeny) American eugenicists were conscious and proud of their impact on legislation in Nazi Germany, recognizing that the German Law on Preventing Hereditarily Ill Progeny was influenced by the California sterilization law and designed after the Model Eugenic Sterilization Law developed by Harry Laughlin in 1922.[40]

After the beginning of sterilization in Germany on January 1st, 1934, American *Eugenic News* printed the translation of a German propaganda article about the successful steps undertaken to implement racial hygiene in

Nazi Germany. The author of the article argued that the 'Law on Preventing Hereditarily Ill Progeny... had created a "tremendous sensation all over the world. Scientists and laymen... greeted it enthusiastically as a milestone in the history of mankind and as return from a hitherto wrong path." The law would ensure that "healthy, happy generations can now live and develop with the protection of the state." The article concluded with a quote from an unnamed American scientist: "Germany has made world history with her sterilization law!"[41] American eugenicists were all for the German plan of sterilization, Marion S. Norton, the leading figure of the Sterilization League of New Jersey, who defended the Nazi law against attacks by the American Catholic Church and declared it a model for the United States.

In 1934, Charles Davenport and Harry Laughlin reported that in "no country of the world is eugenics more active as an applied science than in Germany" and praised the Nazi sterilization law: One may condemn the Nazi policy generally, but specifically it remained for Germany in 1933 to lead the great nations of the world in the recognition of the biological foundations for national character. It is probable that the sterilization statutes of the several American states and the national sterilization statute of Germany will in legal history constitute a milestone which marks the control by the most advanced nations of the world of a major aspect of controlling human reproduction, comparable in importance only with the state's legal control of marriage."[42]

The German's didn't stop there; the sterilization law was later extended, with Amendment laws passed on June 26th, 1935, and February 4th, 1936 ...which now included legalized abortion if the pregnant woman had already been singled out for sterilization. Furthermore, a decree dated February 26th, 1936, allowed for the sterilization of women by radiation.[43]

Starting in 1937, criminals and repeat offenders were now being systematically relocated to concentration camps. That practice was followed by orders for "welfare units" to arrest "vagrants, alcoholics, work dodgers, welfare recipients and even already sterilized, feeble-minded women." Eventually, the Law for the Prevention of Genetically diseased Children laid the foundation for a large-scale witch hunt, culminating in the euthanasia program... Nazi psychiatrists extended genetic theories on feeble-minded to include completely normal people and to justify eliminating them for political reasons.[44] The rest of Germany's eugenic history is well known.

Only after the secrets of Nazi eugenics horrified the world, only after Nuremburg declared compulsory sterilization a crime against humanity, did

American eugenics recede, adopt an 'enlightened' view and then resurface as "genetics" and "human engineering."[45]

UNESCO

Three years after World War II as the full extent of the Nazi Eugenic holocaust was realized, Director-General of the United Nations Educational, Scientific and Cultural Organization (UNESCO) and President of the British Eugenics Society (now the Galton Institute) Sir Julian Huxley, wrote in UNES-CO: It's Purpose and its Philosophy: Thus, even though it is quite true that any radical eugenic policy will be for many years politically and psychologically impossible, it will be important for UNESCO to see that the eugenic problem is examined with the greatest care, and that the public mind is informed of the issues at stake so that much that now is *unthinkable may at least become thinkable.*[46] [Emphasis added] In other words, after the Hitler debacle - how can we get Eugenics back on the table?

The problem was 'examined with the greatest care,' abortions, sterilization and vaccinations could now be made 'thinkable' again under the new banner of 'family planning.' The new disguised eugenic movement was now in a position to promote anti-fertility campaigns, or 'population control' measures without raising the suspicions of the public.

Margaret Sanger was still around and the recent Nazi genocide hadn't deterred her from promoting her own brand eugenic propaganda. To stop the 'unfit' from breeding after the war (under the banner of 'family planning'), Sanger raised $150,000 to fund the development of the first human contraceptive pill, first invented by Carl Djerassi at a laboratory in Mexico in 1951. Later, it was Frank Colton, an American chemist, who invented the first commercially available oral contraceptive named Enovid in 1960 and produced by GD Searle and Co. In 1964 Searle took in $24 million in net profits from Pill sales.[47]

A year later in 1952, Margaret Sanger's Planned Parenthood, established in 1921, changed its name to the International Planned Parenthood Federation (IPPF), now with support from eight founding member associations which included the British Family Planning Association (FPA) and the Planned Parenthood Federation of America (PPFA). The IPPF now collaborates with the World Health Organization (WHO), the United Nations Development Program (UNDP), the United Nations Children's Fund (UNICEF), the United Nations Population Fund (UNPF), and the Organization for Economic Co-operation and Development (OECD) to achieve its goals of population reduction.

In 1966, the International Planned Parenthood Federation began award-ing the Margaret Sanger Award annually to honour, in their words: "individu-als of distinction in recognition of excellence and leadership in furthering reproductive health and reproductive rights." In the first year, it was awarded to four men, Carl G. Hartman, William H. Draper, Lyndon Baines Johnson, and Martin Luther King. Later recipients have included John D. Rockefeller III, Jane Fonda, Hillary Rodham Clinton, and Ted Turner. In June 1976, CNN founder and United Nations supporter Ted Turner quoted in the McAlvany *Intelligence Advisor*: "A total population of 250-300 million people, a 95% decline from present levels, would be ideal."

In 1952, 'convinced of their fundamental significance for human well-be-ing, and undeterred by the sensitivity then associated with birth control,' John D. Rockefeller III convened a group of scientists to discuss the implications of a dramatic demographic change. They met in Williamsburg, Virginia, under the auspices of the National Academy of Sciences, and after two and a half days agreed on the need for a new institution that could provide 'solid science' to guide governments and individuals in addressing population questions.[48] This resulted in the birth of the Rockefeller funded Population Council.

Rockefeller appointee Frederick Henry Osborne was the first president of the Population Council; he also helped found the American Eugenics society, now the Society for the study of Social Biology (1946-1952). In his book 'The *Future of Human Heredity*,' Osborne, understanding the eugenics questionable past stated: "Eugenic goals are most likely to be attained under another name than eugenics."[49]

The Population Council and International Planned Parenthood Federa-tion were extremely active in implementing measures for the universal ac-ceptance of contraceptives and 'family planning.' In 1969, Frederick S. Jaffe, Vice-president of Planned Parenthood World Population, sent a Memorandum to Bernard Berelson, President of the Population Council, recommending 'Proposed Measures to Reduce U.S. Fertility.' The memo suggests: restructuring the family unit through the postponing or avoidance of marriage, alter image of ideal family size, compulsory education of children, encourage increased homosexuality, education for family limitation, fertility control agents in the water supply, encourage women to work, compulsory abortion of out-of-wed-lock pregnancies, compulsory sterilization of all who have two children except for a few who would be allowed three, confine childbearing to only a limited number of adults, stock certificate type permits for children, abortion and sterilization on demand, payments to encourage sterilization, contraception and abortion, allow certain contraceptives to be distributed non-medically and available and accessible to all.[50]

Berelson later proposed in his paper '*Beyond Family Planning*,' that the US should go beyond contraception in the U.S., and include contraception for Third World countries, but with the extra stipulation that the U.S. should insist on using 'population control as the price of food aid,' and use all necessary diplomatic and economic pressures on governments and religious groups impeding the 'solution' of the population problem, meaning... food aid will only be given to poor countries if U.S. sterilization, abortion and vaccination policies are adopted.

The United Nations Population Commission November 12th, 1971, adopted a resolution urging, among other things, that all member states... cooperate in achieving a substantial reduction of the rate of population growth [in the countries where it is needed] ...ensure that information and education about family planning, as well as the means to effectively practice family planning, are made available to all individuals by the end of the Second United Nations Development Decade [1980]. The Commission further designated 1974 as World Population Year, invited all member states to participate in the event, and requested the UN-Secretary-General to study the possibilities of developing a global population strategy, including population movements, for promoting and co-ordinating population policies in Member States with the objective of achieving a balance between population and other natural resources...[51]

Alan F. Guttmacher, president of Planned Parenthood-World Population (PPWP) stated in an article in the *New York Times*, on the subject of birth control, "Each country will have to decide its own form of coercion, determining when and how it should be employed... The means presently available are compulsory sterilisation and compulsory abortion." Guttmacher had asserted that an effective program of contraception could offer a "significant contribution" to a new world order.[52]

Standing Room Only American Future

On July 18th, 1969, President Richard Nixon stated: "One of the most serious challenges to human destiny in the last third of this century will be the growth of the population." On March 27th, 1972, the Report of the Commission on *Population Growth and the American Future* with John D. Rockefeller III as Chairman concluded that 'no substantial benefits would result from continued growth of the [US] nation's population' and that the 'population problem' is long run and now requires a long-run response. Population growth was bringing with it a deterioration of the environment, if we don't do something, it will seriously affect our lives in future decades, and the current population growth will lead to "standing room only," the consequences of our actions are important for the welfare of future generations.

The report continues that at some point in the future, the finite earth will not satisfactorily accommodate more human beings, and in the longer perspective, it is both proper and in our best interest to participate fully in the worldwide search for the good life, *which must include the eventual stabilization of our numbers... freedom from unwanted childbearing would contribute significantly to the stabilization of population.* To improve the quality of our existence while slowing growth, will require nothing less than a basic recasting of American values.

The Rockefeller Population Council echoed that the population growth will lead to "standing room only," and must be avoided at all costs. In solving the 'population problem,' w*e will not like some of the solutions we will have to adopt.* 'The United States needs to undertake much greater efforts to understand these problems and *develop international policies to deal with them... the question is when it will happen, and how?'*[53] [Emphasis Added]

NSSM 200

On the recommendations of John D. Rockefeller III, President Nixon commissioned Rockefeller protégé Henry Kissinger to complete the National Security Study Memorandum 200: *'Implications of Worldwide Population Growth for U.S. Security and Overseas Interests'* or NSSM 200 for short. The report was finished on December 10th, 1974 by the United States National Security Council, and adopted as official U.S. policy by President Gerald Ford in November 1975. The NSSM 200 document was de-classified in 1989, and acknowledged by researchers that its purpose was 'population control,' which served U.S. strategic, economic, and military interest at the expense of developing countries. The report put forth that LDC's (Lower developed countries) were growing fast, leading to unprecedented growth rates. Urgent and immediate measures must be taken to globally reduce fertility.

The report advocates the promotion of education, contraception and other population control measures under the guise of 'family planning,' which must be agreed to as a prerequisite for help from the United States. Thirteen countries were targeted in the report for strategic population reduction, which included India, Bangladesh, Pakistan, Indonesia, Thailand, the Philippines, Turkey, Nigeria, Egypt, Ethiopia, Mexico, Colombia, and Brazil.

In the 1980's, Brazil launched an inquiry into United States population activities of a U.S. sponsored program that resulted in the sterilisation of nearly half of Brazil's women, it was sponsored by more than 165 legislators from every political party that is represented in the Brazilian legislature. The investigation was initiated before the U.S. 'family planning' objectives from the Rockefeller NSSM document were released and published in Brazilian major newspapers.

Brazil's Ministry of Health began the investigation into the sterilisation program, which revealed 44 percent of all Brazilian women between the ages of 14 and 55 had been permanently sterilised. The older women had the operation done when the program started. News reports charge that many of these women underwent the operation without their knowledge or consent. The massive sterilisation activities were mainly orchestrated by BEMFAM, the Brazilian affiliate of Margaret Sangers International Planned Parenthood Federation, and several private U.S. population contractors, operating with funds from the U.S. Agency for International Development. These include the Pathfinder Fund, the Johns Hopkins University Population Communication Services project, Family Health International, the John Snow 'Enterprise' program, the Program for the Introduction and Adaptation of Contraceptive Technology (PIACT), and the Association for Voluntary Surgical Contraceptive. All have current activities both in Brazil and in numerous African nations. Some of the Brazilian programs funded through these groups are subcontracted to BEMFAM, while other projects are run by the USAID contractors through paid contacts at Brazilian universities, family planning clinics, firms, and individuals.

In recent years, Brazilian officials have begun to raise objections to the level of population activities in their country. A large shipment of condoms from USAID was held up in customs for over a year and then seized by Brazilian agents as contraband, according to a report released in late 1989 by the Office of the Inspector General at USAID. The same report advised that Brazilian authorities had complained that the level of U.S. population assistance had become "overwhelming and unnecessary."

One of Brazil's most respected journalists and columnists Heraclio Salles said: "They [U.S.] have given and are giving millions of women procedures that do not differ in their final objectives from those employed by the Nazis under the Hitler regime to affect the removal of the Jewish population."[54]

Stealth Sterilization

It may just be a coincidence that Nigeria also targeted for population reduction in the NSSM 200 document reported that the United Nations Children's Fund (UNICEF) campaign to vaccinate Nigeria's youth against polio may have been a front for sterilizing the nation. Dr. Haruna Kaita, a pharmaceutical scientist and Dean of the Faculty of Pharmaceutical Sciences of Ahmadu Bello University in Zaria, took samples of a vaccine to labs in India for analysis.

Using World Health Organization-recommended technologies like Gas Chromatography (GC), Dr. Kaita found evidence of serious contamination. In an interview with Kaduna's *Weekly Trust*, Dr. Kaita said: "Some of the things we discovered in the vaccines are harmful and toxic; some have direct effects on the human reproductive system... I and some other professional colleagues who are Indians who were in the Lab could not believe the discovery."

Dr. Kaita was asked why he felt the drug manufacturers would have contaminated the Oral Polio Vaccine; he gave three reasons: "These manufacturers or promoters of these harmful things have a secret agenda which only further research can reveal. Secondly they have always taken us in the third world for granted, thinking we don't have the capacity, knowledge and equipment to conduct tests that would reveal such contaminants. And very unfortunately they also have people to defend their atrocities within our midst, and worst still some of these are supposed to be our own professionals who we rely on to protect our interests" Dr. Kaita demanded that "those who imported this fake drug in the name of Polio Vaccines...be prosecuted like any other criminal."

The United Nations Children's Fund (UNICEF) has been caught-out many times and embroiled in controversy over sterilizing agents in vaccines. *LifeSiteNews*.com reported that in 1995, the Catholic Women's League of the Philippines, another nation on the NSSM 200 hit-list, won a court order halting a UNICEF anti-tetanus program because the vaccine had been laced with B-hCG, which when given in a vaccine, permanently causes women to be unable to sustain a pregnancy. The Supreme Court of the Philippines found the surreptitious sterilization program had already vaccinated three million women, aged 12 to 45. B-hCG-laced vaccine was also found in at least four other developing countries.[55]

A BBC '*Horizon*' documentary, aired in 1995 showed Sister Mary Pilar Verzosa, who was suspicious of the vaccine program in the Philippines. The government would announce one or two days a year for immunization, which they called national immunisation days, and only women aged 14 to 45 were allowed to come to the health centres for their tetanus shots. It was strange that only women should receive Tetanus shots as records show two-thirds of tetanus deaths in the Philippines were amongst men. She was even more suspicious when she discovered the jabs were to be given five times in three years. (Tetanus shots are given once every ten years in the US).

In the slum areas of the Philippines, women reported their fertility cycles were 'fouled up,' some women experienced bleedings and miscarriages, some losing their babies at a very early stage. The symptoms came soon after the tetanus vaccination - some the following day, others within a week. The vaccines contained Beta-HCG, part of a hormone necessary for pregnancy. This Beta-HCG stimulates antibodies so that if a woman's egg becomes fertilised her own natural HCG will be destroyed and pregnancy will not occur.

Sister Mary began to suspect that the tetanus vaccines were laced with Beta HCG. Through her connections in the Catholic network, a friend removed some of the vials unnoticed, which were sent to an independent laboratory. The report revealed three out of those four vials tested, registered positive for HCG. Sister Mary's suspicions were confirmed that they are not only giving plain tetanus toxoid vaccination to women, they were also injecting anti-fertility hormones.

Sister Mary was not alone, many women and doctors reported similar findings. Dr. Vilma Gonzaga became suspicious when she had two miscarriages, both times after receiving the tetanus jab. She is now suing the government since tests showed she had very high levels of antibodies to Beta-HCG. The government denied allegations, calling the test results 'hogwash,' but Dr Reynaldo Echavez said: "We in the Philippine Medical Association don't believe in what the government is saying. The tests that were made were all positive for HCG ...this can now neutralise the HCG that a woman will produce during pregnancy and abortion will set in."

Dr Fays Schrater stated: "If there is a conspiracy to immunise the women of the Philippines with chorionic gonadotropin (hCG) rather than tetanus, then it requires the knowledge of some member of a government, or two. It requires the participation of a manufacturer to link the chorionic gonadotropin physically to the tetanus toxoid - you can't just throw it in the vial and expect it to do its work. And it requires that it be mislabelled and that it be shipped... who knows what's in it and who is going to distribute it in a guise of tetanus vaccine... All it takes is money and desire and the willingness to lie."[56]

Four years after the NSSM 200 was written in 1974, the United Nations World Health Organization Task Force on Immunological Methods for Fertility Regulation, Special Programme of Research, Development and Research Training in Human Reproduction released a paper on 8th, February 1978 stating: '...one method of fertility regulation which might have wide appeal as well as great ease of service delivery would be an *anti-fertility vaccine*.' The paper goes on to say evidence has been accumulated from work in animals and humans that there exist proteins specific to the reproductive system. If the action of physiologically active proteins could be blocked by immunological techniques, new methods of fertility regulation would become available. The paper goes on to say that anti-fertility vaccines may: (a) prevent sperm transport and/or fertilization; (b) prevent or disrupt implantation; and (c) prevent blastocyst development (Blastocyst formation begins at day 5 after fertilization in humans).[57] [Emphasis added]

Immunize Every Child

The 1974 NSSM 200 document recognized that in most countries, especially the LDC's (Lower Developed Countries), 'population stability cannot be achieved until the next century.' One such organization leading the charge into the next century, which launched in 1999, is the Global Alliance for Vaccination and Immunization (GAVI), a program with the goal to immunize the world via vaccines, 'to make the world a better place.' GAVI will help the United Nation's 'Millennium Development Goals' (MDG's), which are eight international 'development goals,' (we have already seen how the World Bank has 'Developed' third world nations) that all 192 United Nations member states and at least 23 international organizations have agreed to achieve by the year 2015.

The first board meeting of GAVI was held 28th, October 1999, the partners include: national governments, the Bill and Melinda Gates Children's Vaccine Program, the International Federation of Pharmaceutical Manufacturers Associations (IFPMA), research and technical health institutions, the Rockefeller Foundation, the United Nations Children's Fund (UNICEF), the World Bank Group and the World Health Organization (WHO).

In a press release Tuesday 11th, April 2000, the international vaccine alliance calculated that within five years it will be possible to reach nearly half of the 25 million children born every year in poor countries who are not currently being immunized... Global Alliance for Vaccines and Immunization has the long-term goal of ensuring *universal immunization and accelerating the development of new vaccines.*

The Bill and Melinda Gates Foundation provided the initial commitment to the Vaccine Fund with a grant of $750 million over five years. In addition to the possible U.S. funding, governments, corporations and other donors are being approached to provide the additional resources required to reach the goal of $1.75 billion in five years... 50 developing countries have indicated their interest in becoming involved in the global vaccine effort.

GAVI plans to use part of the resources from the vaccine fund for a *performance-based system* under which governments of countries with low current immunization coverage will receive financial incentives to strengthen their health systems to deliver 'immunization.' The basic principle will be to calculate support based on increases in the number of children immunized in a given country. It is hoped that if successful, this approach can become a model for other international health programs... the Vaccine Fund will emphasize the use of safe and simple delivery techniques, such as combination vaccines – *'grouping more than one antigen in a single injection.'* The GAVI strategies to improve immunization services have been outlined in a paper entitled, *"Immunize Every Child."*[58] [Emphasis Added]

In New York, April 14th, 2010, the United Nations announced with only five years left until the 2015 deadline to achieve their Millennium Development Goals, they were concerned they were not going to achieve their targets, so United Nations Secretary-General Ban Ki-Moon took it up a notch, launching a new global effort on women's and children's health, named *"Every Woman, Every Child."* The GAVI Alliance announced it will be supporting the new global strategy over the next 5 years, along with the World Health Organization, UNFPA, UNICEF, UNAIDS and the World Bank, which will focus on women's and children's 'health' in 35 countries.

Other United Nations supporters for the project include the David and Lucille Packard Foundation with $120 million, the Ford Foundation with an estimated $18 million per year for the next 4 years; the United Nations Foundation committing $400 million, through the HAND to HAND Campaign – which is associated with the International Planned Parenthood Federation, the Guttmacher Institute is also involved in the project, named after Alan F. Guttmacher, who was president of the Planned Parenthood Federation of America and a leader in the International Planned Parenthood Federation in the 1960's and early 1970's.[59] Jacqueline Kasun writes in her book *The War Against Popu-*

lation, that the Guttmacher Institute has masterminded the public manipulation of reproduction in the United States, promoting abortion, sterilization, amniocentesis, and genetic screening, as well as foreign population control.[60]

The Bill & Melinda Gates Foundation committed $1.5 billion and through a partnership with Boston's Children's Hospital the Bill & Melinda Gates Foundation will additionally provide $2.4 million to support the development of a neonatal HIV vaccine and $50 million for improving nutrition and health in south eastern Mexico and Central America.[61]

A year previous to the United Nation's "*Every Woman, Every Child*." Campaign, Bill Gates - founder of *Microsoft* and a member of the Council on Foreign Relations, whose father William H. Gates Sr, served on the board of Sangers Planned Parenthood - held a secret meeting in Manhattan on May 5th, 2009 with David Rockefeller, Warren Buffett, Oprah Winfrey, George Soros and Ted Turner at the home of Sir Paul Nurse, a British Nobel prize biochemist and president of the private Rockefeller University. The meeting was to consider how their wealth could be used to *'slow the growth of the world's population.'* The global cabal discussed many topics, but following Gates lead, they all agreed *'overpopulation was a priority.'* One of the guests had stated: "This is something so nightmarish [global population] that everyone in this group agreed it needs big-brain answers," "They need to be *independent of government agencies,* which are unable to head off the disaster we all see looming." When asked why all the secrecy, the guest replied: "They wanted to speak rich too rich without worrying anything they said would end up in the newspapers, painting them as an *alternative world government*."[62] [Emphasis Added]

The following year at the Technology, Entertainment and Design Conference (TED) in 2010, Long Beach, California, Gates reduced the world's problems down to a simple formula: CO_2 (total population emitted CO_2 per year) = P (people) x S (services per person) x E (average energy per service) x C (average CO_2 emitted per unit of energy). After presenting this equation, Gates explained that the goal was to "look at each one of these and *see how we can get this down to zero.*" While discussing 'P', he said: "*Now if we do a really great job on new vaccines, healthcare, reproductive health services*, we could lower that by perhaps 10 or 15 percent."

As of 2011, the Bill & Melinda Gates Foundation officially launched a new program, '*Saving Lives at Birth*,' which is a new program that seeks to treat pregnant women and their new-borns in rural, low-resource settings. The '*Saving Lives at Birth*' program will combine resources from the US Agency for

International Development or USAID, the Government of Norway, the Bill & Melinda Gates Foundation, Grand Challenges Canada and the World Bank. Together, the combined grant funds for the '*Saving Lives at Birth*' program should total around $14 million. Over the course of five years, the sponsors expect to invest about $50 million to '*transform the lives of pregnant women and their babies*' in the most underserved portions of the world.[63] [Emphasis Added]

Chinese Abortion

The United Nations 'family planning' campaigns are not just tied to Third World countries. The Communist Chinese have some of the worst anti-child laws in the world, but in January 2006, that didn't stop the United Nations Population Fund from funding a $27 million Chinese 'family planning' program.

In a report issued by the International Population Assistance and Family Planning Programs: Issues for Congress, July 8th, 2010, The United Nations Population Fund (UNFPA) Executive Board approved the new five-year program for China on January 30th, 2006, prior to the signing, U.S. Deputy Representative to the United Nations, Ambassador Alejandro Wolff, expressed disappointment and argued that the United Nations Population Fund assistance to China provided a "defacto United Nations 'seal of approval'" to Chinese "abhorrent" practices.

In the Hearing on the *Human Rights in China: Improving or Deteriorating Conditions?* ...held before The Subcommittee on Africa, Global Human Rights and International Relations House of Representatives, 109th Congress, Second Session, April 19th, 2006, Human Rights Advocate, and former political prisoner Ms Rebiya Kadeer stated that China's coercive family planning policy has slaughtered more innocent children than any war in human history. Coercive family planning has wounded Chinese women by the millions, and one of the psychological consequences is that some 500 Chinese women commit suicide every day.

China's one child per couple decreed in 1979 has killed hundreds of millions of babies, by imposing draconian fines up to 10 times annual salaries on their parents to force them to abort. Brothers and sisters are illegal, sex selection and abortions are a direct consequence of allowing only one baby per couple, which has led to gendercide, and approximately one hundred million girls are missing in China. One Chinese demographer has admitted that by the year 2020, 40 million Chinese men won't be able to find wives because Beijing's weapon of mass destruction—population control—has destroyed all the girls.[64]

Ms Kadeer spoke of the forced family planning policy that the Chinese Government has forced upon the Uighurs [Pron: Wee-gurs] started in 1987. The forced family planning policy is unacceptable and beyond reason, and very hard on the uneducated women who live in rural areas. As a result, they continue to become pregnant and end up going through three or four abortions, this number of forced abortions affects their health; there is basically no health care system that prevents or helps with a mother's recovery from all of these forced medical procedures. Various female diseases related to female organs are very common amongst women aged 35 to 50 as a result of poor medical attention prior or after the forced abortion. As a result of this ongoing persecution, a gradual ethnic provincial cleansing is going to result in the Uighurs to be wiped out from the face of the earth if this continues in the next 20 years.

Kadeer goes on to say the Genocide Convention couldn't be clearer that when people are targeted in whole or in part because of their ethnicity for destruction, that that is what constitutes the crime of genocide. And it seems that when there is a systematic effort to displace the Uighurs by using migration policies, coupled with depopulating family planning policies that include forced abortion, it would seem to rise clearly to that level. She also added that in Nuremberg, forced abortion was construed to be a crime against humanity when practiced against Polish women by the Nazis. It is no less a crime against humanity today when practiced by the Chinese against a vast array of women in China, including the Uighurs.[65]

But not only is China controlling the birth of its citizens as a means of controlling its population size, but it is also controlling the death of its elderly. In a government report entitled *Communist Persecution of the Church in Red China and North Korea*, dated March 26th, 1959, it is reported that: "All the elderly people 60 years of age and above who cannot work are put in the old people's 'Happy Home.' After they are placed in the home they are given shots. They are told these shots are for their health. But after the shots are taken, they die within two-weeks.[66]

In 1973, *The New York Times* reported that David Rockefeller had stated "Whatever the price of the Chinese Revolution, it has obviously succeeded not only in producing more efficient and dedicated administration, but also in fostering high morale and community of purpose. The *social experiment* in China under Chairman Maos' leadership is one of the most important and successful in human history."[67] [Emphasis Added]

The Australian Stork

Anti-human treatment is not just confined to second and third world countries. Melissa Ohden tells the story of how she was born in August 1977 in the U.S., her biological mother underwent a saline infusion abortion, the abortion took place over five days, and the intent was of course to end her life. She was delivered by a nurse on the fifth day of the abortion procedure; she was believed to be dead and left on the bedside table as they tended to her mother. The nurses noticed the foetus started to make noises and small movements; the nursing staff stepped in and started to provide medical care. The staff did what they were supposed to do which was to provide medical care. Melissa was lucky; laws were in place to provide medical care for her at the time.

In October 2008, the Victorian Parliament in Australia passed what is arguably the worst piece of legislation in Australia's history, the most radical extreme pro-abortion legislation in the world - the Victorian Abortion Law Reform Act 2008. This Act removed any rights for unborn children right up to the time of birth. The new law ensured that children that are aborted and survive are now to be left to die.

Peter Kavanagh MLC, DLP for Western Victoria, Australia said: "One of the Amendments made it clear that once a baby is aborted, if it is born alive, that all medical personnel have a duty of care to that baby, that Amendment was rejected by the majority of members." The public was not informed of this part of the Bill; instead government spin was used to deflect public concern. Other parts of the Bill include: Abortion allowed right up to birth, partial birth abortion allowed, Doctor's freedom of conscience denied, No independent counselling provided, Pain relief (for child) not required. Unborn children can be 'snuffed out' with impunity at any time in its first nine months of life. People are appalled by the truth on finding out that innocent and unprotected babies are aborted each day and survive, but left to die.[68]

WAR ON THE FAMILY

The New World Order means exactly that, a new ordering of the world, which implies the destruction of the 'old' world, the world you and I know today. Part of our old world involves the family, of which Karl Marx wanted to destroy, as anything that holds people together is targeted for destruction. As Confucius once said: 'As Go the Home, So Go the Nation,' the strength of a nation depends upon fixed moral laws and strong family values. The family unit is the heart of a meaningful life; children who grow up knowing the difference between right and wrong establish strong communities, and gain a strong moral compass. In the 21st century Marxism has sought to erode, and ultimately destroy through psychological warfare, long held traditional beliefs and values, attacking 'out-dated' concepts such as a strong family that rallies together. John Robison's *Proofs of a Conspiracy*, published in 1798 had observed that if they [Illuminati] were to govern the world, they '... must acquire the direction of education.'...to root out all religion and ordinary morality, and even to break the bonds of domestic life, by destroying the veneration of marriage vows, and by taking the education of children out of the hands of the parents.'[1]

Subverting children is not unique to the United Nations, Hitler understood the pre-dominant value system of an entire culture could be overturned in one generation if given unlimited access to children; German children belonged to the state, not the parents. Hitler Youth underwent a social transformation; the State installed a compliant servitude and a politically correct attitude from birth. In a speech delivered in 1939, Hitler proclaimed: "When an opponent declares: 'I will not come over to your side,' I calmly say, your child belongs to us already. What are you? You will pass on. Your descendants, however, now stand in the new camp. In short they will know nothing else but this new community."[2]

Another Brick in the Wall

In 1945, Julian Huxley became Director-General of the United Nations Educational, Scientific, and Cultural Organization (UNESCO); one of the chief objectives called for the social engineering of politically correct, emotionally conditioned children for a new future society. Elizabeth S. Force referred to UNESCO as an initiator of family life programs, a school system designed for global citizenship. As director of family life education for the American Social Health Association, she cooperated extensively with various U.N. agencies. In the February 1964 issue of *Journal of Marriage and the Family*, Mrs Force wrote of a UNESCO conference at which she delivered a paper entitled *The Role of the School in Family Life Education*. Commenting on this paper, the editor of the journal wrote: "We think the paper performs an important service for family life teachers in the United States by linking them and their efforts to a movement *which is world-wide in scope*."[3]

UNESCO's role for the New World was revealed in *The Saturday Review* in 1952, which stated: "If UNESCO is attacked on the grounds that it is helping to prepare the world's peoples for world government, then it is an error to burst forth with apologetic statements and denials. Let us face it: the job of UNESCO is to help create and promote the elements of world citizenship. When faced with such a 'charge,' let us by all means affirm it from the housetops."[4]

Julian Huxley wrote in *UNESCO: It's Purpose and its Philosophy*, "The task before UNESCO... is to help the emergence of a single world culture, with its own philosophy and background of ideas, and with its own broad purposes." These 'broad purposes' were revealed in 1947, when President Truman's Commission on Higher Education gave its official blessing to a Nine-Volume UNESCO study - *Towards World Understanding* which became... the blueprint for conditioning American children for the day when their first loyalty will be to a socialistic one-world government under the United Nations.[5]

The belief system of the UNESCO blueprint can be seen in the opening pages of Volume V, *In the Classroom with Children under Thirteen Years of Age:* Before the child enters school his mind has already been profoundly marked, and often injuriously, by earlier influences first gained in the home. On page 58 it states that it is the family that infects the child with extreme nationalism.[6] [Emphasis Added]

G. Brock Chisholm, Director-General of the World Health Organization (WHO), which became a permanent United Nations fixture in April, 1948, 'specialized' in the mental health of children and developed strong views that children should be raised in an intellectually free environment, independent of the prejudices and biases - political, moral and religious ideals of their parents. On September 11, 1954, at the Conference on Education; Asilomar, California, Chisholm stated that children who have been taught to believe what they were told by their parents or their teachers were a *menace to the world*. He also stated: "To achieve world government, it is necessary to remove from the minds of men their individualism, *loyalty to family tradition, national patriotism, and religious dogmas.*" The notion that children are not 'well' and 'infected' with traditional family values has become a constant theme amongst educational circles.

At the Childhood International Education Seminar for teachers in Denver in 1973, Chester M. Pierce, M.D., a professor of education and psychiatry at Harvard, told educators: "Every child in America entering school at the age of 5 is mentally ill because he comes to school with certain allegiances to our founding fathers, towards our elected officials, towards his parents, toward a belief in a supernatural being, and toward the sovereignty of this nation as a separate entity. It's up to you as teachers to make all these *sick children* well - by creating the *international* child of the future.[7] [Emphasis Added]

In 1989, A New Philosophy of Education by Dr. Shirley McCune, Sr. Director, MCREL U.S. Department of Education's objectives for education, stated quite clearly that: "What we are into is the *total restructuring of the society...* the issues for the children, and the issues for society is that what is changed in education *today we no longer see the teaching of facts and information as the primary outcome of education...* we have to prepare students not for today's society, but for a society that's 20, 30, 40, 50 years down the road, and so we have to anticipate what the future is, then move back and figure out what it is that we need to do today, that's called anticipatory socialization or the social change function of schools."

Schools of the Future

Former communist Joseph Z. Kornfeder explained that "UNESCO corresponds to the agitation and propaganda department in the Communist Party. This department handles the strategy and method of getting at the public mind, young and old.[8] To get at the 'public mind,' it was the responsibility of Teachers College at Columbia University, home of Humanist John Dewey, to transmit the UNESCO party line to the educational establishments of America.

John Dewey was the '*Father of Progressive Education*' who redefined the purpose of 'education' in the West. Dewey was amongst the first to promote school as a mechanism for the creation of a Socialist world order, and as a forum for enforcing 'conformity' of the masses rather than as a place to learn the three 'R's.[9] (Reading, wRiting and aRithmetic) The Dewey belief system hypothesised that the environment was constantly changing, therefore the teaching of fixed moral laws and ethical truths to children were all a waste of time. He believed literacy promoted intelligence and independent thinking which was anti-social. In 1899 Dewey said: "Children who know how to think for themselves spoil the harmony of the collective society which is coming where everyone is inter-dependent."[10] The promotion of the group mentality and destruction of a child's individualistic traits is the primary goal of *"Progressive Education,"* no child is permitted to forge ahead of another, all children are equal.

Dewey wasn't the originator of behavioural science or social engineering; he was following in the psychological footsteps developed by German psychologist Wilhelm Maximilian Wundt, the founder of experimental psychology at the University of Leipzig in 1875. Wundt had echoed the philosophy of Jean Jacques Rousseau who believed 'philosopher kings' or elitists should rule the masses through social engineering with a socialist form of government. (Wundt's grandfather is documented as having been a member of the Illuminati secret society...)[11]

Wundt's idea was that schools were orientated more toward the socialization of the child than toward the development of intellect; and for the emergence of a society more and more blatantly devoted to the gratification of sensory desires at the expense of responsibility and achievement.[12] He believed that through a stimulus-response approach (such as Pavlov, who also studied under Wundt) students could be conditioned to exhibit the 'right' kind of responses. Wundt's 'science' based man as an animal without a soul that could be trained to obey and not to think; individualism was to give way to social conformity as education is redefined as 'well-adjusted' children. Wundt's ideas can be seen almost a century later, with a report issued on February 9th, 1993, entitled *Task Force on High School Restructuring*, which doesn't state ... what students should 'know' or 'be able to do,' the report sees schools shaping what students should 'be like.'[13] How did Wundt's ideas emigrate from Germany to be disseminated throughout western culture?

Monopoly on Philanthropy

At the turn of the twentieth century, the name John D. Rockefeller was well known and what he stood for, with targeted investigations by various committees into Rockefeller activities, public opinion was at an all-time low. Apart from hiring Madison Avenue guru Ivy Lee to clean up his image, who advised him to give away dimes to children when out in public, Rockefeller gave $600,000 to the University of Chicago where he met Frederick Taylor Gates, who he hired to take 'philanthropic burdens' of his shoulders. It was Gates who set about organizing the 'monopoly on philanthropy,' funnelling large sums from the fortunes of Rockefeller and the other industrial barons, distributing the money in a way guaranteed to ensure respect for the Rockefellers. One of those 'philanthropic' deeds led to establishing the General Education Board in 1902.

While Rockefeller masqueraded under the facade of philanthropy towards his fellow man, Frederick Taylor Gates expressed the real motivations behind establishing the General Education Board when stating: "In our dreams, we have limitless resources and the people yield themselves with perfect docility to our molding hands. The present education conventions fade from their minds, and unhampered by tradition, we work our own good will upon a grateful and responsive rural folk. We shall not try to make these people or any of their children into philosophers or men of learning, or men of science. We have not to raise up from among them authors, editors, poets or men of letters. We shall not search for embryo great artists, painters, musicians nor lawyers, doctors, preachers, politicians, statesmen, of whom we have an ample supply... The task we set before ourselves is very simple as well as a very beautiful one, to train these people as we find them to a perfectly ideal life just where they are. So we will organize our children and teach them to do in a perfect way the things their fathers and mothers are doing in an imperfect way, in the homes, in the shops and on the farm."[14] Board Trustee Walter Hines Page also stated: "The world lies before us. It'll not be the same world when we get done with it that it was before."[15] Raymond Fosdick's memorial history of the Rockefeller General Education Board was more open when he indicated that it will be part of John D. Rockefeller, Jr.'s effort towards "this goal of social control."[16]

Behaviourism Comes To America

G. Stanley Hall was the first of Wundt's students to bring the new behavioural 'science' from Germany to the United States where upon he organized the psychology laboratory at John Hopkins University in 1887. Hall's attitude toward education is revealed in 1898 when proclaiming the benefits of illiteracy, stating that: "Illiterates escape much eye strain and mental excitement... and certain temptation."[17] Dewey enrolled as a student at Hopkins University and it was here that he was mentored with Hall's wisdom. Dewey went on to become the head of the prestigious Teachers College at Columbia University in New York, where he developed the term '*Progressive Education*.'

The Dewey philosophy was taking hold just about the time John D. Rockefeller established The General Education Board, it was Rockefeller money that financed the Columbia Teachers College, promoting the Wundtian, Dewey, socialist school of education. With unlimited funds available to the psychologists to spread their 'science' throughout America, Dewey put together a group of young educationalists, namely Dr. George Counts and Dr. Harold Rugg, who referred to themselves as *Frontier Thinkers*. In his book, *The Great Technology*, written for teachers in 1933, Rugg stated: "A new public mind is to be created. How? Only by creating tens of millions of new individual minds and welding them into a new social mind. Old stereotypes must be broken up and new 'climates of opinion' formed in the neighbourhoods of America."[18] It was Counts and Rugg who added the concept of using the schools as an instrument for 'building a new social order'... they were also to play a major role in the rewriting of textbooks and curriculum materials to produce the "new philosophy of life and education."[19] Rene Wormser in his book *Foundations: Their Power and Influence* tells us that five million copies of the books were poured into American schools up to 1940.[20] It was the Rockefeller General Education Board... which provided over $50,000 for the production of these books, taken over and intensively promoted by The National Education Association (NEA).[21] The State of California barred these books from its schools after the Dilworth Committee investigated the textbooks by Rugg and concluded they were subtle attempts to play up Marxism and to destroy our [American] traditions.[22]

The work of Counts and Rugg laid the foundation for the eventual destruction of the U.S. Constitution and the free market system so that America could be easily merged into a socialistic world federation under UNESCO guidelines.[23] By the 1950's fully 20% of all American school superintendents and 40% of all teacher college heads had received advanced degrees under Dewey at Columbia.[24]

Dennis Cuddy reveals that the 'progressive educators' (largely from Teachers College, Columbia University) had obtained key positions in Colleges of Education and as school superintendents and principles around the nation, from which they could appoint teachers to their liking. By the early 1960's, sufficient 'progressive' teachers were in place throughout the land, so that education in general shifted from an emphasis on the cognitive academic basics to the affective domain of feelings and relationships.[25]

The '*Frontier Thinkers*' also gained the prestige of the largest professional teacher's organizations and captured and controlled the top jobs of the National Education Association (NEA). In the 1940's, the NEA set up a think tank, the National Training Laboratory (NTL), in which their training manual for teachers says of children: "Although they appear to behave appropriately and seem normal by most cultural standards, they may actually be in need of mental health care in order to help them change, adapt, and conform to the planned society in which there will be no conflict of attitudes or beliefs."[26] In a later report, entitled *Education for the 70's,* the NEA wrote: Schools will become clinics whose purpose is to provide individualised, psycho-social treatment for the student, and teachers must become psycho-social therapists. This will include biochemical and psychological mediation of learning, as drugs are introduced experimentally to improve in the learner such qualities as personality, concentration and memory.[27]

The ultimate goal of behavioural science is the establishment of scientific control over individuals and society, now commonly known as sociology. Its advocates define human behaviour as fixed and determined by material circumstances, without any control by 'free will.' It claims people are pawns of their environment, and therefore should be "understood" and excused for any wrongdoing. The ultimate goal of behavioural science is the establishment of scientific control over individuals and society.[28]

Full Frontal Assault

In a letter to Congressional colleagues, Henry Hyde, Chairman of the U.S. House of representatives Judiciary Committee stated: "Behaviour modification is a significant part of restructuring our schools. School children will be trained to be 'politically correct,' to be unbiased, to understand diversity, and to accept 'alternative lifestyles.'[29] The 'diversity' and 'alternative lifestyles' is the new concept of sex education that was hatched in 1964 with the UNESCO sponsored International Symposium on Health Education, Sex Education and Education for Home and Family. Birgitta Linner, author of *Sex and Society in Sweden*, reported at the United Nations conference that a universal sex education program was "put forth by two Swedish delegates... [and] was accepted by the majority of the delegates." The Swedish Program outline for sex education was:

- Differences between the sexes (anatomical, physiological, emotional, psychological, genetic), structure and function of genitals, menstruation, and masturbation.
- Boy-girl relationships...
- Childbirth, conception...
- Sterility, impotence, and frigidity...
- Abortion...
- Birth control...
- Venereal disease...
- Sexual deviations.[30]

Shortly after the symposium was held in 1964, the Sex Information and Education Council of the United States (SIECUS) was born. The SIECUS concept of sex education is identical to the Swedish program put forward which is now adopted by UNESCO. SIECUS is nothing more than a programme of social engineering through sex education in schools... to erase the traditional moral values of the Judeo-Christian code and replace them with situation ethics and the 'new morality.'[31] Congressman John Rarick of Louisiana, speaking in the House of Representatives on June 25th, 1968, on the topic of SIECUS-generated sex education stated: "Through the promotion of pornography, drug use and the "New Morality," the will to resist the International Communist Conspiracy is being awakened... 'Situation ethics' and the idea that there is no longer any 'right or wrong' way to act, along with the downgrading of the influence of the family and religion play right into the hands of the Communists.[32]

As Claire Chambers tells us in *The SIECUS Circle*, that since its inception, the SIECUS orbit has expanded to envelop publishing houses, film producers, governmental and private agencies, foundations, medical societies, educational institutions, and religious bodies. This massive network of interlocking organizations is the power structure through which SIECUS operates to exert pressure on local schools and an unsuspecting public to adopt its sex education program.[33] She goes on to explain how the SIECUS-generated public school sex education helps further the New World Order Communist cause:

1. The very concept of teaching sexual morality on a mass scale is collectivistic. The American tradition reserves this fundamental right for parents within the privacy of the home.
2. Sensitivity training is employed; this, in essence, is a form of "brainwashing."
3. Darwinism is the prevailing theme. Most sex education materials consistently speak of man as an animal, omitting any reference to him as a spiritual being.
4. The program blatantly teaches students to formulate their values on the basis of Humanism's "situation ethics," rather than on the laws of God.
5. Some of the materials pit the child against his parents, in an effort to break down parental authority and redirect the child's obedience to the authority of the State.
6. A negative outlook toward traditional family life is promoted. The abolition of the family as we know it is another Communist objective.
7. Other home and family living materials pit race against race, another tactic used in Communism's "divide and conquer" strategy.
8. Often injected into the curriculum is pornography, which ultimately debases man.
9. Individualism is discouraged by an emphasis on "group conformity," a concept that "ripens" human beings for eventual subjugation.
10. Birth control is treated in such a way as to prepare youth for world population control - another collectivist concept.
11. Materials designed to stimulate sociological discussion usually deride the free enterprise system and promote instead the socialistic concepts of a Marxist State.[34]

John Stormer's *None Dare Call It Education* outlines texts developed by SIECUS for sex education classes, to demonstrate to parents what their children are to be 'taught' in schools:

AGES 5-8: Both girls and boys have body parts that feel good when touched (p. 11); Sexual intercourse occurs when a man and a woman place the penis inside the vagina (p. 12); some men and women are homosexual, which means they will be attracted to and fall in love with someone of the same gender (p. 15); touching and rubbing one's own genitals is called masturbation. (p. 32).

AGES 9-12: Sexual intercourse provides pleasure (p. 12); there are ways to have genital intercourse without causing pregnancy (p. 12); Homosexual love relationships can be as fulfilling as heterosexual relationships (p. 15); Members of the same family may have different values (p. 25); Masturbation is often the first way a person experiences sexual pleasure (p. 32); Many boys and girls begin to masturbate for sexual pleasure during puberty (p. 32); Masturbation does not cause physical or mental harm (p. 32).

AGES 12-15: Some of the reproductive organs provide pleasure as well as reproductive capability (p. 12); some young people have brief sexual experiences with the other gender but mainly feel attracted to their own gender (p. 15); It is common for people to feel some attraction to men and women (p. 15); Sexual orientation cannot be changed by therapy or medicine (p. 15); Gay men, lesbian women, and bisexuals can lead fulfilling lives (p. 15); Masturbation, either alone or with a partner, is one way a person can enjoy and express sexuality without risking pregnancy or an STD/HIV (p. 33).

AGES 15-18: Teenagers who have questions about their sexual orientation should consult a trusted and knowledgeable adult. (P. 16); the telephone number of the gay and lesbian switchboard is 1-212... (p. 16); for most people, sharing a sexual experience with a partner is the most satisfying way to express sexuality (p. 33); Some common sexual behaviours shared by partners include kissing, touching, caressing, massage, sharing explicit literature or art, bathing/showering together, and oral, vaginal, or anal intercourse (p. 33); Individuals are responsible for their own sexual pleasure (p. 33).[35]

Humanism

Much of the sex education material currently available to young people describes sexual intercourse in terms of 'boy' and 'girl' activity, rather than 'husband' and 'wife.' It is difficult to find any mention of marriage as a positive relationship to aim for.[36] Nowhere is it taught the age old wisdom that a man can make a house, while the woman can make a home. Young people are given no concept of right and wrong, and presented with the moral absolutes of - use contraceptives when you have sex and don't worry if you get pregnant - you can always get an abortion. It's all part of the John Dewey system of education to break down the family unit.

The value system or philosophy the younger generation are exposed to and persuaded to adopt for the New World Order is humanism, which received an update in 1933 and 1973, when the Humanist Manifestos I and II were drafted respectively, signed by leading humanists of the day, John Dewey, B. F. Skinner and Sir Julian Huxley of UNESCO. These two documents define and underpin the philosophy that is helping to reshape society.[37]

Humanists believe in the Darwinian theory of evolution, a theory that is often presented as fact in many schools and textbooks. Humanists believe that everyone has a right to full sexual freedom, the right to express their individual sexual preferences as they desire. They believe that everyone, regardless of age or condition, has a right to determine the values and goals that affect their lives. They believe in the right to suicide, abortion and euthanasia. They adhere to situation ethics morality, meaning they do not live by or believe in absolute standards of morality. They recognize no immutable rights or wrongs as revealed in the Ten Commandments. They believe everyone has a right to maximum individual autonomy, meaning the right of each to do his own thing, whatever it may be. Humanists do not believe in national sovereignty, but in a world government.[38]

Humanism substitutes moral absolutes for arbitrary absolutes or 'situational ethics.' Children are taught to reject a moral code of conduct, that there is no such thing as absolute truth, and that lying, cheating, stealing or committing fraud, etc., are totally acceptable within society, as the end justifies the means. The new morality obscures the line between what a Christian would instinctively know to be right or wrong.

In Allyn and Bacon's 1978 high school psychology book, *Inquiries in Sociology* students read: There are exceptions to almost all moral laws, depending on the situation. What is wrong in one instance may be right in another. Most children learn that it is wrong to lie. But later they may learn that it's tactless, if not actually wrong, not to lie under certain circumstances. (Page 45)[39]

To give an example of a 'situational ethic,' consider a 1985 conference of the Society for the Scientific Study of Sex (SSSS, a SIECUS front), Dr. Mary Calderone, the first executive director of SIECUS, [who was also closely linked to Planned Parenthood] participated in a panel discussion on child sex abuse. Some of the participants were startled when Calderone contributed a kind word for paedophilia: "I... have a question that is... almost the reverse of what we've been talking about. What do we know about situations in which young children and older people, stronger people, have had a sexual relationship of one kind or another that has been pleasant, and the child feels good about it because it's warm and seductive and tender?... If the child really enjoys this, it may be the only time the child ever gets a loving touch."[40] Tried and tested value systems that have evolved over thousands of years that have kept the social order together are slowly, systematically being attacked in favour of the 'new morality.'

For several generations schools and even churches have promoted "situational ethics" rather than the concept that there are absolute values of right and wrong that do not change. As a result, research by George Barna and Associates in 1994-95 found that 71% of Americans surveyed reject the concept of absolute truth. Even more disturbing, 61% of those who claimed to be born again Christians concluded that "there is no such thing as absolute truth."[41] "Humanism is the denial of God and the total affirmation of man... Humanism is really nothing else but Marxism."[42]

Condoms, Masturbation and Abortion

Peter Dawson, OBE wrote in the forward to Valerie Riches' book *Sex Education or Indoctrination* that the key to good sex is not self-gratification and self-service but the tender loving care of one person for another. But during [his] eight years as the leader of an Ofsted team of school inspectors [in England]; such a proposition had never reached his ears. Dawson also explains the focus of most sex education lessons had to do with what sort of contraceptives are available, and how to obtain a sufficient supply for one's 'teenage needs.' The glorious future promise of the morning-after pill being made available from the school nurse was frequently offered.[43]

Valerie Riches' had become interested in the subject of school sex education when her 14 year old came home from school, overwhelmed by the content of a sex lesson by a Family Planning Association trained biology teacher. She says the full range of contraceptives had been demonstrated to the students with the message that party-going inevitably led to sexual intercourse, and that a means of birth control was therefore a prerequisite. If, however, a pregnancy resulted, an abortion could always be arranged.[44] As a spokesman stated on behalf of the FPA's Education Service in 1969: "Contraceptive education has to be given very young, it is almost too late when the children get to puberty... children in school are a captive audience."[45]

Public opinion is formed through carefully crafted propaganda campaigns to accept sex education in schools. Valerie Riches' *Sex Education or Indoctrination* writes that to soften public opinion, headlines such as 'Fourteen-year-old dies after giving birth in churchyard' is ideal material to sensationalize the cause of sex education in the classroom. Slogans are used like 'every child a wanted child,' 'safe sex for teenagers,' 'meeting the needs of young people' and 'the right to confidentiality,' to suggest that if underage girls were given sex education, with free access to contraceptives without fear of their parents knowing, they would not end up pregnant. Following such spurious propaganda we are then confronted with proposals, articles and studies to reinforce the arguments, none of which bears too much scrutiny for scientific validity.[46]

Right to Sexual Freedom

Dr. Richard Farson, a psychologist and author is president of the Western Behavioural Sciences Institute, who heads the International Leadership Forum (ILF), a core group of 'Fellows' of the International Leadership Forum which included former president of Planned Parenthood Gloria Feldt[47] wrote Birthrights: *A Bill of Rights for Children* in 1974, in which he writes that parents perceive it is their fundamental right to have children and to raise them as they see fit, the 1970 White House Conference on Children, however, offered a different view. The conference held that the rights of parents cannot infringe upon the rights of children. As a society we may soon come to a similar conclusion, that the ability to conceive a child gives one no right to raise that child, and that raising a child gives one no right to dominate or abuse him. The decisions about a child's home environment should not belong to his parents alone. The child must have some rights to choose also. And if he is too young to choose, his rights must be protected by having an advocate acting in his behalf.

Although the child cannot choose his parents in the genetic sense, he should be able to choose them in an environmental sense. The child cannot avoid deriving his genetic makeup from his parents, but he should have the opportunity, if he chooses, to avoid their daily influence. He must be provided with alternatives to his parents' home environment.[48] He later tells us in spite of our romantic myths about natural families; parents are not all that necessary or beneficial for children.[49]

Farson also believes the right to sex information implies the right to a straightforward answer from a parent or teacher, advocating the elimination of all forms of censorship which keep children ignorant about sex and giving them access to all of the information to which adults have access... [And] include the right to enter stores and theaters where 'adult only' films, magazines, and other sexual entertainment are presented. He also writes that as far as pornography is concerned we must recognize it as an important source, even if we find it personally distasteful... [It can] provide many answers which the child simply does not get from adults... If it is information available to adults, it must also be available to children.[50]

Another propagandist in the same camp was author of *Escape from Childhood*, John Holt, who writes: I urge the law grant and guarantee to the young the freedom that it now grants to adults... This means, in turn, that the law will take action against anyone who interferes with the young people's right to do such things. He further states... What we can and should do is leave to the child the right to decide how good his home seems to be and give him the right if he does not like it to choose something else. The state may decide to provide or help provide some of these other choices... It should give the child the right to say no to it as well as to his parents.[51]

The rights of the child to do what they please and tell parents where they can stick it is making its way through the United Nations Conventions on the Rights of the Child (UNCRC), the state education system that will provide the framework to completely destroy parental authority. The United Nations International Children's Emergency Fund (UNICEF), even has the slogan. *"UNICEF, because every child is our own."*

The United Nations Convention on the Rights of the Child is a human rights treaty that set out the civil, political, economic, social, health and cultural rights of children worldwide. Nations that ratify this convention are bound by international law to comply. It came into force on 2 September 1990, as of November 2009, 194 countries have ratified the treaty, including every member of the United Nations except Somalia and the United States of America. Somalia's cabinet ministers have announced plans to ratify the treaty. Governments of countries that have ratified the Convention are required to report to the United Nations Committee on the Rights of the Child periodically to be examined on their progress with regards to the advancement of the implementation of the Convention and the status of child rights in their country.

Colossians 3:20 states: "Children, obey your parents in all things: for this is well pleasing unto the Lord." Writing for the majority, Chief Justice Burger made this comment... The law's concept of the family rests on a presumption that parents possess what a child lacks in maturity, experience, and capacity for judgement required for making life's difficult decisions. More important, historically, it has been recognized that the natural bonds of affection lead parents to act in the best interests of their children. [1 W. Blackstone, Commentaries 447; 2 J. Kent, Commentaries on American Law 190][52] He goes on to say that some parents "may at times be acting against the interests of their children" [which] creates a basis for caution, but it is hardly a reason to discard wholesale those pages of human experience that teach that parents generally do act in the child's best interest... The statist notion that government power should supersede parental authority in all cases because some parents abuse and neglect children is repugnant to American tradition.[53]

The United Nations Convention is designed to transfer parental rights and responsibilities to the State, giving children the right to disregard parental authority, undermining the family with rights that the child can ignore parental guidance.

Ingrid J. Guzman's *Parent Police* explains that Article 3 of the UNCRC concerning all actions of the child, that the courts, social service workers, and bureaucrats are empowered to regulate families based on their *subjective* determination of the "best interest of the child."[54] The responsibility is to shift from parental judgement and decision making to the state, and ultimately to the United Nations. Article 4 goes on to say these rights must be enforced; the United States would be required to "undertake measures to the maximum extent of available resources... within the framework of international cooperation in order to *restructure society* in accordance with the implementation of these rights."[55] [Emphasis Added]

Article 7 states all children should be registered at birth, insuring control over development by the State and the United Nations. There are severe limitations on the parent's right to direct and train their children as they see fit, under Article 13... Parents could be subject to prosecution for any attempt to prevent their children from interacting with material they deemed unacceptable. Children are vested with a "freedom of expression" right which is virtually absolute.

Article 14 states children are guaranteed "freedom of thought, conscience and religion." Children have a legal right to object to all religious training. Alternatively, children may assert their right against parental objection to participate in occult, Muslim or Buddhist worship services.

Article 15 declares... parents could be prevented from forbidding their child to associate with people deemed to be objectionable companions. Under Article 15, children could claim a "fundamental right" to join gangs, cults, and racist organizations over parental objection.

The United Nations wants to establish the child's 'right' to purchase and use contraceptives, the 'right' to heterosexual and homosexual promiscuity, and the 'right' to pornography in the home.[56] With Senate ratification, this will become the "law of the land." Children cannot escape their 'right' to have sex pushed on them by the United Nations and the government. Even on the street, children as young as eight playing in the park are handed free condoms.[57]

At present, parents have the right to intervene, if UNCRC is ratified by the Senate, the "law of the land" will give children their 'right' to make homosexuality, bestiality, tantric sex and all base pornography the new normal in the home, and for parents that don't comply with the wishes of the child, they will be prosecuted as 'violating' the child's 'right' to sexual freedom. An intensive bureaucracy will be set up for the purpose of... identification, reporting, referral, investigation, treatment, and follow-up of parents who, in violation of the child's 'rights,' treat their children negligently.[58]

UNESCO Dirty Sods

The child's right to masturbate, to watch porn, engage in gay, straight, anal or bestiality sex received an update on September 3rd, 2009, when UNESCO released a new draft proposal for their international Sexuality Education guidelines. UNESCO pulled an earlier draft of the guidelines from its website after they sparked international controversy and criticism from conservative and religious groups: Conservative commentators in America were particularly vocal about that draft's suggestion of discussion about masturbation for children as young as 5 years old.

UNESCO guidelines promote sex education as a "demonstrably effective programme for young people." UNESCO's guidelines argue that sex education helps to postpone the onset of sexual activity among young people, reduce the number of sexual partners and unprotected sex they are having, and decrease the rate of sexually transmitted infection and unplanned pregnancy.

The new UNESCO guidelines place emphasis on condom use, frank discussions of masturbation, homosexuality, and abortion. UNESCO explains Sexuality Education guidelines, coordinated with other U.N. agencies including UNICEF and the World Health Organization, are intended to help U.N.

member countries improve sex education and sexual health, particularly among young people and in the developing world, to reduce illegal abortions, and to reduce the spread of sexually transmitted infection, including HIV and AIDS.[59]

On March 3rd, 2011, the Catholic Family and Human Rights Institute in New York held an event for the Commission on the Status of Women (CSW). Diane Schneider, representing the National Education Association (NEA), now the largest teachers union in the US, told a panel on combating homophobia and transphobia that "Oral sex, masturbation, and orgasms need to be taught in education." Schneider advocated for more "inclusive" sex education in US schools, with curricula based on liberal hetero and homosexual expression. Comprehensive sex education is "the only way to combat hetero-sexism and gender conformity," Schneider proclaimed, "and we must make these issues a part of every middle and high-school student's agenda." "Gender identity expression and sexual orientation are a spectrum," she explained, and said that those opposed to homosexuality "are stuck in a binary box that religion and family create."

The CSW also promoted the U.N. system, a panel sponsored in part by the United Nations Population Fund (UNFPA) advocated for "comprehensive sex education" not only as a tool to combat "gender oppression," but also as the key to achieving all of the Millennium Development Goals. The panellists presented the UNESCO guidelines on Sex Education, as well as a new International Planned Parenthood Federation-sponsored curriculum as the gold standard for comprehensive sex education. The panellists also insisted that these programs be implemented in schools in order to reach as many students as possible, and they also recommended they start as soon as possible, given the fact that many girls in developing countries leave school before the age of sixteen.[60]

It is only too well known that Britain has the highest teenage pregnancy rate in Europe.[61] But this fact hasn't stopped the implementation of further plans to educate the young people of Britain with even more explicit measures for sex education. In 2011, the UK newspaper *The Dailymail* reveals vulgar and graphic materials cleared for schools to teach sex education, which include adult language and sexual intercourse to schoolchildren as young as five. The materials are to be promoted by local councils and the BBC. The *Primary School Sex and Relationships Education Pack* by HIT UK includes material to allow children aged five to 11 to learn about different sexual positions. It also encourages primary aged children to learn about 'oral sex,' 'prostitution' and 'anal intercourse.' The dossier, compiled by the Christian Institute, also pin-points a book called *Let's Talk About Sex*, by Robie H Harris, which includes a chapter on heterosexuality called 'Straight and Gay.' Norman Wells, of the Family Education Trust, said the use of explicit teaching tools was 'deeply concerning' and eroded 'traditional moral standards.'[62] As former Secretary-General of the United Nations U Thant once stated: "The world will not change and find peace if there is not a new education."[63]

UNITED NATIONS OF RELIGION

"You will know the truth and the truth will set you free." John 8:32. The Bible warns that in the last days people would be deceived in such a way, that they would turn from God's truth to mythology. Time was when faith ruled. It is no accident the 21st century has witnessed a spiritual transformation as we move from the Age of Pisces, towards the dawning of the New Age of Aquarius.

Moving into the Aquarian Age, Kathy Newburn in *A Planetary Awakening* explains the old and outworn ways of living and being that may have been suitable to the earlier time and generation must be cleared away as they no longer meet humanity's needs and clash with the new time and generation that are coming... Under the influence of the energies of Aquarius, the focus is shifting from religion to a 'broad-based spirituality' and to recognition of the authority of the soul, the master within.[1] Newburn later reveals that what we are preparing for is a 'planetary awakening of such magnitude that it will transcend... all the world's faiths.'[2]

The 'planetary awakening' of the Aquarian Age has nothing to do with what we would associate with Western Judeo-Christian family values and morals. Christians are enemies of the globalist goals because they do not believe in pantheistic nature worship, the pagan spiritualism behind the environmental movement. Brannon Howse, in *The Battle for Your Faith, Family and Freedoms,* describes that by destroying the influence of Biblical Christianity within a culture, globalists remove their main obstacle to socialism, radical environmentalism, active euthanasia through socialized medicine, compulsory abortion, the end of parental authority, the elimination of an armed populace, private property, homosexuality (homosexuals are favoured because they do not reproduce and add to world population), and the indoctrination of our children with their worldview. Peter Singer, who teaches ethics at Princeton University, makes this clear: "Christianity is our foe.... we must destroy the Judeo Christian religious tradition."[3] Our New Age teachers of the new philosophy have been described as 'supreme spiritual executives,' men and women of extraordinary capacities who will be able to implement sweeping changes in the direction of our planetary civilization.[4]

Society's new spiritual makeover comes complete with a new set of common values. In the name of tolerance, diversity, and understanding, society is to accept a new spiritual consciousness, a hodgepodge mix of New Age Mysticism, Socialism, Collectivism, Humanism, Occultism, Pantheism (Earth Worship), Hinduism, Communism and many other ism's, all wrapped up in a trendy, feel-good package of an 'Earth Centered, We Are All One, Planetary Consciousness,' a United Nations of Religion. As the mystics have always said, a new world is a new mind.[5]

To help formulate the 'New Mind,' the United Nations built the 'Temple of Understanding,' constructed on 50 acres by the Potomac River in Washington, DC... sponsors included many of the usual suspects, such as John D. Rockefeller IV (CFR), socialist leader Norman Thomas, and Robert S. McNamara (CFR).[6] The priesthood which helped create and operate the Temple of Understanding is the United Lodge of Theosophists of New York, through the tax-exempt Lucis Trust.[7] The United Nations also has a Meditation Room maintained by the Lucis Trust at their headquarters in New York, designed in 1952 by Dag Hammarskjold, the same loving 'humanitarian' to personally oversee the Katanga operation in the Congo. The shrine contains no symbols of the world's major religions.

The spiritual life of the United Nations advocates the worship of Christ the divine 'light-bearer,' who is Lucifer, not Jesus Christ. As the late Bill Cooper describes the philosophy: "...here's their metaphor, Adam and Eve were held prisoner in the Garden of Eden by an unjust, cruel and vindictive God, until Lucifer, through his agent Satan set man free from this Garden by giving him the gift of intellect. Through the use of intellect, man will conquer the earth, will conquer nature and will himself become God, [this is] taught in every masonic temple in this land, every secret brotherhood, every secret society, every mystical temple, every occult organization teaches the Luciferian philosophy."

The 'Great Work' seeks to perfect that which was left imperfect through the understanding of science and nature. With the help of the United Nations, Jesus Christ, and 'out-dated' Christianity will not make it into the New World, the Money-Lenders are driving Jesus from the United Nations Temple. As researcher Dr. Scott Johnson remarked: "Satan's good at what he does."

The Lucis Trust is a direct descendent of the 'Mother of the New Age,' Helena Blavatsky's Theosophy Society, the 'practical occultism' of many individuals and groups, including Adam Weishaupt's Bavarian Illuminati,[8] and later Hitler's Nazi Party. Blavatsky's Theosophical concepts of a spiritual hierarchy attracted successor Alice Bailey, who joined the society, moving to the headquarters at Krotona in 1917, where she edited the society's periodical, *the Messenger*, and later marrying Foster Bailey in 1920.

While out walking in the hills in November 1919, Alice Bailey was contacted by a 'spiritual master,' Djual Khul, who came to be known as 'The Tibetan.' Khul dictated a series of books telepathically to Alice Bailey. The first book *Initiation, Human and Solar*, was 'channelled' in 1920, over the next 30 years some 18 other books were produced.[9] The books 'channelled' through Bailey detailed the uniting of Eastern Religion with Western occult practices, which has since become the foundation of what we know today as the modern day 'New Age Movement.'

Bailey originally set up the Lucis Trust in New York in the 1920's as the Lucifer Publishing Company, for organising and promoting her occult books, but the name Lucifer Publishing Company had to be changed as Lucifer gave away too much of the true nature of 'The Plan.'

New Age teaching informs us of a spiritual dimension we can tap into beyond the physical realm, and through meditation, we can channel higher powers to attain knowledge. New Age thinking also believes in all forms of monism, 'All is One,' and the underlying belief that 'Man is God.' New Age thinking has since become main-stream, as Alice Bailey said it would in the *Externalization of the Hierarchy*; writing: "The new era is coming; the new ideals, the new civilization, the new modes of life, of education, of religious presentation and of government are slowly precipitating and nothing can stop them."[10]

The 'channelled' books of Alice Bailey showed a tenacious hatred for orthodox Christianity and fierce loyalty to the cause of occultism and Eastern mysticism.[11] Along with husband Foster Bailey, she devoted her life to giving directions for the new era, and the infiltration of all religions... step by step they plotted the coming 'New Age.'[12]

What is not quite so common knowledge is the New Age philosophy has the same Aryan roots Hitler believed would give him occult power. As Constance Cumbey wrote in *The Hidden Dangers of the Rainbow*: "Those who induced Germany to embrace the swastika are not dead. They are still among us, just as they have been in every era, and doubtless will continue to be until the Apocalypse. National Socialism was for them but a means, and Hitler was but an instrument. The undertaking failed. What they are now trying to do is revive the myth using other means."[13] She goes on to say that both Nazism and the New Age Movement are programs for expediting the 'path' to 'transcendental consciousness,' for the transformation of the masses through initiation into the 'mysteries.'[14] Just as occult teachings and pagan practices were injected into the mainstream of a nation during Hitler's reign,[15] occult teachings have been injected into modern western society for the 21st century.

World Goodwill

Lucis Trust set-up World Goodwill in 1932, an accredited non-governmental organisation with the Department of Public Information of the United Nation's. World Goodwill was founded to 'initiate action to prepare for the new world order.' Based on 'principles of brotherhood, human unity, sharing and cooperation; and the fundamental freedoms embodied in the United Nations Universal Declaration of Human Rights,' World Goodwill believes the UN is the 'main hope for humanity's future.' World Goodwill is on the Roster of the United Nations Economic and Social Council and represented at regular United Nations briefing sessions in New York and Geneva.

World Goodwill believe the 'immediate spiritual problem is offsetting selfish separateness,' and look to 'introduce *new values for living, new standards of behaviour, new attitudes* of *non-separateness* and *cooperation*.' Alice Bailey's '*Externalization of the Hierarchy*,' reveals: 'the fusion of many minds into one directed activity is today of supreme importance... Unity of directed thought and purpose is the guarantee of inevitable and future success. The power of *massed thought* is omnipotent.' She continues, to 'create a new world... and the new way of life... seperativeness must be superseded by unity.'[16] [Emphasis Added] High Priestess Alice Bailey views 'separation' as evil, of which Christianity is considered a 'seperative' religion.

World Goodwill believes 'this is a time of preparation not only for a new civilisation and culture in a new world order, but also for the coming of a new spiritual dispensation... Humanity is not following an uncharted course, but there is a divine 'Plan' in the Cosmos of which we are a part... Today the reappearance of the World Teacher, the Christ, is expected by millions, not only by those of Christian faith but by those of every faith who expect the Avatar under other names - the Lord Maitreya, Krishna, Messiah, Imam Mahdi and the Bodhisattva.' 'The coming World Teacher will be mainly concerned... with the requirements of a new world order and with the reorganisation of the social structure.' World Goodwill's main purpose is to 'cooperate in the work of *preparation for the reappearance of the Christ*.'[17]

On April 25th, 1982, a $500,000-plus ad-campaign ran the headlines: 'THE CHRIST IS NOW HERE.' The announcement was for 'Maitreya the Christ,' who was coming soon. The ads were sponsored by the Tara Center, a front organization for Benjamin Creme, a disciple of Blavatsky and Bailey. The false Christ was intended to usher in the new world government and a new world religion. Creme had been on a global speaking tour since 1975, and when the new Christ was to appear, Creme would be doing the speaking for 'The Christ.' Creme had the full support of United Nations officials.[18]

When Benjamin Creme spoke in Detroit on November 4th, 1981, he was asked if he had ever met the Christ. He said: "No, I've never met the Christ, but I've met the human body he is inhabiting several times – but never as the Christ."[19] Through transmissions to Benjamin Creme, Maitreya has claimed that Jesus is one of his disciples. This can be documented in Creme's books, *The Reappearance of Christ,* and *the Masters of Wisdom*.[20]

Unfortunately for Creme, 'Maitreya the Christ' wasn't quite ready and failed to materialize, this hasn't dampened Creme's spirit [no pun intended]; he still prepares the ground for when Lucifer arrives and can be found at UN Conferences and programs where the power elite of the Club of Rome, Aspen Institute, Council on Foreign Relations, World Federalists, World Bank, etc., mingling with New Agers of every description.[21]

Acid Dreams

In preparation for the 'Light-Bearer's' return, many minds were to be made receptive, which is why the 1960's saw the rise of the hippie 'flower power' counterculture, who were to experience an 'altered state' of awareness through the use of drugs, especially LSD. (LSD was developed in 1943 by Albert Hoffman; a chemist at Sandoz A, B., a Swiss pharmaceutical house owned by S. G. Warburg,[22] the same Warburg family to give America the Federal Reserve System) The groundwork for the movement had been prepared from as early as the 1930's, when the first Director-General of UNESCO, Sir Julian Huxley's brother Aldous Huxley, author of *Brave New World*, was sent from

Britain to prepare America for the mass dissemination of drugs.[23] Aldous Huxley was a lifelong collaborator with Arnold Toynbee, who was on the Council of the Round Table's Royal Institute of International Affairs, and was the head of British Intelligence's Research Division.[24]

The counterculture that was foisted on the 1960's adolescent youth was a descendent of the pagan cult ceremonies dating back to the Egyptian Isis priesthood of the third millennium B.C., even down to the popularization of the Isis cross as the counterculture's most frequently used symbol.[25]

Aldous Huxley was introduced to the 'most evil man in the world' Aleister Crowley, who helped form the Isis-Urania Temple of Hermetic Students of the Golden Dawn. The Isis Cult was organized around the 1877 manuscript *Isis Unveiled* by Blavatsky, in which she called for the British aristocracy to organize itself into an Isis priesthood... Huxley founded a nest of Isis cults in southern California and San Francisco... teaming up with pederast Christopher Isherwood, who during the California period, translated and propagated ancient Zen Buddhist documents, inspiring Zen-mystical cults along the way... [26] Huxley and Isherwood both laid the foundations for the new psychedelic movement which would invade the student campuses of America.

Some had doubts about the usefulness of psychedelics, in his 1964 book *Nova Express*, William Burroughs - one time active in Scientology wrote: Who monopolized Cosmic Consciousness? Who monopolized Love Sex and Dream? Who monopolized *Time, Life* and *Fortune*? Who took from you what is yours? ...Listen: Their Garden of Delights is a terminal sewer... Their immortality Cosmic Consciousness and Love is second-run grade-B shit... Stay out of the Garden of Delights... Flush their drug kicks down the drain – they are poisoning and monopolizing the hallucinogenic drugs - learn to make it without any chemical corn.[27]

Pete Townsend of The Who was one of the few musicians who found LSD politically and spiritually useless stating: "The trips are just a side street, and before you know it you're back where you were. Each trip is more disturbing than the one that follows until eventually the side street becomes a dead end. Not only spiritually, which is the most important, but it can actually stop you thinking." ...Townsend blamed Woodstock: "a field full of six-foot-deep mud laced with LSD. If that was the world they wanted to live in, then fuck the lot of them."[28]

Drugs were only the stepping stone into the world of occult mystical experiences; the real power was to be experienced through Eastern Mysticism. As one chronicler of the sixties remarked: "LSD gave a whole generation a religious experience." But chemical *satori* is... too overwhelming to integrate into everyday life... For whatever glories the mushrooms and saturated sugar cubes contained, they were only the glimpse – coming attractions, but not the main feature. [29] Toynbee said in 1935 that a creative minority, "turning to the inner world of the psyche," could summon the vision of a *new way of life* for our troubled civilization. He also predicted that the most significant development of the age would be the influence of the *Eastern spiritual perspective* on the West. [30] [Emphasis added]

All You Need Is Love

An advertisement in *The Times* in late 1959 announced the Indian guru Maharishi Mahesh Yogi who was on tour, devoting his life to changing the world through 'Transcendental Meditation' (TM), establishing branches of his movement throughout the world - was heading for the shores of Great Britain.

On arrival to the West, Maharishi openly taught Transcendental Meditation as a Hindu religious practice, but exposed its real purpose was to produce "a legendary substance called Soma in the meditator's body so the Gods of the Hindu pantheon could be fed and awakened." But when he was denied access to public schools and government funding on the grounds that he was promoting religious practices, Maharishi quickly deleted all reference to religion and began presenting TM as a *science*. [31]

Maharishi made it clear to those on the inside: It doesn't matter if you lie teaching people... [because] TM is the ultimate, absolute spiritual authority on the face of the earth. [TM'ers] are the only teachers and upholders of genuine spiritual tradition on the face of the earth. They're running the universe. They are controlling the gods through the soma sacrifice. [32] It wasn't until 1967 that Maharishi Mahesh Yogi began to gain public interest in his 'Transcendental Meditation,' when he became associated with *The Beatles*.

The Beatles attended a Maharishi event and met the Yogi backstage, and eventually travelled to India to learn the secrets of Transcendental Meditation from the 'master.' They were each given a personal mantra and initiated into the movement, where they were instructed to use their mantra while meditating for 20 minutes, twice a day. Its repetition, the Maharishi claimed, would enable initiates to attain a "deeper level of consciousness" and "harmonise with the infinite." The exercise was the linchpin of the Transcendental Meditation system, which claimed that meditators could have "the ability to perceive things which are beyond the reach of the senses, the development of profound intimacy and support from one's physical environment, and even such abilities as disappearing and rising up or levitating at will." George Harrison, interviewed by David Frost explained the system: "The energy is latent within everybody. It's there anyway... meditation is a natural process of being able to contact that, so by doing it each day you contact that energy and give yourself a little more. Consequently, you're able to do whatever you normally do just with a little more happiness." Although the mantra is usually in Sanskrit, Harrison revealed that his was an English word that is included in the lyrics of *'I am the Walrus.'*

It became fashionable to be associated with the Maharishi, celebrities such as Mick Jagger, Marianne Faithfull, the Beach Boys, Mia Farrow, Kurt Vonnegut and Vidal Sassoon became involved in the movement, it was at a TM meeting that The Doors first met.[33]

It is not an accident that *The Beatles* paved the way for oriental gurus to move from the East and take up residence in the West, introducing Hindu concepts such as karma, reincarnation and meditation to Westerners for a more 'enlightened' spiritual path. They raised social awareness of Transcendental Meditation, Eastern spirituality, and Hinduism, inspiring youth culture to embrace mystical experiences as something they should incorporate into their lives.

Caryl Matrisciana tells us that the mystical power of Yoga meditation was launched on the American campuses as a relaxation technique and as a stress management benefit, but had been completely separated from its Hindu roots, and that Eastern Mysticism continued to grow as the hippie generation recognized similarities in Yoga's altered states, and those obtained by drug use.[34]

Yoga Uncoiled

Yoga in Hindu philosophy includes Raja Yoga, Karma Yoga, Bhakti Yoga, and Hatha Yoga. The Hare Krishna movement was formed to spread the practice of bhakti yoga, in which aspirant devotees (bhaktas) dedicate their thoughts and actions towards pleasing the 'Supreme Lord,' Krishna. George Harrison became a dedicated member of Hinduism's Hare Krishna Consciousness movement established by Swami Prabhupada. George Harrison's *'My Sweet Lord'* effectively blended Eastern Religion with traditional western thought, becoming the first to successfully merge New Age Mysticism into contemporary pop music. He created spiritual fusion by interchanging the names of Eastern deities like Krishna and Rama, with the Biblical worship names of Hallelujah and Lord God.[35]

Unknown to the public the practise of TM and Yoga are known to have extremely terrifying and uncontrollable spiritual experiences, as Kathy Newburn explains... safeguards are essential on the path of spiritual development as we are brought into contact with fiery energies that can wreak havoc in our lives if precautions are not undertaken.[36] As actor Richard Chamberlain credited with realigning his "psychic force" [stated]: Not one person knows what [psychic power] is or all of its aspects and no one has ever known, despite attempts over thousands of years to master this knowledge. Tapping these energies is fire, and the consequences... can be psychosis, aggravation of neurosis, acceleration of disease processes and suicide.[37]

Yoga's end result has similar effects to drug induced states with psychological changes in the body and brain... mysticism and substance abuse have remarkable similarities, yet despite the dangers, Yoga devotion is promoted as a beneficial body-mind exercise.[38]

Yoga is the very heart of Hinduism; the physical cannot be separated from the spiritual. Just as UNESCO promotes a humanist ideology, the whole philosophy behind Hinduism is relative; there are no moral absolutes, no standard morals on which to act. Freedom in the east is freedom from individuality. Since the 1960's, Yoga teachers have become the leading missionaries for Hinduism, finding their way into movies, magazines, DVD's, CD's, Church halls, hospitals, and fitness clubs, etc.

Most self-improvement techniques being adopted throughout society-by public educators, psychologists, psychiatrists, medical doctors, and success, motivation seminar leaders – employ varying forms of Eastern meditation and self-hypnosis similar to TM's variation on Yoga. [39]

The goal of Yoga is to shut down from life's reality; it's all an illusion, which is the perfect cover for the United Nations global plan – to ignore what's happening in reality. The revolution of the 1960's had planted the seeds of apocalypse; the psychedelic drugs, however abused, had given a visionary experience of self-transcendence to a sufficient number of individuals, so that they might well determine the future of human development – "not a Utopia, but a collectively altered state of consciousness."[40] 'There is a way which seems right to a man and appears straight before him, but at the end of it is the way of death.' Proverbs 14:12

Esalen

In 1962, Aldous Huxley helped found the Esalen Institute in Big Sur, California, which became a mecca for hundreds of Americans to engage in weekends of Training Groups modelled on behaviour group therapy for Zen, Hindu, and Buddhist transcendental meditation, and "out of body" experiences through simulated and actual hallucinogenic drugs.[41] Its purpose from the very beginning has been to bring about a merger of Eastern mysticism with Western culture. It has played that role to the hilt, serving as the major think tank of the human-potential movement.[42]

As described in the Esalen Institute Newsletter: "Esalen started in the fall of 1962 as a forum to bring together a wide variety of approaches to enhancement of the human potential... including experiential sessions involving encounter groups, sensory awakening, gestalt awareness training and related disciplines. Our latest step is to fan out into the community at large, running programs in cooperation with many different institutions, churches, schools, hospitals, and government." Esalen's catalogue offers: T-Groups, Psychodrama Marathon, Fight Training for Lovers and Couples, Religious Cults, LSD Experiences and the Great Religions of the World, Are You Sound, a weekend workshop with Alan Watts, Creating New Forms of Worship, Hallucinogenic Psychosis, and Non-Drug Approaches to Psychedelic Experiences."[43]

Also in 1962, considered by many as the birthplace of planetary spirituality was Findhorn in Scotland, often referred to as the 'Mecca' of the 'New Age Movement,' who were developing a new way to live to tune in with the laws of nature and the universe. They were trying, in the spirit of "The Great Invocation," to be "Centers of Light," or focal points in a network from which spiritual illumination would eventually spread out and encompass the globe.[44]

An original member of Findhorn was David Spangler, an important man in the New Age Movement who once remarked: "...the Aryan race is the first race in evolutionary progression of man to come into full grips with its power of mind..."[45] In 1965, Spangler claimed he 'worked clairvoyantly with a group of non-physical beings from the inner worlds of spirit.'[46] Spangler wrote the book which purported to be a transmission from unearthly sources – or "his higher self." *Revelation: the Birth of a New Age* quickly became mandatory reading for Findhorn residents,[47] as did the reading of Blavatsky and Bailey. Referring to the kind of New World they want to bring about, Spangler stated...You will have to pledge loyalty to Lucifer or Maitreya to get a permit to do business in the New Age.[48]

Spangler is now part of the Lorian organization, who originally met at Findhorn in Scotland in 1971. Leaving Findhorn, they created Lorian as an informal organization linking several independent projects, each fostering a new and growing awareness of the 'Sacred in the world.' In 1974 Lorian Association was formally incorporated, and in 2003 they created the Lorian Center for Incarnational Spirituality (LCIS), which offers long-term study programs with a Masters-degree option, with home-study educational books and materials, and to build a worldwide network to teach 'Incarnational Spirituality' through active online interaction.[49]

Occult practices entering academia has become the norm with Harvard University in Cambridge, Massachusetts, lending its immense prestige to New Age beliefs by hosting the 1987 Iyengar Yoga Convention. A few months earlier at highly regarded Claremont Graduate School in Southern California, a symposium of university professors seriously discussed out-of-body experiences, extrasensory perception, spirit survival of bodily death, and reincarnation... one of the professors remarked: "This kind of conference couldn't have been held in a university setting ten years ago."[50]

Bio-Hinduism

No religion has placed more emphasis on environmental ethics, preservation of environment and ecological balance than Hinduism. Ecology is an inherent part of the Hindu spiritual world view, forbidding man from exploiting nature. Hinduism teaches man to live in harmony with nature and recognize that 'divinity' prevails in all elements; 'including plants and animals.'[51]

Eastern Hindu philosophy began to get its political foot in the door in 1965 when the General Assembly of the United Nations established the Unity-and-Diversity World Council who believe Christianity and other religions are fighting each other, with many people turning away from religion, feeling that it is irrelevant to today's world, suggesting we need to look at 'alternative spiritual movements.' To provide leadership in achieving peace, justice, and a 'sustainable environment,' science also has to play a role in the process of unification among religions, especially as it bridges between the religions and other 'dimensions of consciousness.' We need to cooperate for a 'global society' to emerge. Instead of plundering the earth, we must come to see the 'earth as sacred,' a step forward in the emergence of a 'global civilization that works for all.'[52]

The Unity-and-Diversity World Council objectives were to help realize our connection to the 'Source of All Life' and to 'all life forms,' and to facilitate personal and social transformation, and to act as... an international coordinating body devoted to linking metaphysical and New Age groups. The council also seeks to coordinate cultural and religious organizations that "...foster the emergence of a *new universal person* and a civilization based on unity in diversity among all peoples."[53]

Gaia

The United Nations 'alternative spiritual movement' to view the 'Earth as Sacred' was given wings in 1972 when British chemist James Lovelock proposed the 'Gaia hypothesis,' which views the Earth as a living organism. Blavatsky also described the Earth as a *'living* organism.'[54] Gaia is seen as a way to clean up the environment and promote an "ecofeminism" that balances Earth as mother against God as father.

Henry Lamb's *eco-logic* Special Report, *The Rise of Global Green Religion* tells us apart from being a living organism, Gaia is the source of all life, which has the capacity to regulate, or 'heal' itself under 'natural' conditions. Lamb further explains Lovelock's contention is that the human species has developed the technology to overwhelm Gaia's capacity to 'heal' itself, and is therefore doomed to destruction unless the human species stops its technological assault... global warming is the result of the human assault on the earth, and likened it to a fever in humans, but is worried that humans are not allowing Gaia to recuperate. He said: "She may be unable to relax because we have been busy removing her skin and using it as farm land, especially the trees and forests of the humid tropics...we are also adding a vast blanket of greenhouse gases to the already feverish patient."[55]

In his 1979 book *Gaia: A New Look at Life on Earth*, James Lovelock tells us this new interrelationship of Gaia with man is by no means fully established; we are not yet a truly *collective* species *corralled* and *tamed* as an integral part of the biosphere, as we are as individual creatures. *It may be that the destiny of mankind is to become tamed,* so that the fierce, destructive, and greedy forces of tribalism and nationalism are fused into a compulsive urge to belong to the commonwealth of all creatures which constitutes Gaia.[56] [Emphasis added]

United Religions supporter, former Advisory board member of the Unity-and-Diversity World Council, and Assistant Secretary General of the United Nations Robert Muller wrote in his book *New Genesis: Shaping a Global Spirituality*: 'on a universal scale, humankind is seeking no less than its reunion with the 'divine,' it's transcendence into ever higher forms of life. Hindus call our earth Brahma, or God, for they rightly see no difference between our earth and the divine. This ancient simple truth is slowly dawning again upon humanity ... as we are about to enter our cosmic age and to become what we were always meant to be: the planet of God.'[57] Muller was asked to explain the word 'gaiaphily,' and responded: "It comes from Gaia, the Greek name of the goddess Earth (hence gaiagraphy, gaialogy, gaiametry, gaiaphysics, etc. distorted later by male scientists into geography, geology, geometry, geophysics, etc.) meaning the description, the science, the measurement and the physical aspects of the Earth, words all derived from Greek. Phily is also a Greek word which means love. Thus philanthropy means the love of anthropos (man or humanity). I coined the word gaiaphily because in our time we must also love Gaia, our precious Mother Earth."[58]

Muller took the Gaia concept to the classroom in the late 70's and early 80's when he developed the Robert Muller School 'World Core Curriculum.' Robert Muller Schools are to bring 'the world's children to a consciousness which is inclusive in nature... emphasizing the Unity underlying the evolutionary process, and the Brotherhood of all Humankind,' which he believes is vitally important for the 'future relationships of humankind.'

To implement the 'World Core Curriculum' philosophy, the first Robert Muller School was started in Arlington, Texas, in 1979. Berit Kjos tells us in *Brave New Schools*, that she took a visit to the School in Arlington, where upon she was handed the *Robert Muller World Core Curriculum Manual* which states: 'The underlying philosophy upon which the Robert Muller School is based will be found in the teaching set forth in the books of Alice A. Bailey by the Tibetan teacher, Djwhal Khul...' The back of the manual contained a certificate that announced The Robert Muller School "is a participating institution in the United Nations Educational, Scientific and Cultural Organization (UNESCO) Associated Schools Project in Education for International Cooperation and Peace."[59] Individual achievement and personal responsibility are counter to the value of 'mutual respect.' In the *World Core Curriculum Manual* (November, 1986) it states: 'The idea for the school grew out of a desire to provide experiences which would enable the students to become true planetary citizens through a global approach to education.' The first principle of the curriculum is to: 'Promote growth of the group idea, so that group good, group understanding, group interrelations and group goodwill replace all limited, self-centered objectives leading to group consciousness.'[60] For his contribution, Muller was awarded the UNESCO Peace Education Award in 1989, earning him the nickname "father of global education."[61] Muller believes in the idea that "If Christ [Lucifer] came back to earth; his first visit would be to the United Nations to see if his dream of human oneness and brotherhood had come true."[62]

The United Nations Online tells us the World Core Curriculum is 'dedicated to the idea of the new education... Schools around the world will vary in size and also in the ages of students served... school will begin at birth, with the parents having used the 'Balanced Beginnings Program' prenatally; and will continue through the secondary level. In this structure, the student will move directly into college with no break in the continuity of presented perspective. By that time, there will be an *understanding which overrides all false concepts which are still held among much of the general populace of the world,* concepts which have bred seperative and prejudiced behavior for most of human history. The Staff and supporters will be recognized as those who are bringing about a needed and radical change in the consciousness of the world's children. A School can begin with any age group of children; however it is hoped that children will be taught the Curriculum from birth and throughout life; the interdependence of all existence will be *foundational to their 'thinking' for a lifetime.* [Emphasis added]

The UN Online also states the 'student will have a picture of her/himself as one Cosmic Unit, [as] part of the human species, existing for a limited period of time on the planet Earth, and contributing to the entire planetary scheme. The student will have a clear realization that he/she plays a definite part, however minuscule, in creating or damaging harmonious relationships in this magnificent 'inter-dependent system.'[63]

Our Common Future

In the 1970's, billionaire socialist and outspoken proponent of hardcore New Age paganism Maurice Strong and wife Hanna, bought more than 200,000 acres of land in the Colorado valley.[64] Strong's Colorado ranch, Baca Grande, is home for a Babylonian Sun God Temple. The association advances the [Blavatsky] theosophical idea of one universal religion that teaches that the kingdom of God is the kingdom of nature.[65] The area now has a Buddhist monastery, a holistic center based on ancient Hawaiian spirituality, a conservation-minded Indian ashram, and a multi-religious retreat center. The community that live in the San Luis Valley are into crystals, tarot, astrology, intuition, Buddhism, divine intervention, angels and channelling. In 1988 the Strong's established the Manitou Foundation and later conceived the idea of a "refuge for world truths," to grant land to spiritual groups and organizations, it is now considered 'one of the most sacred places on the planet.' Strong deals with stress by meditating for 20 minutes every morning and does yoga morning and night. Hanna Strong said she once took her husband to Tibet to study meditation with a teacher there.[66] Who is Maurice Strong?

Maurice Strong was the Trustee of the Rockefeller Foundation from 1971-77 and a member of the Council at the Rockefeller University between 1972-76.[67] He was also a major player in the United Nations 'think tank' the Club of Rome. Canadian attorney and author Ezra Levant points out, Strong has "never stopped pressing for a world where the UN's resolutions would be enforced as the law in every corner of the Earth."[68]

Strong was chosen as Secretary-General of the first UN environmental Conference in 1972, the United Nations Conference on the Human Environment (also known as the Stockholm Conference) held in Sweden, June 5th-16th. This was the beginning of the Big 'Red' Green juggernaut now known as the environmental movement. A year later in 1973, Strong became the first executive director of the United Nations Environment Programme (UNEP), an international body designed to be the overseer of a future monitoring system of the world's environment.

In 1980, Strong 'restructured and revitalized' the International Union for the Conservation of Nature, a Non-Governmental Organization (NGO) that now has 743 government agency and NGO members in 68 nations. In his lifetime, Strong has found time to be President of the World Federation of United Nations Associations; Co-chair, World Economic Forum; member of the Club of Rome, Trustee, Aspen Institute, Director, World Future Society, Director of Finance for the Lindisfarne Association, founder of Planetary Citizens, convener of the Fourth World Wilderness Congress, founder of the World Economic Forum, and involved with the Business Council for Sustainable Development, Petro-Canada, Dome Petroleum, and Hydro-Canada.[69]

It was Strong who helped create the concept of "sustainable development" as a member of the United Nations-aligned Brundtland Commission. Strong informed us that sustainable development "...will require the development of an effective and enforceable international legal regime." Strong - referring to the United Nations stated: "...to prepare for the vastly increased role it must have as the primary multi-lateral framework of a new world order."[70]

In December 1983, the General Assembly of the United Nations, asked Prime Minister of Norway Gro Harlem Brundtland, Secretary-General of the United Nations to establish and chair a special, independent commission to address 'A global agenda for change, which became known as The Brundtland Commission, formally the World Commission on Environment and Development (WCED). In establishing the commission, the UN General Assembly recognized that environmental problems were global in nature and determined that it was in the common interest of all nations to establish policies for 'Sustainable Development'[71] - the deceptive title of the global agenda for the future control of all human activity on the planet.

The Brundtland Commission produced the *Brundtland Report* in 1987, referred to as *Our Common Future*, used as the basis for the 4th World Wilderness Congress, where Maurice Strong introduced Edmond De Rothschild with a proposal for a World Conservation Bank. The report called for "... 'major changes' . . . *in attitudes and in the way our societies are organized*"[72] [Emphasis Added]

The Brundtland Commission's *Our Common Future* deals with sustainable development and the change of politics needed for achieving its objective. The definition of this term in the report is quite well known and often cited: "Sustainable development is development that meets the needs of the present without compromising the ability of future generations to meet their own needs." Or as Stanley Monteith at *Radio Liberty* tells us - any time you hear the phrase 'Sustainable Development,' you should substitute the term 'socialism' to be able to understand what is intended.[73]

Our Common Future has placed environmental issues firmly on the political agenda; it aimed to discuss the environment and its development as a single issue. In conjunction with the work of the World Commission on Environment and Development, they would lay the groundwork for the convening of the 1992 United Nations Earth Summit in Rio.

Prior to the release of the *Our Common Future/Brundtland Report*, 10,000 people participated in the UNEP World Environment Festival, as part of an 'Environment Awareness Week' [read as Propaganda Week] in New York, held at United Nations Headquarters from the 1st – 5th June, 1987. The celebration was part of UNEP's 15th anniversary, with children from more than 200 American schools who created some 300 works of art to illustrate the environment and shelter theme. Two dozen bands, orchestras, choirs, dance groups and soloists made special presentations emphasizing global concerns about the environment. An outdoor concert by the international music and dance group, "Up With People," was sponsored by the United States Mission to the United Nations.[74]

In April of 1988, representatives of Christianity, Buddhism, Hinduism, Islam, and Judaism met with political leaders from over forty nations to 'solve the world's problems.' This Global Conference of Spiritual and Parliamentary

Leaders on Human Survival was sponsored by the [UN] Temple of Understanding... the Temple has become a "hotbed of international dialogue and outright promotion of eastern mysticism." Among its recent guest speakers were New Age advocates David Spangler and Benjamin Creme who still continues to herald the coming of Lord Maitreya, 'The Christ.'

Washington began to move into the Green picture, supporting cosmic environmentalism with Vice President Al Gore, who believes "...we should actively search for ways to promote a new way of thinking about the current relationship between human civilization and the earth.[75] Gore has made it no secret he worships the mother goddess Gaia and advocates "reliance upon a Higher Power, by whatever name." In his plenary address to the 1990 Global Forum in Moscow, cosponsored by the Soviet Academy of Science (which drew from 83 countries participating scientists as well as religious leaders from among Hindus, Muslims, Buddhists, "Christians," et al), Gore advocated a "new spirituality" common to all religions.[76] Gore also addressed the Mass as a Baptist and environmentalist in 1991, stating: "If God is within us, is God not also within other living things?" He then added: "God is not separate from the Earth."[77] Christians recognize these Gaia concepts as pagan; God's universe does not see God's fullness in plants and animals. God *created* the Earth; He is not part of it.

Media propaganda never ceases with the Green Agenda; the United Nations Environment Programme (UNEP) featured 42 astronauts and cosmonauts from 14 different countries at its Earth Day ceremony at the United Nations on April 22nd, 1990. Entitled '*Only One Earth*,' the theme of the ceremony was the inter-relatedness of the planetary environment and its entire people.[78]

Her Name is Rio

1992 was the media event of the millennium with the United Nations Conference on Environment and Development (UNCED), or the Rio Earth Summit, organized by Maurice Strong who said he was looking for nothing short of a "historic civilizational change," a transition in which both rich and poor will turn away from the craze for consumption and begin to live within their environmental means. The world had never seen anything like it. In his opening address to the UNCED plenary session... Strong directed the world's attention to the declaration of the Sacred Earth Gathering, which was part of the pre-Summit ceremonies. "[T]he changes in behaviour and direction called for here... must be rooted in our deepest spiritual, moral and ethical values."

According to the declaration, the ecological 'crisis' "transcends all national, religious, cultural, social, political, and economic boundaries... The responsibility
of each human being today is to choose between the force of darkness and the
force of light. We must therefore transform our attitudes and values, and adopt
a renewed respect for the superior law of Divine Nature."[79] Only a few years
later in his 2000 book *Where on Earth Are We Going?* Strong declared: "We are
all gods now, gods in charge of our own destiny," a line he recycled from the
serpent in the Garden of Eden.[80]

The Earth Summit was a first of its kind; the meeting of world leaders
focused on the global environment and how nasty-man has ruined it. There
was no shortage of propaganda with Olivia Newton-John and her Hollywood
pals making a six-minute video appeal to deliver to the White House, amid
much publicity.[81] Washington's own Al Gore led the U.S. Senate delegation to
Rio, having just released his book *Earth in the Balance: Ecology and the Human
Spirit*, in which he writes: "We must make the rescue of the environment the
central organizing principle for civilization... Use every policy and program,
every law and institution, every treaty and alliance, every tactic and strategy,
every plan and course of action... to halt the destruction of the environment
and to preserve and nurture our ecological system."[82] Gore's book talks about
the future of the human race and of the Earth with an 'enviro-spiritual focus.'
The League of Conservation Voters applauded Gore as '...a future-minded
leader [who understands] the dangers facing our life support systems, namely
ozone depletion and global warming."[83] Although not everyone agreed, as
newspaper columnist George Will called for Gore's book "...to be thrown in the
wastebasket."[84]

The Rio Earth Summit had an accompanying Global Forum, a 'people's
summit,' which drew 15,000 participants from 165 nations; the Forum was a
coming together of Eastern and Western religious beliefs and ideas. To impart
a spirit of hope to the Earth Summit, a replica of a Viking ship named Gaia
docked at the Global Forum, carrying thousands of messages from children
around the world to leaders who are gathering to chart the planet's environmental future. "We will not be forgiven if we leave future generations to cope
with global changes that we have left undone," Prime Minister Gro Harlem
Brundtland of Norway said.

Symbolism, spiritualism and pragmatism were among the wares of the
700 exhibitors at the Global Forum. In a plaza outside the center, Edwina
Sandys put finishing touches on a massive red and white sculpture made en-

tirely of recycled aluminium, depicting a person, hands upstretched between two trees pierced by hearts, fish and birds. Ms Sandys, the granddaughter of Sir Winston Churchill, said the statue symbolizes the purity of nature and dangers facing the environment. Mr Peixoto of Orlando Peixoto, a stand devoted to propagating Mahikari, a Japanese healing art stated: "Our goal is to purify man by purifying his energy particles," he also said that using transfers of light, he could purify houses or fields and "make telephones work better."[85]

The Washington Post described the Global Forum as a kind of Counter-Earth Summit designed to allow nongovernmental organizations (NGOs) to get in on the Rio action. Every conceivable breed of environmentalist and quasi-environmentalist was there: the one-worlders, the neo-humanists, the anti-rationalists, the Esperanto speakers, the pseudo-Vikings, the enviro-feminists, the eco-architects, and various label-resistant people who seriously want to 'rescue' the planet.[86]

The real purpose of the Rio conference was that it did much to lay the legal, intellectual, and institutional groundwork for a concerted drive to achieve sustainable development.[87] Maurice Strong was to reveal what is not 'sustainable:' "...*current lifestyles* and consumption patterns of the affluent middle class," also "high meat intake, use of fossil fuels, appliances, home and workplace air-conditioning, and suburban housing [is] ...not sustainable. A *shift* is necessary which will require a vast strengthening of the multilateral system, including the United Nations..."[88] [Emphasis Added]

The blueprint for the 'Sustainable' future was produced at the Summit in the form of an 800-page, forty chapter document named *Agenda 21*, a 'comprehensive plan of action' for control of the world. *Agenda 21* ignores science and naturally occurring phenomena in nature, in favor of radical social engineering projects to be implemented that will limit and restrict human activity, to reduce man to have less value than a tree. *Agenda 21* binds governments around the world to the United Nations plan for changing the way we live, the way we eat, the way we think, what we say, where we go, what is right, what is wrong, where we will work, learn, and communicate etc., everything present in the current ordering of the world is to be totally eradicated, religion, education, private property and human rights will not exist in the New World Order. It's all happening under the banner of 'Saving the Earth.'

The United Nations Environment Program (UNEP) is the catalyst to reorganize and regulate all human activity. UNEP has remapped the whole world into 'bioregions,' and is responsible for virtually all of the environmental policy changes that have occurred globally... Their five-step action plan[89] as presented in UNEP documents is to:

1. Redraw land maps to differentiate biological characteristics rather than political jurisdiction.
2. Regroup human populations into self-sustaining settlements that minimize impact on biodiversity.
3. Educate humans in the "Gaia ethic," which holds that Gaia is the creator of all life and all life is a part of the creator (New World Order Religion).
4. Create a new system of governance based on local decision-making within the framework of international agreements.
5. Reduce the use of natural resources by (a) reducing population; (b) reducing consumption; and (c) shifting to 'appropriate' technology.[90]

On June 29th, 1993, by Executive Order No. 12852, the 'President's Council on Sustainable Development' (PCSD) was established.[91] Between June 1993 and June 1999, the PCSD advised President Clinton on sustainable development, developing 'bold, new approaches to achieve economic, environmental, and equity goals.'[92] The Clinton Administration side-stepped Congress to approve the sustainable development agenda and implement its policies in America: All cabinet officials had to do was change some wording of existing programs and reroute already-approved funding to begin to implement the agenda-without Congress and without debate. Former Commerce Secretary Ron Brown told a meeting of the President's Council that he could implement 67% of the Sustainable Development agenda in his agency with no new legislation. Other agencies like Interior, EPA, HUD and more did the same thing. To help it all along, Clinton issued a blizzard of Executive Orders.[93] (Many politicians talk in terms of 'bold new approaches,' descriptive titles such as Smart Growth, Greenways, Pathways or Vision, these are all euphemisms for the United Nations sustainable future, of which every county in America has its own *Agenda 21* programme (*Agenda 21* is a global document).

The Rio Earth Summit also produced the Global Biodiversity Assessment (GBA) report, funded by the Global Environment Facility and UNEP, a document designed to help '...limit the range of options that people will have in the future.'[94] The language is deliberately vague, warm and fuzzy, but ultimately designed for governments to takeover private lands, dissolve political boundaries and help establish new 'bioregional boundaries.'

The report says that '...all humanity could uphold the core values of respect for life, liberty, justice and equity, mutual respect, caring, and integrity.' 'Respect for life' is not limited to human life, it actually means equal respect for *all* life. The Global Biodiversity Assessment (Section 9), prepared under the auspices of the United Nations Environment Programme (UNEP), describes in great detail the biocentric view that 'humans are one strand in nature's web,' consistent with the biocentric view that all life has equal intrinsic value.[95] This means trees, insects, birds, mice, weeds, fish eggs, etc., have the same respect and status as that of human beings. We are to abide by multitudes of laws and restrictions, show 'mutual respect' for everything on the planet, including the planet – all defined as tolerance. They understand that some may be against losing all their rights, having a lower standard of living, more taxes, less food, a total globalization and homogenized world; but those people will simply be labelled as 'bigots' or 'intolerant.'

Spearheading these new 'bioregional boundaries' is Dave Foreman, involved in the environmental movement since 1971 in radical efforts to reduce population. He was the co-founder of Earth First! Their motto is *No Compromise in the Defense of Mother Earth!* Foreman believes 'the less humans the better,' and sees "eating, manufacturing, travelling, warring and breeding" by humans as causes of "the greatest crisis in 4 billion years of life on Earth."[96] It was Foreman's 'vision' in his book *Confessions of an Eco Warrior* of a 'Rewilded' America, a radical environment program seeking to 'preserve biological diversity' in the United States.

The 'Rewilding' of America goes under the name The Wildlands Project (TWP), of which Foreman is the founder, serving as its Chairman from 1991 to 2003 and as Executive Editor or Publisher of the journal *Wild Earth* during that same period.[97] According to Ron Arnold's book *Undue Influence,* funding comes from the Ted Turner foundation and the Rockefeller Brothers Foundation.[98]

The Wildlands Project will restructure human society around nature, setting aside limited areas for human habitation. The project was embraced by the United Nations Environmental Programme (UNEP), UNESCO, The Nature Conservancy, the U.S. Department of Interior, the EPA, and the Sierra Club, who elected Dave Foreman to its Board of Directors. The Project will turn at least *fifty percent* of the land of America to 'core wilderness areas' where human activity is barred. This huge portion of the rewilded U.S. mainland will be home to large carnivorous predators such as grizzly bears, jaguars, panthers, pumas and packs of wolves.

Matt Bennett of the Citizens with Common Sense stated: "Wildlands will be core reserves of millions of acres connected by vast corridors following rivers and other migratory paths from west to east, from Central America and Mexico through the U.S. and Canada, using national forests and other government lands." Bennett calls TWP a "rethinking of science, politics, land use, industrialization and civilization. It requires a new philosophical and spiritual foundation for Western civilization." He also calls it nature worship "on a mission from God or Gaia." He also warns when you see a river, tract of land or whole region designated as a U.S. Heritage site, U.N. Biosphere Reserve, greenway, trail, path or some other special name conferred by environmentalists and their legislative and bureaucratic allies, "think Wildlands in the making."

Carol LaGrasse, president of the Property Rights Foundation of America believes making these areas environmentally unique will create "...the impression that the area has some sort of holiness, some sort of mystical significance and really should be protected in a special way." LaGrasse lives in Stony Creek, N.Y., a rural hamlet in the heart of the Adirondack Mountains ordained a U.N. Biosphere Reserve without so much as local consultation. The spiritual aura that she sees implied in these designations discourages normal human uses of the land such as "modern home life, farming, forestry, mining, industry and commerce..."

Although *Agenda 21* and the *Global Biodiversity Assessment* report are being implemented throughout America; they are Global plans for ultimate domination, anywhere UNEP goes, those reports are sure to follow. As an example in 2002, a report compiled by UNEP World Conservation Monitoring Center (UNEP-WCMC) said 'Mountains worldwide need urgent measures of protection,' the report was a contribution to the 'International Year of Mountains.'[99]

In 2008, a five year $26 million scheme by the United Nations Environment Programme, funded by the Global Environment Facility and also coordinated by the UN Food and Agriculture Organisation are taking over to protect bees, bats, birds and others that are essential to global crop production and biodiversity. The scheme is to be introduced worldwide.[100] There are literally hundreds, if not thousands of similar schemes in operation all over the globe. The United Nations is gradually taking control of the entire planet, simultaneously narrowing where humans will be allowed to live and work.

GREATEST SCIENTIFIC FRAUD IN HISTORY

Mankind is well understood by the rulers of the world, they understand very well that men in times of crisis forget their differences and pull together as a team. The Club of Rome (COR), an organizational tentacle or *'think tank'* of the United Nations specializes in the fabrication of scenarios the Money-Lenders want to bring about. In the COR's *The First Global Revolution* published in 1991, they had worked on the idea of how 'to bring the divided nation together to face an outside enemy,' and as far as they were concerned, it didn't matter whether the threat to mankind was *'...a real one or else one invented for the purpose...'*[1] [Emphasis Added] The 'purpose' being the New World Order.

The threat of the Aliens, asteroids, planets colliding, acid rain, ozone depletion, etc., have all been tried at one time or another but didn't quite stick with the public. The Club of Rome understood that new enemies had to be identified, new strategies imagined, and new weapons devised. So the Club of Rome's new enemy they came up with that threatens the existence of the whole human race was: '...pollution, water shortage, famine, malnutrition, illiteracy and unemployment.' However, it appears that awareness of the new enemies were 'insufficient to elicit world cohesion and solidarity for the fight.'[2] The report then goes on to say that they had found the perfect solution: 'In searching for a new enemy to unite us, we came up with the idea that *pollution, threat of global warming, water shortages, famine and the like would fit the bill...* All these dangers are caused by human intervention and it is *only through changed attitudes and behaviour* that they can be overcome. The real enemy, then, is humanity itself.[3] [Emphasis Added] The imagined crisis for the whole world to pull together is obviously global warming, however, since the planet has actually been cooling since the late 90's, global warming had to be changed to Climate Change – with the new term, whatever the forecast for the future, they are pretty much covered.

The politically minded manipulator often is rewarded with eminent status, whether he is a true scholar or not. The symbol of academic prestige is not necessarily evidence of learning or of sound social judgement. Once an academician is selected to act as an "expert," he becomes one in the public eye because he has been so chosen.[4] One such chosen 'politically minded manipulator' is former 'I invented the Internet' pathological liar, Gaia worshipping Al Gore, who on March 21st, 2007, as Chairman of the Alliance for Climate Protection Governing Council, Senate Environment Committee, stated: "This is not a normal time. We are facing a planetary emergency. The relationship between human kind and planet earth has been radically altered in a short period of time, and what makes us believe we can go through these changes and not have an impact."[5] In his speech at the Copenhagen Summit 2009, Gore declared that the Arctic could be completely ice-free in five years; he followed with: "These figures are fresh. Some of the models suggest to Dr Maslowski that there is a 75% chance that the entire north polar ice cap, during the summer months, could be completely ice-free within five to seven years."[6] According to Al and his cronies, selfish man is to stand trial for his selfish desire for big-screen TV's, mobile phones, cars, houses, automatic carpets and gadgets that are consuming the earth's resources at an alarming rate, and also for causing air pollution, water pollution, loss of forests, degradation of coastlines, mass starvation, mass extinctions, rising sea levels, and hurricanes etc.

While Gore campaigns around the globe informing people of the danger to humanity of using too many light bulbs, back home, his eight-bathroom house in the Tennessee city consumed nearly 221,000 kilowatt-hours of electricity in 2006, which was more than twenty times the national average.[7]

Recent propaganda informs us that it's not too late to 'Save the Earth' from man, as the United Nations can avert this nightmare scenario if all countries sign a new 'Cap and Trade' bill into law, designed for nations to lower their CO_2 emissions. It's amazing; the planet can be 'saved' with the stroke of a pen by putting a price on the cost of a recently reclassified new 'pollutant' – carbon, one of the basic elements of life.

The real story is that the only threat 'Climate Change' poses the world is the introduction of monumental new taxes for everyone, and a lower standard of living for the whole world. With the new imaginary 'carbon crisis,' everyone and everything on the planet is contributing an imaginary amount of extra carbon; everything you buy will have used a certain amount of imaginary carbon - *which will have a price tag*, which is not imaginary. As Ben Lieber-man, Senior Policy Analyst for Energy and Environment in the Thomas A. Roe Institute for Economic Policy Studies at The Heritage Foundation stated: "It is clear that cap-and-trade is very expensive and amounts to nothing more than an energy tax in disguise... [it is] the most convoluted attempt at economic central planning this nation has ever attempted - the bottom line is that cap and trade works by raising the cost of energy high enough so that individuals and businesses are forced to use less of it. Inflicting economic pain is what this is all about. That is how the ever-tightening emissions targets will be met."[8] U.S. Senator James M. Inhofe (republican, Okla) said in 2005, January 4th, on the Senate floor: "much of the debate over global warming is predicated on fear, rather than science." He called it the "greatest hoax ever perpetrated on the American people..."[9]

Population Bomb

The environmental eco-mania, save the earth apocalyptic doom train has chugged steadily forward with the help of the United Nations for at least the past four decades. An onslaught of environmental social engineering, earth centered propaganda from books, magazines, cartoons, films, TV documen-taries, public speakers, all designed to induce guilt about poor beaten Mother Earth, have scared the public into eco-fanatics to have fewer children and ac-cept ever increasing governmental controls as the new normal.

Paul Ehrlich of Stanford University helped kick-off propaganda in 1968, when releasing his controversial book *The Population Bomb*, which begins with the statement: 'The battle to feed all of humanity is over... in the 1970's hundreds of millions of people will starve to death in spite of any crash pro-grams embarked upon now. At this late date nothing can prevent a substantial increase in the world death rate.' The modern day Malthusian Ehrlich went on to say that reckless human reproduction had overwhelmed the Earth and that massive famine would result, which would destroy one fifth of humanity by the end of the seventies and then the planet was sure to follow. He concluded that we must have population control, hopefully through a system of incen-tives and penalties, but by compulsion if voluntary methods fail... "We can no longer afford merely to treat the symptoms of the cancer of population growth; the cancer itself must be cut out."[10] Ehrlich also believed that "the birth of each American child is 50 times the disaster for the world as the birth of a child in India."[11] Ehrlich also predicted that in 1973, 200,000 Americans would die from air pollution, and that by 1980 the life expectancy of Americans would be 42 years. In an interview in *Mademoiselle Magazine,* April 1970, he also predicted "...the population will inevitably and completely outstrip whatever small increases in food supplies we make."[12]

Ehrlich was also a big eugenics fan who praised abortion as 'a highly effective weapon in the armoury of population control' and urged the creation of a federal population commission "with a large budget for propaganda." Pleading his case, he said: "It must be made clear to our population that it is socially irresponsible to have large families." He further stipulated the necessity for "federal laws making instruction in birth-control methods mandatory in all public schools" across the nation. "If all these steps fail to reverse today's population growth, we shall then be faced with some form of compulsory birth regulation." "We might institute a system whereby a temporary *sterilant would be added to a staple food or to the water supply.* An antidote would have to be taken to permit reproduction." He suggested that the distribution of the antidote be under government control.[13] [Emphasis added] Dr. Melvin M. Ketchel of Tufts University also recommended: "If the birth rate cannot be controlled by voluntary means, then it is a necessary and proper function of the government to take steps to reduce it. He further stated that "...drugs could be developed which can be administered to a whole population to statistically reduce the number of children born."[14]

Ehrlich's predictions of 'overwhelming the earth' were soon followed by mainstream CFR media and academia. Washington's University's biologist Barry Commoner stated: "We are in an environmental crisis which threatens the survival of this nation, and of the world as a suitable place of human habitation."

The January edition of *Life* Magazine, 1970 wrote: "Scientists have solid experimental and theoretical evidence to support…the following predictions: In a decade, urban dwellers will have to wear gas masks to survive air pollution…by 1985 air pollution will have reduced the amount of sunlight reaching earth by one half…."

Ecologist Kenneth Watt told *Time* magazine that, "At the present rate of nitrogen build-up, it's only a matter of time before light will be filtered out of the atmosphere and none of our land will be usable."

Barry Commoner cited a National Research Council report that had estimated "that by 1980 the oxygen demand due to municipal wastes will equal the oxygen content of the total flow of all the U.S. river systems in the summer months." Translation: Decaying organic pollutants would use up all of the oxygen in America's rivers, causing freshwater fish to suffocate.[15]

Peter Gunter, professor of North Texas State University stated: "Demographers agree almost unanimously on the following grim timetable: by 1975 widespread famines will begin in India; these will spread by 1990 to include all of India, Pakistan, China and the Near East, Africa. By the year 2000, or conceivably sooner, South and Central America will exist under famine conditions....By the year 2000, thirty years from now, the entire world, with the exception of Western Europe, North America, and Australia, will be in famine."[16]

Environmental indoctrination was reaching the public, but environmental concerns needed a political spotlight, Senator Nelson Gaylord was the man for the job. Speaking publicly across the nation with talks along the lines: "... that in 25 years, somewhere between 75 and 80 percent of all the species of living animals will be extinct," he hoped to 'organize a huge 'grassroots' protest over what was happening to the environment.'[17]

Pollution of the environment by man was driven home in 1969, when the Union Oil Company's drilling platform off the Santa Barbara coast suffered a blowout, resulting in thousands of gallons of crude oil seeping into the Pacific Ocean, washing up on the coastline, with pictures of blackened beaches filling the news. The cameras of the world media rushed to the scene to focus on oil-coated birds stuck in the same muck that was used to power American cars... the relentless coverage of America's pollution issues in '69 made it to the floor of the United Nations, with Secretary General U Thant predicted that the planet had only ten years to avert environmental disaster.[18]

At the same time period, anti-Vietnam War demonstrations called "teach-ins," had spread throughout college campuses in the US. Senator Gaylord had the idea that '...if we could tap into the environmental concerns of the general public and infuse the student anti-war energy into the environmental cause, we could generate a demonstration that would force this issue onto the political agenda.'[19]

The 'anti-war energy' became the fuel for the environmental movement which, in April 22nd, 1970, provided the world's first Earth Day, which just happens to be the birthday of Vladimir Lenin. Today, Earth Day is coordinated globally by the Earth Day Network, celebrated in more than 175 countries every year. In 2009, the United Nations designated April 22nd International Mother Earth Day.[20] Earth Day is a day of propaganda, a reminder of how man

is destroying the earth, lest we should forget.

Chief organizer of Earth Day was Denis Hayes, who sadly announced: "It is already too late to avoid mass starvation." Hayes was so committed to his anti-capitalist cause that he made sure his organization did not even produce any Earth Day bumper stickers. "You know why?" he explained to the *Times*, because "they go on automobiles."[21]

Before, during and after Earth Day, the usual environmental propaganda had begun to do the rounds in the mainstream CFR media and academia. The *New York Times* editorial wrote: "Man must stop pollution and conserve his resources, not merely to enhance existence but to save the race from intolerable deterioration and possible extinction." Biologist George Wald of Harvard University, April 19th, 1970 said: "…civilization will end within 15 or 30 years unless immediate action is taken against problems facing mankind,"

Paul Ehrlich's interview with *Mademoiselle Magazine*, April 1970 said: "…air pollution…is certainly going to take hundreds of thousands of lives in the next few years alone," and biologist Barry Commoner, University of Washington, writing in the journal *Environment,* April 1970 wrote: "We are in an environmental crisis which threatens the survival of this nation, and of the world as a suitable place of human habitation."[22] Academia, politicians, celebrities and the media have all 'predicted' every doom and gloom scenario imaginable for nearly half a century.

The first Earth Day and following propaganda paved the way for the United Nations Conference on the Human Environment (the Stockholm Conference) held in Sweden, June 5th-16th, 1972, which marked the beginning of the modern political and public awareness of global environmental problems. Just prior to the convening of the conference, U.N. Secretary-General Kurt Waldheim expressed the opinion that the conference's leaders "must surely link the increasing pollution of the planet with the increasing population of the planet." Accordingly, the Stockholm conference urged, among other things: "That special attention be given to population concerns as they relate to the environment during the 1974 observance of World Population Year."[23]

New Ice Age

On April 25th, 1975, environmental propaganda took a new turn when a CFR *Newsweek* article warned: 'There are ominous signs that the Earth's weather patterns have begun to change dramatically and that these changes may portend a drastic decline in food production… The evidence in support of these predictions has now begun to accumulate so massively that meteorologists are hard-pressed to keep up with it. In England, farmers have seen their growing season decline by about two weeks since 1950, with a resultant overall loss in grain production estimated at up to 100,000 tons annually. During the same time, the average temperature around the equator has risen by a fraction of a degree – a fraction that in some areas can mean drought and desolation. Last April, in the most devastating outbreak of tornadoes ever recorded, 148 twisters killed more than 300 people and caused half a billion dollars' worth of damage in 13 U.S. states.'

'To scientists, these seemingly disparate incidents represent the advance signs of fundamental changes in the world's weather. *The central fact is that after three quarters of a century of extraordinarily mild conditions, the earth's climate seems to be cooling down.*'[24] [Emphasis Added] The CFR prophets of doom were all espousing *global cooling;* we were all going to freeze to death. In the same year a group of distinguished scientists wrote a letter to U.S. President Richard Nixon, expressing their fear that the world was entering a new Ice Age.[25]

This should have come as no surprize as *Time* magazine had reported earlier in Jun 24th, 1974 that in Africa, drought had continued for the sixth consecutive year, adding terribly to the toll of famine victims, and during 1972 record rains in parts of the U.S., Pakistan and Japan causing some of the worst flooding in centuries. Canada's wheat belt, a particularly chilly and rainy spring has delayed planting and may well bring a disappointingly small harvest. Rainy Britain, on the other hand, has suffered from uncharacteristic dry spells the past few springs. A series of unusually cold winters has gripped the American Far West, while New England and northern Europe have recently experienced the mildest winters within anyone's recollection.

As they review the bizarre and unpredictable weather pattern of the past several years, a growing number of scientists are beginning to suspect that many seemingly contradictory meteorological fluctuations are actually part of a global climatic upheaval. However widely the weather varies from place to place and time to time, when meteorologists take an average of temperatures around the globe they find that the atmosphere has been growing *gradually cooler* for the past three decades. The trend shows *no indication of reversing*. Climatological Cassandra's are becoming increasingly apprehensive, for the weather aberrations they are studying may be the harbinger of *another ice age*.[26] [Emphasis Added] Speaking at Swarthmore University, Kenneth Watt said the world will be "…eleven degrees colder in the year 2000. This is about twice what it would take to put us into an ice age,"[27] In November 1974, BBC1 chipped in with *The Weather Machine*, stating that there was now '…the ever present threat of the big freeze.'

Global Warming

Scientists were right about temperatures declining from around 1940 to the mid-seventies, this was known as the 'Little Cooling' period, but less than a decade after the world was threatened with a new ice age that 'experts' warned shows *'no indication of reversing,'* the US NBC *'Nightly News,'* 23rd, June 1988 reported: "…and some 'experts' are now saying that the whole world is heating up because of a global greenhouse effect - that is heat caught in the atmosphere by air pollution that prevents its escape."

The UK's *News at Ten,* 11th, April 1989 reported: "Information from satellites has convinced most scientists that average temperatures will rise by two to five degrees Celsius over the next one hundred years."

With scenes of children playing on the beaches of a small island in the Maldives, *Channel 4 News* in the UK, 4th, April 1989, reported: "As the children play, year by year the waters are rising around them. They will be adults by the time the Pacific swamps the nine sandy stubs that are the Islands of Tuvalu. If forecasts are correct the seas around here will rise by about two feet over the next fifty years."

A British Channel 4 documentary *The Green Conspiracy*, aired on SBS Television in Australia in 1990, saw Dr. Sherwood IDSO stating that: "A lot of people are getting very famous and very well-funded as a result of promoting the disastrous scenario of greenhouse warming." Professor Reginald Newell also stated: "My suspicion is that if you have a crisis like this it's easier to gain funds for the profession as a whole." Dr. Roy Spencer of the NASA Space Flight Centre followed with: "It's easier to get funding if you can show some evidence for impending climate disasters. In the late 1970's it was the coming ice age and now it's the coming global warming. Who knows what it will be ten years from now. Sure, science benefits from scary scenarios." He later went on to say: "If you don't jump on the environmental bandwagon to stop the inevitable warming of the Earth, then you will be ostracised from the scientific community and from everybody else's community, because it's not fashionable to disagree with the environmentalists these days."[28]

The same documentary shows Professor of Meteorology Reginald Newell, at MIT, Boston, when asked if there is any real evidence of a forthcoming environmental disaster who states: "No, I would not think there is any evidence for a catastrophic change in our climate at the present time." The interviewer then asked: "No evidence at all?" Newell replied: "There is no evidence at all."[29]

No evidence at all of an impending apocalypse didn't stop the World Meteorological Organization (WMO) and the United Nations Environment Programme (UNEP) in 1988, from establishing the Intergovernmental Panel on Climate Change (IPCC), an arm of the United Nations to create 'special reports' to promote the environmental global warming issue. It is interesting to note that with the impending disaster that threatens the planet, a 'political' organization is set up to deal with the situation.

United Nations Conference on Environment and Deception

As seen in the last chapter, 1992 saw the United Nations Conference on Environment and Development (UNCED), or 'Earth Summit' held in Rio which paved the way for *Agenda 21* and the *Global Biodiversity Assessment*. The Summit also paved the way for measures to tackle 'Global Warming.'

One attendee of the conference was author and expert on the United Nations games of deception, William F. Jasper, who witnessed the event firsthand. He told of eminent scientist Dr Dixy Lee Ray, who challenged the absurd claims and dangerous proposals of the environmental fanatics, pointing out holes in the Establishment's argument, but was virtually ignored, as were other noted scientists and scholars, while the CFR establishment press drooled over every sacred syllable uttered by the likes of Fidel Castro, Mikhail Gorbachev, Jerry "Governor Moonbeam" Brown, then-senator Al Gore, Jacques Cousteau, and Maurice Strong.[30]

As a distinguished professor of Zoology, Dr Ray remarked on the UN conference that she had "never seen a bigger zoo." Dr Ray had stated: "First, we must recognize that the environmental movement is not about facts or logic. More and more it is becoming clear that those who support the so-called 'New World Order' or World Government under the United Nations have adopted global environmentalism as a basis for the dissolution of independent nations and the international realignment of power."[31]Jasper also reveals that more than 250 distinguished scientists, including 27 Nobel Laureates, released a statement called the *Heidelberg Appeal to Heads of States and Governments*, who wrote: "We are... worried at the dawn of the twenty-first century, at the emergence of an irrational ideology which is opposed to scientific and industrial progress and impedes economic and social development."[32] They were also ignored; there was no debate on merit.

The 1992 Earth Summit produced the United Nations Framework Convention on Climate Change (UNFCCC), a global response to tackle global warming, to stabilise greenhouse gas emissions. The Convention is to be complemented by the Kyoto Protocol, which will be established in 1997. Under this new treaty, industrialized nations and the European Community commit to reduce their carbon emissions. 154 countries queued up to sign the UN Framework Convention on Climate Change (UNFCCC). The Intergovernmental Panel on Climate Change (IPCC) 'special reports' are frequently used as the basis for decisions made under the Convention.

The Intergovernmental Panel on Climate Change (IPCC) 'special reports' are often cited as the 'consensus,' claiming the world's top 2,500 scientists agree with IPCC conclusions. When looking through the bibliography of members, there are a number of non-scientists, reviewers, government workers, and anyone else that happened to walk past the building once. In 2007 the IPCC 2,500 scientists blamed 'human activities for climate changes ranging from more heat waves to floods.'[33] Professor Richard Lindzen of M.I.T. remarked about scientific 'consensus' amongst IPCC members: "...none of them are asked to agree, many of them disagree."

The IPCC published a 'special report' in 1995, '*The Science of Climate Change*.' The report was held in high regard largely because it was peer-reviewed, meaning it has been read, discussed, modified and approved by an international body of experts. But as Professor Frederick Seitz stated this is not the version that was approved by the contributing scientists, and that the IPCC had censored the most important statements of the scientists. Professor Seitz stated: "In my more than 60 years as a member of the American scientific community, including service as president of both the National Academy of Sciences and the American Physical Society, I have never witnessed a more disturbing corruption of the peer-review process than the events that led to this IPCC report." Passages that were originally approved in the report were deleted from the peer-reviewed published version. Deleted lines included:

"None of the studies cited above has shown clear evidence that we can attribute the observed [climate] changes to the specific cause of increases in greenhouse gases."

"No study to date has positively attributed all or part [of the climate change observed to date] to anthropogenic [man-made] causes."

"Any claims of positive detection of significant climate change are likely to remain controversial until uncertainties in the total natural variability of the climate system are reduced." If they lead *to carbon taxes and restraints on economic growth, they will have a major and almost certainly destructive impact on the economies of the world.* Seitz says that whatever the intent was of those who made these significant changes, their effect is to *deceive policy makers and the public into believing that the scientific evidence shows human activities are causing global warming.* Professor Seitz also stated: "If the IPCC is incapable of following its most basic procedures, it would be best to abandon the entire IPCC process or at least that part that is concerned with the scientific evidence on climate change, and look for more reliable sources of advice to governments..."[34] [Emphasis Added] Sir John Houghton, first chairman of the IPCC Scientific Working Group 1994 stated: "Unless we announce disasters, no one will listen."[35]

The report was designed to provide the underpinning for the Kyoto Protocols in 1997, to enable practical foundations to tackle global warming. Under the Protocol member countries now give general commitments to cut carbon emissions to 5.2 percent below 1990 levels. The Protocols were eventually adopted on 11th, December, 1997 in Kyoto, Japan and entered into force on 16th, February 2005. As of July 2010, 191 states have signed and ratified the protocol.[36] Patrick J. Michaels, a professor of environmental sciences at the University of Virginia and senior fellow in environmental studies at the Cato Institute wrote that: 'The Kyoto Protocol will have no discernible effect on global climate, in fact, it is doubtful that the current network of surface thermometers could distinguish a change on the order of .19 degree from normal year-to-year variations. The Kyoto Protocol will result in no demonstrable climate change but easily *demonstrable economic damage*.'[37] [Emphasis Added] Those commitments are due to expire at the end of 2012 and, if there is to be a second round of legally binding pledges, they would need to be made at the UN's climate summit in Durban (2012).

The treaty introduced the idea of 'emissions trading' (Also known as Cap and Trade), whereby countries or firms which were failing to meet their reduction targets could buy 'carbon credits' to carry on trading.

Hockey Sticks

The United Nations undeterred by missing evidence in the IPCC report received another potential 'Green' light in 1998, when US scientist Michael E. Mann revealed the MBH98 graph, or the 'Hockey Stick Curve,' which showed estimated computer reconstruction models of temperature records of the past 1000 years, indicating an alarming sharp rise in temperatures during the second half of the 20th century. Mann had fed data into a computer program to predict the extent of global warming, even thou realistic computer models or predictions of what earth may or may not do are difficult to compute because of the complexity and uncertainty of the weather, oceans, the atmosphere, the surface of the earth, and the millions of other variations in the way they interact at any one moment, etc. Any desired result can be generated by putting selective or biased information into a computer system, as Dr Patrick J. Michaels of the University of Virginia put it, "The entire global climate change hysteria is driven by computer models, it is not driven by reality. Reality is not warming up like those models said it would!"

Professor Richard Lindzen in the UK's *Daily Mail* quoted: "Future generations will wonder in bemused amazement that the early 21st-century's developed world went into hysterical panic over a globally average temperature increase of a few tenths of a degree, and on the basis of gross exaggerations of highly uncertain computer projections contemplated a roll-back of the industrial age."[38]

Stephen McIntyre of the Northwest Exploration Co, Ontario, Canada, and Department of Economics at the University of Guelph's Professor Ross McKitrick, recompiled and analysed the data by Mann and got quite different answers. They then revealed that the Hockey Stick graph was incorrect, they were very polite when putting the false data down to a computer programming error. The hockey stick curve has since become one of the most discredited artefacts in the history of science.

An Inconvenient Truth about CO$_2$

From the turn of the century, climbing CO$_2$ levels caused by man have been in the news media practically every day. The UK's *The Guardian* newspaper, 11th, October 2004, leads with 'Climate fear as levels soar,' scientists 'bewildered' by sharp rise of CO$_2$ in atmosphere for second year running. Scientists are 'baffled,' 'unexplained and unprecedented' rise in carbon dioxide in the atmosphere two years running has raised fears that the world may be on the brink of 'runaway global warming.' *USA Today* on August 1st, 1999 ran with 'Arctic temperature rise spurs carbon dioxide increase.' 'An increase in arctic temperatures as a result of global warming could result in significantly higher levels of carbon dioxide being released into the atmosphere; this could fuel global warming even more,' and a million other articles with more of the same.

The crowning glory of propaganda came in 2006, when ex-Vice President Al Gore proclaimed in his Academy Award winning documentary *An Inconvenient Truth,* "When there is more carbon dioxide, the temperature gets warmer because it traps more heat from the sun inside." This is a complete untruth, disproved by 1000's of scientists worldwide, whose voices you will never hear because they don't conform to UN theory, and besides - facts don't matter.

Let's back up a little, history records have shown hotter, as well as colder periods throughout recorded history, the climate continually changes without any assistance from man. Going back 8000 years during the Bronze Age, the 'Holocene Maximum' period had temperatures higher than today, for more than three millennia. Around 900 AD, the 'Medieval Warm Period' lasted for about four centuries until around 1350, the earth experienced the 'Little Ice Age.' Reports of the Thames River in London would freeze over, resulting in ice fairs, skating, and vendors selling their wares on the ice. Professor Tim Patterson of the Dept. of Earth Sciences, Carlton University, testifying before Canada's House of Commons, Subcommittee on the Environment and Sustainable Development, Feb 10th, 2005 stated: "The paleoclimatic data that I and others have collected, it is obvious that climate is and always has been variable. In fact, the only constant about climate is change. It changes continually. CO_2 has an influence but is certainly not significant enough for us to worry about."[39]

The Post War Economic Boom (PWEB) is blamed for the current global warming 'crisis.' The earth has risen 0.5 degree in the last 100 years; long before industry was 'polluting' the planet; most of the warming had occurred before 1940. After World War II, or the PWEB, industry boomed with mass produced washing machines, appliances, cars and fridges, etc. With the start of the PWEB, the temperature records should indicate a rising in temperatures due to the rise of heavy industry polluting the atmosphere, but they don't, records show that for the next four decades, temperatures started to *decline.* Carbon dioxide was increasing, but temperatures were falling, indicating CO_2 does not rise because of man's activities. These facts can be proved in many different ways from many different sources, which again, CFR establishment media ignore.

Al Gore's argument is carbon-dioxide is the major green house gas that is driving the temperature of the earth upwards. The reality is that CO_2 *follows* a rise in temperature, *it doesn't precede it.* It is important to understand this distinction as the United Nations Establishment and Gore have used this argument to spearhead the global warming agenda. CO_2 does not cause temperature to rise as Gore would have us believe, but *temperature* causes CO_2 levels to rise. As Dr. Ian Clark, Department of Earth Sciences University points out, looking at "...the ice core record from Vostok... we see temperature going up from early time... and then we see the CO_2 coming up, CO_2 *lags* behind that increase by *800 years*, so temperature is *leading* CO_2 by *800 years*." [Emphasis Added] Or as Professor Tim Ball, Dept. Of Climatology, University of Winnipeg stated: "...the ice core records from Vostok show exactly the opposite, the whole fundamental assumption of theory of climate change, due to humans is shown to be wrong."

Al Gore and the U.N.'s Intergovernmental Panel on Climate Change went on to win the 2007 Nobel Peace Prize for their 'sterling work to humanity' and were even congratulated by President Bush. Receiving the award, Gore took the opportunity to remind everyone that global warming is "the greatest challenge we've ever faced... a true planetary emergency. The climate crisis is not a political issue; it is a moral and spiritual challenge to all humanity."[40] Gore didn't take any questions.

Al Gore's film was distributed with four other short films to 3,500 schools in the UK. A father accused the Government of 'brainwashing' with propaganda by showing it to children. A judge indicated schools should issue a warning before they show pupils Gore's controversial film about global warming. Stewart Dimmock said the former U.S. Vice-President's documentary, *An Inconvenient Truth*, is unfit for schools because it is politically biased and contains serious scientific inaccuracies and 'sentimental mush.'[41]

What's even more incredible is that CO_2 is only a very small part of the earth's atmosphere, to understand how small, Brian Sussman describes Michael Crichton's visual representation to assist us in wrapping our minds around the components of Earth's atmosphere... he likens the atmosphere to a football field. The goal line to the 78 yard-line contains nothing but nitrogen. Oxygen fills the next 21 yards, stretching to the 99 yard line. The final yard, except for about two and a half inches, is argon, a wonderfully mysterious inert gas useful for putting out electric fires. About half of the remaining inches are crammed with a variety of minor, but essential gases. And the last 1.37 inches? Carbon dioxide. The equivalent of 1 inch out of a 100-yard field… how much of that last inch is contributed by human activities? The equivalent of a line as thin as a dime standing on edge.[42]

Any person who has conducted a smidgen of research would find that human beings are partly made of carbon, and carbon dioxide is a natural part of life, and plants that receive more CO_2 than normal are usually 'found to be in a vigorous state of development.'[43] But since 'global warming' was declared a 'crisis,' carbon-dioxide is now officially described as a pollutant. The whole debate has become detached from reality, and taken a trip into unreality with an incredible weak-lemon drink of well-funded laughable 'science.'

John Gibbons of the *Sovereign Independent* put it this way: "I came to the conclusion after a period of self-analysis and rehabilitation combined with my own rediscovered power of critical thinking, that I and many of my friends had been duped by the IPCC and other so called 'green' organisations over a long period of time. It was actually my daughter that pointed out to me that CO_2 was actually essential for life and that if we stopped CO_2 production then all the plants and fluffy animals, of which I love very much, would all die. Then I had that 'eureka' moment when I realised that she meant humans too."

When another reporter asked him how he felt when realising that an international unelected organisation such as the United Nations had lied to the world for decades on the subject of 'global warming,' he replied: "I didn't believe it at first and even refused point blank on many occasions on the national airwaves to look at the scientifically peer reviewed evidence against my religious belief that manmade climate change was real and the earth was heading for catastrophe. Little did I know that the opposite was the case and that a warmer planet would create an abundance of food supplies and green-ery across the world."[44] The whole of the United Nations argument for more governmental control over man and everything in it rests on the theory of too much CO_2. In simple terms as former editor of *New Scientist*, Nigel Calder said: "Man-made global warming is just propaganda."[45]

ClimateGate

In 2009, December 7th – 18th, the United Nations Climate Change Con-ference or the Copenhagen Summit (COP15), was held in Denmark, this was the big one. The Copenhagen summit was to produce an agreement limiting greenhouse gases, but according to 'experts,' the conference had generated the same carbon footprint as a medium-sized African country such as Malawi. There were 34,000 delegates attending the event, and the grander among them were forced 'to park their private jets in Norway because Denmark had run out of Tarmac, and had to procure their gas-guzzling limousines from Germany.'[46]

Days before the Conference began, the propaganda machines were turned on full steam, to remind the public of what is going to happen to the earth if the new Global Warming treaty isn't signed. The public mind was prepared for the Summit with an article appearing on the front page of the UK's *Guardian* newspaper, the article then proceeded to run in *56 newspapers in 45 countries at the same time!* Alan Rusbridger, editor-in-chief of the *Guardian* said: "No individual newspaper editorial could hope to influence the outcome of Copenhagen but I hope the combined voice of 56 major newspapers speaking in 20 languages will remind the politicians and negotiators gathering there what is at stake and persuade them to rise above the rivalries and inflexibility that have stood in the way of a deal."[47]

Ministers of Foreign Affairs on the 4th December 2009 stated: 'Only days before the UN Climate Change Conference in Copenhagen, humankind is confronted with the consequences of its past actions, 'scientific evidence' clearly shows that anthropogenic greenhouse gas emissions contribute significantly to global warming. The prospects are grim: rising temperatures will cause major crop declines in entire regions and significant changes in the availability of water resources. At the same time, as some areas experience major water shortages, rising sea levels will threaten some of the world's largest cities and may even cause loss of territory and give rise to border disputes. Entire ecosystems, from glaciers to rain forests, 'could' collapse, and many species would face extinction. Storms, droughts, forest fires and floods will cause irreversible environmental degradation and desertification, affecting the food security of millions and causing massive migration flows.'[48] The same eco-fear nonsense used in the *Newsweek* article on Global Cooling in 1975.

All the stops had been pulled out; they placed their bets on everything, so they may get lucky that one of the disasters might happen, they thought there should be enough there to scare everyone into signing the treaty, as the scare had followed an imminent swine flu pandemic that was supposedly rife at the time, the flu virus was about to go viral across the whole world at any moment, killing millions in its path. But the pandemic had to be put on hold for another time while COP15 was in session. The swine flu pandemic was just another attempt at forced vaccination to advance the de-population program, which is important, but not as important as compared to the profits the Money-Lenders will receive from a signed treaty at Copenhagen. But I am sure swine flu is getting a new makeover, and will be back for a new season in the near future.

Prince Charles had stated previously that "The grim reality is that our planet has reached a point of crisis and we have only seven years before we lose the levers of control." The President of Gabon chipped in with "The door to our future is closing..."[49] So concerned was the Prince about the environment, that he personally commandeered a jet belonging to the Queen's Flight, generating an estimated 6.4 tons of carbon dioxide, 5.2 tons more than if he had used a commercial flight.[50] Gordon Brown the then Prime Minister of Britain, who a few months earlier claimed we only had "50 days to save to earth," chartered a luxury 185-seat Airbus to take him and 20 aides to the Copenhagen Conference. Apocalyptic doom or not, old habits die hard.

Unfortunately for the world's elite, the United Nations conference began under the knowledge that the University of East Anglia's Climatic Research Unit (CRU) website had been the victims of hackers, which revealed email correspondence between two top United Nations scientists, revealing damaging evidence that the UN's own scientists manipulated data to corroborate the story of human beings causing global warming. Some 1,000 e-mails and 3,000 documents from the Climate Research Unit at the U.K.'s University of East Anglia had been leaked.[51]

Not only did the emails from the university's climate unit reveal that some of the world's leading scientists discussed how they could shield data from the public eye, but also how to suppress independent scientist's findings that didn't match their own. The revelations of all the new information and data surrounding the leaked emails put a dark cloud over the talks. The United Nations desperately tried to pretend that the leaked emails, or 'Climate Gate' as it was called didn't happen. Most of the mainstream media ignored it, and those that did touch on it didn't state the content of the emails. The media, the United Nations and the scientists all practically ignored the unfortunate incident, and had no time for questions or anyone's opinion about the matter and just pressed on with the agenda. When they did confront the emails, instead of looking at the content of the emails to look for evidence of a conspiracy, the media and the United Nations diverted attention away from the issue by using a Cold War tactic, Pascal van Ypersele, vice-chairman of the IPCC blamed

'Climate-Gate' on a fiendish Russian plot! Achim Steiner, the director of the United Nations Environment Programme (UNEP), said the theft of thousands of emails from the CRU were first published on a small server in the city of Tomsk in Siberia, which is a world-renowned centre for climate research. It all had similarities with the Watergate scandal which brought down US President Richard Nixon... But: "This is not Climate gate, its 'hacker gate'. Let's not forget the word 'gate' refers to a place [the Watergate building] where data was stolen by people who were paid to do so.... So the media should direct its investigations into that."[52] The investigation was to focus its attention on where the emails had come from instead of the actual content. Jean-Pascal van Ypersele went on to say the exposed emails were making it more difficult to persuade the 192 countries going to Copenhagen of the need to cut carbon emissions, which was the only truth stated in Copenhagen, because it is more difficult to persuade nation states to sign away their sovereignty when your only evidence for global warming is found to be based on lies, deception and propaganda. When asked whether they still have to justify the science Rajendra Pachauri, Chairman of the Intergovernmental Panel on Climate Change (IPCC) remarked... "I don't think so because the IPCC has 21 years of unblemished record of performance and these emails don't change anything."[53]

Even thou we only have a few years before we lose the 'levers of control' of the planet, an even bigger problem occurred at the conference, if the end of the world isn't big enough. The biggest disagreement at the United Nations Climate Change Conference was not how to reduce Global Warming or how to cut carbon emissions - but once all nations have signed the treaty, WHO'S GOING TO COLLECT ALL THE MONEY? Which institution is going to look after all this new found 'carbon' money? Fifty African countries, so disgusted with the event, walked out of the negotiations, their main protest point being they don't want any of the established Rothschild private banks to handle adaptation cash. Sudanese Chief Negotiator, Lumumba Di–Aping stated: "We have no desire at all to have the World Bank and the IMF & GEF manage this. We have trusted them with our economies and I don't think anyone of you can tell us how much development or economic instability and financial instability we have achieved." The African nations and other developing countries called for a whole new institution to be developed and funded with public money, not private money, to take away the profit motive for climate change.

Carbon Neutral Humans - Do Not Exhale

If global warming is not the villain Al Gore and the United Nation's makes it out to be, why repeat the mantra of the destruction of the planet from CO_2? In July 2006, Environment Secretary David Miliband gives us a clue when he states: "Imagine a country where carbon becomes a new currency... We carry bank cards that store both pounds and carbon points. When we buy electricity, gas and fuel, we use our carbon points, as well as pounds." In the same month, the BBC Breakfast program in the UK aired the story of 'Would you live a greener lifestyle, if you could make money from it?' Personal carbon allowances (PCA's) could be implemented with everyone in the UK allocated with an annual carbon allowance: "...rather like a supermarket loyalty card, points would be deducted every time you buy or use non-renewable energy. Any points left over could be sold back to the central bank, and people who need more, like motorists who have used their allocation could then pay for a top-up."[54] Carbon trading is not only designed for big business and industry to cut emissions; carbon trading is to come down to the individual level.

In June 2009, the UK Energy Research Centre released a working paper exploring what people would need to know 'if' a Personal Carbon Allowance (PCA) scheme was introduced. PCA is to be a mandatory carbon 'Cap and Trade' policy for all individuals to receive an annual carbon emissions 'budget,' or 'Carbon Credits' for personal use, covering household energy use, such as electricity, gas and private transport.

Under a PCA policy, a deduction will be made from your personal carbon budget for each carbon-unit you buy. If you emit more carbon than your allowance, you will need to buy more carbon credits. Those who emit less carbon than their allowance can sell the excess into the carbon market. A 'pay as you go' option could be offered to those who do not wish to trade. Individuals will have to learn how to *live within their carbon budget; which will be reduced each year* to meet the UK's 80% cut in emissions by 2050. The wording is very clever – Question: How do you cut your personal emission by 80%? Answer: You lower your already struggling standard of living by 4/5's. The paper goes on to say carbon literacy needs to be improved so that individuals know their actual carbon footprints and the corresponding 'carbon income' and expenditure from their budgets. The plans are also to prompt *carbon conscious behaviour... by helping to prepare individuals and society for a *carbon-constrained world.*[55] [Emphasis Added]

Tina Fawcett, of the Environmental Change Institute, Oxford University, writes that the administration of carbon allowances could be straightforward, with each person issued an electronic card containing that year's carbon credits. The card would have to be presented on purchase of energy or travel services, and the correct amount of carbon would be deducted. The technologies and systems already in place for direct debit systems and credit cards could be used. There are relatively few sellers of gas, electricity, petrol, diesel and other fuels, and flows of fossil fuels are already very well recorded and tightly regulated in the economy – both these factors would ease introduction of such a system.[56]

In November 2009, Lord Smith of Finsbury stated that everyone should have a unique number... which they could use like a bank account, a statement would be sent out each month to help people keep track of what they are using. If their "carbon account" hits zero, they would have to pay to get more credits.[57]

Andrew Revkin, who reports on environmental issues for *The New York Times*, floated an idea for combating global warming: Give carbon credits to couples that limit themselves to having one child. Revkin said: "...probably the single-most concrete and substantive thing an American, young American, could do to lower carbon footprint is not turning off the lights or driving a Prius, it's having fewer kids, having fewer children..." Revkin is saying "should you get credit... for having a one-child family when you could have had two or three?"[58] Revkin is the same guy who asked "Are Condoms the Ultimate Green-Technology?" Citing an August 2009 study by the London School of Economics that highlighted having fewer children could be a solution to diminishing your carbon footprint. It is not a stretch of the imagination to float the idea that paper money in the not-too-distant future is on its way out, that the world is getting a new economic system, a cashless society with a new carbon currency.

Low Carbon Future Economy

The transition to the 'low carbon future economy' will involve monitoring and controlling the consumption of electricity through new technology known as 'Smart Meters' in the home. Smart meters are sold under the pretext of saving the customer money; but smart meters underway in the US are already experiencing problems. California residents are already experiencing 40-50% increase in their bills. Rob States, M.S., of the San-Francisco Tesla Society said on October 10th, 2010: "Smart meters are responsible for zero energy savings, zero reduction." Savings do not come from the meters; savings come from a change in *customer behaviour*, from using less energy. These are new control measures through *behaviour modification*.

On October 27th, 2009, President Obama announced a $3.4 Billion investment to spur the transition to a new 'Smart Energy Grid.'[59] The UK is not far behind with the Department of Energy and Climate Change (DECC), who plan to roll out 53 million 'Smart Meters' in 30 million homes and businesses across the UK. The Government's mass roll-out is to start in early 2014 and to be completed in 2019.[60] Smart meters will replace current analogue meters; including gas meters, which are wirelessly connected to the 'Smart Grid,' different rates will be charged throughout the day known as 'time of day' rates. It is a system of incentives so you don't use excessive amounts of energy.

Smart meters are wireless, designed to monitor all electrical appliances in the home. Smart meters know which appliances you are using, when you are using them, how much and for how long. All appliances in 5 years will have to have wireless connections that *talk* to the smart meter, there will be no choice, your appliances will have to be wireless enabled to work with the smart meter. All modern technology appliances, cookers, kettles, lighting, hairdryers, etc., will have microchips that can be 'remotely connected and disconnected.'[61] with Cap and Trade in place, you may reach your limit before the end of the calendar month and be *remotely* cut-off.

In the US, Fanny Mae was granted the patent (monopoly) for the future outlet sockets in the wall, which are lockable – when you plug in your small appliance, if it's not compatible with the grid network, the appliance won't work. Two major players in the US for the new generation of appliances are General Electric and Whirlpool, who are working "...to address how appliances will interact with the Smart Grid." Bracken Darrell, president of Whirlpool Europe recently announced that by 2015, the company will "make all the electronically controlled appliances it produces—everywhere in the world—capable of receiving and responding to signals from smart grids..." General Electric is introducing appliances that are capable of receiving pricing increase signals and adjusting their functions to reduce power consumption until prices goes back down. They currently have a pilot program in Louisville, KY to determine the effectiveness of the Smart Grid enabled appliances. The utility is providing a pricing plan where prices vary across the day and once customers have established their preferences based on pricing, these smart appliances will adjust their operations automatically.[62]

The government will finally enter your living area and be in control of what you can and can't do within your own home environment, and with 80% reduction targets to meet up to 2050, control measures will become increasingly more severe as the new low carbon future economy becomes a reality, or as John D. Rockefeller, Jr.'s phrased it - just another nail in the coffin towards "this goal of social control."

EPILOGUE

The Illuminati plan for world control has come a long way from the early days of 1776. The New World Order is still a work-in-progress, but with the United Nations as the organizing body, the destiny of the world looks to be in their hands. Mayer Amschel Rothschild could never have imagined that the plan to rule the world could have worked so well, 'modern' society has become a dictator's dream.

The last century has seen the wealth of the world shift from ordinary people and small businesses to a few private international banking families, who use their wealth and power to run a parallel government – the Royal Institute for International Affairs, the Council on Foreign Relations, the Trilateral Commission, the United Nations, etc., and an army of Non-Governmental-Organizations staffed with thousands of bureaucrats. They have installed their central banks one by one in each country, gradually taking control of each nation. They have infiltrated all levels of government and its institutions, the military, media and entertainment, academia, and agriculture, buying Presidents, politicians, celebrities, scientists, professors, doctors, and military personal along the way who use their position to sign over the wealth and power of the world to the few who belong to the 'Establishment' and its myriad of powerful multinational corporations. Any 'authorized' person on the world stage is a frontman for the Illuminati and will do as they are instructed to do. Through secret societies, Brotherhoods and hidden agreements, they pledge their allegiance, all following the party line knowing they will be removed should they say otherwise.

The general public still believe they have a democratic vote when presented with world politics, but these organized groups present the appearance of democracy through their media, whether labour or conservative, Republican or Democrat, left or right, black or white, up and down - it is all a manufactured illusion, it is a circus for the public to talk about while the real world is created in private behind closed doors.

This is how the world really works, the true masters who rule the world, implementing far reaching plans that most people haven't ascribed to their own way of living yet. Within a few generations of indoctrination; the people haven't made the connection that their traditional values upheld for centuries by our forefathers who died on the battlefields are fading from memory, each passing generation is being born into a slightly more distorted version of reality than the previous generation.

Our masters are changing what it means to be human, creating a one size fits all standardized version of man; individuality is to be stamped out as man is led down the garden path, listening to, and fed insane propaganda, nonsense and trivia, worshipping and following pseudo celebrities who know nothing and represent nothing.

Unborn generations of children will be socially engineered for the new hedonistic, humanistic culture of tomorrow, all the 'sustainable' high talk of looking out for the children's future is complete fabrication. The money-lenders, through the United Nations will impoverish all future generations into world slavery. One only needs to look around to see what kind of a controlled, no privacy world children are already being born into - a high-tech world with 24 hour surveillance; scanners and pat downs at airports, face recognition and scanning technology when entering school, cameras in toilets; CCTV in the classroom and fingerprints stored in databases – for their 'protection.' This is a world where every transaction is recorded through credit cards, travel cards, loyalty cards, mobile phone tracking systems and a whole multitude of other real-time tracking devices, including Facebook and Google who collect all your data, etc., to the younger generation, no privacy is the new normal.

We live in a world where the sexualisation of children is normal, where children see many teenage single women who have children, who are barely children themselves, a world of increasingly promoted homosexuality, teaching anal sex to five year olds, abortion, no respect for the elderly, increased taxes for *everything* [but there is never any money for *anything*], both parents of a family out working in low paid dead end jobs, police officers that 'Protect and Serve,' given absolute power over the public to use brute force to stop, search, detain and enter homes for no reason, you can even be detained for crimes you 'may' commit in the future.

It is not just the children; we are all experiencing a shift in our daily experience of 'living,' this new society is being installed in every country. The 'old' culture is giving way to the new, cultural knowledge and wisdom is losing the battle in the push for globalism. Internationalism will eventually destroy every culture and tradition on the planet.

The enemies of the past were easily identifiable by their military uniforms, their armies and weaponry. Today's rulers wear Armani suits, have pearl white teeth, flash friendly warm smiles and are chauffeur driven in limousines around Capitol Hill and Westminster. Their armies of bureaucrats are very skilled in using such weapons as language, education, cultural heritage, human rights, religion and the family unit against society. This is the New World Order, Big Brother is Big Banker.

References

Chapter One: Money Lenders, Usury and Christ

1. Stephen A. Zarlenga, *The Lost Science of Money: The Mythology of Money – the Story of Power*, P. 340. American Monetary Institute, Valatie, New York, 2002.

2. Ellen Hodgson Brown, J.D., *The Web of Debt: The Shocking Truth About Our Money System And How We Can Break Free*, P. 31. Third Millennium Press, Baton Rouge, Louisiana 2008.

3. William Guy Carr, *Pawns in the Game*, P. 12-13. (No Publishing Information).

4. http://www.iamthewitness.com

5. Des Griffin, *Fourth Reich of the Rich*, P. 275. Emissary Publications, Clackamas, OR, 1998 Edition.

6. Ellen Hodgson Brown, J.D., *The Web of Debt: The Shocking Truth About Our Money System And How We Can Break Free*, P. 347.

7. G. Edward Griffin, *The Creature from Jekyll Island: A Second Look at the Federal Reserve*, P. 159-160. American Media, Westlake Village, California, 1998.

8. Ibid, P. 144

9. Ellen Hodgson Brown, J.D., *The Web of Debt: The Shocking Truth About Our Money System And How We Can Break Free*, P. 27.

10. Ibid, P. 71

11. G. Edward Griffin, *The Creature from Jekyll Island: A Second Look at the Federal Reserve*, P. 55.

12. William Guy Carr, *Pawns in the Game*, P. 23.

13. Ibid, P. 21

14. Ellen Hodgson Brown, J.D., *The Web of Debt: The Shocking Truth About Our Money System And How We Can Break Free*, P. 68.

15. William Guy Carr, *Pawns in the Game*, P, 23.

16. G. Edward Griffin, *The Creature from Jekyll Island: A Second Look at the Federal Reserve*, P. 175.

17. William Guy Carr, *Pawns in the Game*, P. 24.

18. Ibid, P. 23-24

19. E. C. Knuth, *The Empire of "The City," The Secret History of British Financial Power*, P. 27. The Book Tree, San Diego, California, 2006.

20. Andrew Carrington Hitchcock, *The Synagogue of Satan: The Secret History of Jewish World Domination*, P. 29. RiverCrest Publishing, Austin, Texas, 2009.

21. Carroll Quigley, *Tragedy and Hope: A History of the World in Our Time*, P. 48-49, First Published in 1966 by The Macmillan Company. GSG and Associates, San Pedro, California.

22. Ellen Hodgson Brown, J.D., *The Web of Debt: The Shocking Truth About Our Money System And How We Can Break Free*, P. 68-69.

23. G. Edward Griffin, *The Creature from Jekyll Island: A Second Look at the Federal Reserve*, P. 183.

24. Eustace Mullins, *The World Order: A Study in the Hegemony of Parasitism,* P. 29. Ezra Pound Institute of Civilization, Staunton, VA, 1985.

Chapter Two: *Brotherhood of Death*

1. Eustace Mullins, *The World Order: A Study in the Hegemony of Parasitism*, P. 8. Ezra Pound Institute of Civilization, Staunton, VA, 1985.

2. Carroll Quigley, *Tragedy and Hope: A History of the World in Our Time*, P. 51-52. First Published in 1966 by The Macmillan Company. GSG and Associates, San Pedro, California.

3. Eustace Mullins, *The World Order: A Study in the Hegemony of Parasitism*, P. 9.

4. John Reeves, *The Rothschilds: The Financial Rulers of the Nations*, P. 104-105. Sampson Low, Marston, Searle and Rivington, 1887.

5. William Guy Carr, *Pawns in the Game*, P. 27-31. (No Publishing Information)

6. Dee Zahner, *The Secret Side of History: Mystery Babylon and the New World Order*, P. 29. LTAA Communications Publishers, Hesperia, California, 1994.

7. Andrew Carrington Hitchcock, *The Synagogue of Satan: The Secret History of Jewish World Domination*, P. 36-37. RiverCrest Publishing, Austin, Texas, 2009.

Chapter Three: *First American Central Bank*

1. Dee Zahner, *The Secret Side of History: Mystery Babylon and the New World Order*, P. 57. LTAA Communications Publishers, Hesperia, California, 1994.

2. Alexander James, *Hidden History of Money and New World Order Usury Secrets Revealed*, P. 37. [Independent Publisher: available through http://www.lulu.com]

3. Antony C. Sutton, *The Federal Reserve Conspiracy: Bankers that Stole America*, P. 7. 1995. (No Publishing Information).

4. Ibid, P. 5

5. William Guy Carr, *Pawns in the Game*, P. 51. (No Publishing Information).

6. Andrew Carrington Hitchcock, *The Synagogue of Satan: The Secret History of Jewish World Domination*, P. 37. RiverCrest Publishing, Austin, Texas, 2009.

7. William Guy Carr, *Pawns in the Game*, P. 52.

8. Ellen Hodgson Brown, J.D., *The Web of Debt: The Shocking Truth About Our Money System And How We Can Break Free*, P. 76. Third Millennium Press, Baton Rouge, Louisiana 2008.

9. William Guy Carr, *Pawns in the Game*, P. 53.

10. Ellen Hodgson Brown, J.D., *The Web of Debt: The Shocking Truth About Our Money System And How We Can Break Free*, P. 77.

11. Ibid, P. 79

12. Des Griffin, *Descent into Slavery*, P. 52. Emissary Publications, Colton, OR, 1980, 2009 Edition.

13. Eustace Mullins, *The World Order: A Study in the Hegemony of Parasitism*, P. 11. Ezra Pound Institute of Civilization, Staunton, VA, 1985.

14. Bill Still, *The Secret of Oz: Solutions for a Broken Economy*, http://www.youtube.com/watch?v=swkq2E8mswI

15. Robert V. Remini, *The Life of Andrew Jackson* (New York: Harper & Row, 1988), pp.227-28. Cited - G. Edward Griffin, *The Creature from Jekyll Island: A Second Look at the Federal Reserve*, P. 338. American Media, Westlake Village, California, 1998.

16. G. Edward Griffin, *The Creature from Jekyll Island: A Second Look at the Federal Reserve*, P. 349.

17.   Andrew Carrington Hitchcock, *The Synagogue of Satan: The Secret History of Jewish World Domination,* P. 51.

18.   Ibid, P. 52

19.   Ibid, P. 52-53

Chapter Four: *The New Banksters*

1.   Antony C. Sutton, *Wall Street and the Bolshevik Revolution*, P. 49. Arlington House Publishers, New Rochelle, New York, 1974.

2.   Carroll Quigley, *Tragedy and Hope: A History of the World in Our Time*, P. 71-72. First Published in 1966 by The Macmillan Company. GSG and Associates, San Pedro, California.

3.   Gary Allen, *The Rockefeller File: The Untold Story of the Most Powerful Family in America*, P. 23. '76 Press, Seal Beach, California, 1976.

4.   Eustace Mullins, *The World Order: A Study in the Hegemony of Parasitism,* P. 100. Ezra Pound Institute of Civilization, Staunton, VA, 1985.

5.   Gary Allen, *The Rockefeller File: The Untold Story of the Most Powerful Family in America,* P. 23.

6.   Ibid, P. 39

7.   Eustace Mullins, *The World Order: A Study in the Hegemony of Parasitism*, P. 108.

8.   Antony C. Sutton, *Wall Street and the Bolshevik Revolution,* P. 50.

9.   Eustace Mullins, *The World Order: A Study in the Hegemony of Parasitism*, P. 101.

10.   Eustace Clarence Mullins, *A Study of the Federal Reserve*, P. 10. Originally Published New York: Kasper and Horton 1952, Martino Publishing, 2009.

11.   International Business Times, '*American Dream' withers as tent cities mushroom in Promised Land*,' November 21st, 2010. http://hken.ibtimes.com.

12.   Antony C. Sutton, *The Federal Reserve Conspiracy: Bankers that Stole America*, P. 12. 1995.

13.   G. Edward Griffin, *The Creature from Jekyll Island: A Second Look at the Federal Reserve*, P. 8. American Media, Westlake Village, California, 1998.

14.   Dee Zahner, *The Secret Side of History: Mystery Babylon and the New World Order*, P. 81. LTAA Communications Publishers, Hesperia, California, 1994.

15.   Eustace Clarence Mullins, *A Study of the Federal Reserve*, P. 10. Originally Published New York: Kasper and Horton 1952, Martino Publishing, 2009.

16.   Ibid, P. 7.

17.   Eustace Mullins, *The World Order: A Study in the Hegemony of Parasitism*, P. 19.

18.   George Armstrong, *Rothschild Money Trust*, P, 132. 1940.

19.   Eustace Clarence Mullins, *A Study of the Federal Reserve*, P. 15.

20.   Stephen Birmingham, *Our Crowd*, P. 400. Dell Publishing Co., New York, 1967. Cited - W. Cleon Skousen, *The Naked Capitalist*, P. 17. Buccaneer Books, Cutchogue, New York, 1970.

21.   Eustace Mullins, *The World Order: A Study in the Hegemony of Parasitism*, P. 94.

22.   G. Edward Griffin, *The Creature from Jekyll Island: A Second Look at the Federal Reserve*, P. 6.

23.   Antony C. Sutton, *The Federal Reserve Conspiracy: Bankers that Stole America*. P. 77. 1995.

24.   Frank A. Vanderlip, "*From Farm Boy to Financier*," the *Saturday Evening Post*, Feb. 9th, 1933, P. 25, 70. The identical story was told two years later in Vanderlip's book bearing the same title

as the article, New York: D. Appleton Century Company, 1935, P. 210-219, Cited - G. Edward Griffin, *The Creature from Jekyll Island: A Second Look at the Federal Reserve*, P. 11.

25. Antony C. Sutton, *The Federal Reserve Conspiracy: Bankers that Stole America*, P. 75. 1995.

26. G. Edward Griffin, *The Creature from Jekyll Island: A Second Look at the Federal Reserve,* P. 438.

27. Antony C. Sutton, *The Federal Reserve Conspiracy: Bankers that Stole America*, P. 82. 1995.

28. Eustace Clarence Mullins, *A Study of the Federal Reserve*, P. 13-14.

29. Antony C. Sutton, *The Federal Reserve Conspiracy: Bankers that Stole America*, P. 81. 1995.

30. Eustace Clarence Mullins, *A Study of the Federal Reserve*, P. 26.

31. Ibid, P. 39-40.

32. Eustace Mullins, *The World Order: A Study in the Hegemony of Parasitism*, P. 95.

33. A. Ralph Epperson, *The Unseen Hand: An Introduction to the Conspiratorial View of History*, P. 186. Publius Press, Tucson, Arizona, 2006.

34. Gary Allen, *None Dare Call It Conspiracy*, P. 51. Concord Press, Seal Beach, California, 1971.

35. G. Edward Griffin, *The Creature from Jekyll Island: A Second Look at the Federal Reserve,* P. 20.

36. Eustace Clarence Mullins, *Secrets of the Federal Reserve System: The London Connection*, P. 14.

37. Dan Smoot, *The Invisible Government*, P, 6. Western Islands Publishers, Boston/Los Angeles, 1965.

38. G. Edward Griffin, *Creature from Jekyll Island: A Second Look at the Federal Reserve*, P. 239-240.

39. A. Ralph Epperson, *The Unseen Hand: An Introduction to the Conspiratorial View of History*, P. 168.

40. Arthur D. Howden Smith, *Mr House of Texas*, P. 70, Cited – James Perloff, *The Shadows of Power: The Council on Foreign Relations and the American Decline*, P. 28. Published by The John Birch Society Through Western Islands, Appleton, Wisconsin, 2008.

41. http://www.library.yale.edu/un/house/hist_sig.htm

42. Gary Allen, *None Dare Call It a Conspiracy*, P. 79.

43. George Sylvester Viereck, *The Strangest Friendship in History*, Cited – James Perloff, *The Shadows of Power: The Council on Foreign Relations and the American Decline*, P. 28.

44. G. Edward Griffin, *Creature from Jekyll Island: A Second Look at the Federal Reserve*, P. 240.

45. Houghton Mifflin, *The Intimate Papers of Colonel House*, Volume I, P. 114.

46. Gary Allen, *None Dare Call It Conspiracy*, P. 49.

Chapter Five: *Secret Un-American Activities*

1. George Armstrong, *Rothschild Money Trust*, P. 44. 1940.

2. Colin Simpson, *The Lusitania*, P. 157. Boston: Little, Brown. 1972 - Cited- James Perloff, *The Shadows of Power: The Council on Foreign Relations and the American Decline*, P. 30. Published by The John Birch Society through Western Islands, Appleton, Wisconsin, 2008.

3. Gary Allen, *None Dare Call It Conspiracy*, P. 63. Concord Press, Seal Beach, California, 1971

4. A. Ralph Epperson, *The Unseen Hand: An Introduction to the Conspiratorial View of History*, P. 257-258. Publius Press, Tucson, Arizona, 2006.

5. Des Griffin, *Descent into Slavery*, P. 100. Emissary Publications 1980. Colton, OR, 2009 Edition.

6. A. Ralph Epperson, *The Unseen Hand: An Introduction to the Conspiratorial View of History,* P. 258-259. Publius Press, Tucson, Arizona, 2006.

7. Dee Zahner, *The Secret Side of History: Mystery Babylon and the New World Order*, P. 90. LTAA Communications Publishers, Hesperia, California, 2004.

8. David Allen Rivera, *Final Warning: A History of the New World Order*, P. 126. Edited and Published by ProgressivePress.com. 2010.

9. Dan Smoot, *The Invisible Government*, P. 86. Western Islands Publishers, Boston/Los Angeles, 1965.

10. Colin Simpson, *The Lusitania*, P. 6. New York: Ballantine Books, 1972. Cited - A. Ralph Epperson, *The Unseen Hand: An Introduction to the Conspiratorial View of History*, P. 259.

11. Carroll Quigley, *Tragedy and Hope: A History of the World in Our Time*, P. 256, First Published in 1966 by The Macmillan Company. GSG and Associates, San Pedro, California.

12. Dr John Coleman, *Diplomacy by Deception: An Account of the Treasonous Conduct by the Governments of Britain and the United States*, P. 12.

13. Carroll Quigley, *Tragedy and Hope: A History of the World in Our Time*, P. 255-256.

14. Robert W. Lee, *The United Nations Conspiracy*, P. 38. Western Islands Publishers, Boston/ Los Angeles, 1981.

15. Ibid, P. 37

16. Lincoln P. Bloomfield, testimony, Subcommittee on International Organizations of the House Committee on International Relations, *The United States In The United Nations,* February 10-11, 1976, P. 12. Professor Bloomfield's statement was given February 10th. Cited - Robert W. Lee, *The United Nations Conspiracy,* P. 38.

17. Dr. John Coleman, *The Conspirator's Hierarchy: The Committee of 300*, 4th Edition, P. 133. Published by World in Review, Carson City, NV, 2006.

18. Gary Allen, *None Dare Call It Conspiracy*, P. 64.

19. Dan Smoot, *The Invisible Government*, P. 6.

20. Ibid, P. 6

21. A. Ralph Epperson, *The Unseen Hand: An Introduction to the Conspiratorial View of History,* P. 109.

22. Eustace Mullins, *The World Order: A Study in the Hegemony of Parasitism,* P. 47. Ezra Pound Institute of Civilization, Staunton, VA, 1985.

23. A. Ralph Epperson, *The Unseen Hand: An Introduction to the Conspiratorial View of History*, P. 261.

24. E. C. Knuth, *The Empire of "The City," The Secret History of British Financial Power*, P. 42. The Book Tree, San Diego, California, 2006.

25. Ibid, P. 100

26. William Guy Carr, *Pawns in the Game*, P. 97. (No Publishing Information).

27. E. C. Knuth, *The Empire of "The City," The Secret History of British Financial Power,* P. 45.

28. James Perloff, *The Shadows of Power: The Council on Foreign Relations and the American Decline*, P. 31.

29. Des Griffith, *Descent into Slavery*, P. 116.

Chapter Six: *The British Secret Society*

1. W. Cleon Skousen, *The Naked Capitalist*, P. 27-28, Buccaneer Books, Cutchogue, New York, 1970.

2. Eustace Mullins, *The World Order: A Study in the Hegemony of Parasitism*, P. 22. Ezra Pound Institute of Civilization, Staunton, VA, 1985.

3. Dennis L. Cuddy, PhD, *The Globalists,* P. 18. Hearthstone Publishing, Oklahoma City, Oklahoma.

4. Carroll Quigley, *The Anglo American Establishment: from Rhodes to Cliveden*, P. 4-5. GSG and Associates Publishers, San Pedro, California, 1981.

5. Ibid, P. 3

6. Ibid, P. 5

7. Ibid, P. 33

8. Joan Veon, *The United Nations Global Straightjacket*, P. 61-62. Hearthstone Publishing, Oklahoma, 2000.

9. Dennis Laurence Cuddy, Ph.D., *Secret Records Revealed: The Men, The Money and The Methods Behind the New World Order,* P. 14. Hearthstone Publishing Ltd, Oklahoma City, Oklahoma, 1999.

10. David Allen Rivera, *Final Warning: A History of the New World Order*, P. 146. Edited and Published by ProgressivePress.com. 2010.

11. International Affairs, *The Trend of International Affairs Since the War,* P. 809. November 1931.

12. Carroll Quigley, *The Anglo American Establishment: from Rhodes to Cliveden*, P. 10.

13. Ibid, P. 35

14. Carroll Quigley, *Tragedy and Hope: A History of the World in Our Time*, P. 132. First Published in 1966 by The Macmillan Company. GSG and Associates, San Pedro, California.

15. Ibid, P. 15

16. Gary Allen, *None Dare Call It a Conspiracy*, P. 79. Concord Press, Seal Beach, California, 1971

17. Eustace Mullins, *The World Order: A Study in the Hegemony of Parasitism*, P. 51.

18. Carroll Quigley, *The Anglo American Establishment: from Rhodes to Cliveden*, P. 151

Chapter Seven: *The Council on Foreign Relations*

1. http://www.cfr.org

2. Edith Kermit Roosevelt, *"Elite Clique Holds Power in U.S.,"* Indianapolis News, December 23rd, 1961, P. 6. Cited - James Perloff, *The Shadows of Power: The Council on Foreign Relations and the American Decline*, P. 5. Published by The John Birch Society Through Western Islands, Appleton, Wisconsin, 2008.

3. James Perloff, *The Shadows of Power: The Council on Foreign Relations and the American Decline*, P. 7.

4. Gary Allen, *The Rockefeller File: The Untold Story of the Most Powerful family in America*, P. 55. '76 Press, Seal Beach California, January 1976.

5.   Ibid, P. 55

6.   Ibid, P. 55

7.   Phyllis Schlafly and Chester Ward, *Kissinger on the Couch*, P. 150-151. New Rochelle, N. Y.: Arlington House, 1975. Cited - Robert W. Lee, *The United Nations Conspiracy*, P. 5- 6. Western Islands Publishers, Boston/Los Angeles, 1981.

8.   Jim Marrs, *Rule by Secrecy*, P. 35. Harper Collins Publishers Inc. New York, 2001.

9.   James Perloff, *The Shadows of Power: The Council on Foreign Relations and the American Decline*, P. 7.

10. Jacques Ellul, *Propaganda: the Formation of Men's Attitudes*, P. 17-18. Vintage Books A Division of Random House, New York, 1973.

11. Ibid, P. 19

12. Type 'Bingo The Clowno' into http://www.YouTube.com or http://www.youtube.com/watch?v=4h-O1R7iXqk

13. Carroll Quigley, *Tragedy and Hope: A History of the World in Our Time,* P. 132. First Published in 1966 by The Macmillan Company. GSG and Associates, San Pedro, California.

14. Ibid, P. 953

15. Congressional Record, Volume 54, P. 2947-48. February 9th, 1917.

16. Gary Allen, *The Rockefeller File,* 76 Press, Seal Beach, California, P. 53. 1976.

17. Ibid, P. 65

18. Ibid, P. 66

19. Ibid, P. 66

20. Ibid, P. 68

21. Ibid, P. 69-70

22. Ibid, P. 70

23. Ibid, P. 72

24. Ibid, P. 72

25. Ibid, P. 73

26. Ibid, P. 74

27. Jacques Ellul, *Propaganda: the Formation of Men's Attitudes*, P. 9-10.

28. Ibid, P. 9-10

29. Ibid, P. 11

30. Dan Smoot, *The Invisible Government*, P. 80. Western Islands Publishers, Boston/Los Angeles, 1965.

31. Ibid, P. 82

32. Ibid, P. 82

33. Jim Keith, *Mass Control: Engineering Human Consciousness,* P. 41. Adventures Unlimited Press, Kempton, Illinois, 2003.

34. George Orwell, *Nineteen Eighty-Four*, P. 35, Penguin Books, Harmondsworth, Middlesex, 1954.

35. James Perloff, *The Shadows of Power: The Council on Foreign Relations and the American Decline*, P. 180.

36. George Orwell, *Nineteen Eighty-Four,* P. 31.

Chapter Eight: *Red Wall Street*

1.   W. Cleon Skousen, *The Naked Communist*, P. 90, Published by The Reviewer, Salt Lake City, Utah. Eleventh Edition, January, 1962. 20th Printing, 1983.

2.   Ibid, P. 91

3.   William Guy Carr, *Pawns in the Game*, P. 67. (No Publishing Information).

4.   Ibid, P. 66

5.   Ibid, P. 68

6.   Gary Allen, *None Dare Call It Conspiracy*, P.69. Published by Concord Press, Seal Beach, California, 1971.

7.   William Guy Carr, *Pawns in the Game*, P. 71.

8.   A. Ralph Epperson, *The Unseen Hand: An Introduction to the Conspiratorial View of History,* P. 102. Publius Press, Tucson, Arizona, 2006.

9.   Antony C. Sutton, *Wall Street and the Bolshevik Revolution*, P. 12. Arlington House Publishers, New Rochelle, New York, 1974.

10. Ibid, P. 72

11. Ibid, P. 72

12. Ibid, P. 73

13. Ibid, P. 81

14. Ibid, P. 22

15. Eustace Mullins, *The World Order: A Study in the Hegemony of Parasitism*, P. 72. Ezra Pound Institute of Civilization, Staunton, VA, 1985.

16. Antony Sutton, *Wall Street and the Bolshevik Revolution*, P. 27-28

17. David Allen Rivera, *Final Warning: A History of the New World Order*, P.149. Edited and Published by ProgressivePress.com. 2010.

18. Antony C. Sutton, *Wall Street and the Bolshevik Revolution*, P. 25

19. Ibid, P. 39

20. Gary Allen, *None Dare Call It Conspiracy*, P. 68.

21. Ibid, P. 69

22. Ibid, P. 68-69

23. David Allen Rivera, *Final Warning: A History of the New World Order*, P. 217

24. Antony C. Sutton, *Wall Street and the Bolshevik Revolution*, P. 45.

25. Ibid, P. 46

26. Donzella Cross Boyle, *Quest of a Hemisphere*, P. 558. Cited - A. Ralph Epperson, *The Unseen Hand: An Introduction to the Conspiratorial View of History*, P. 107.

27. Michel Sturdza, *Betrayal by Rulers*, P. 115, Belmont, Massachusetts: Western Islands, 1976. Cited - A. Ralph Epperson, *The Unseen Hand: An Introduction to the Conspiratorial View of History,* P. 107.

28. William T. Still, *New World Order: The Ancient Plan of Secret Societies*, P. 140. Huntington House Publishers, Lafayette, Louisiana, 1990.

29. A. Ralph Epperson, *The Unseen Hand: An Introduction to the Conspiratorial View of History*, P. 109-110.

30. David Allen Rivera, *Final Warning: A History of the New World Order*, P. 219.

31. A. Ralph Epperson, *The Unseen Hand: An Introduction to the Conspiratorial View of History*, P. 110.

32. Antony Sutton, *Wall Street and the Bolshevik Revolution*, P. 91.

33. Donald McCormack, *The Mask of Merlin*, P. 208. London: MacDonald, 1963; New York: Holt, Rinehart and Winston, 1964. Cited- Antony Sutton, *Wall Street and the Bolshevik Revolution*, P. 93.

34. Antony Sutton, *Wall Street and the Bolshevik Revolution*, P. 94.

35. Dr John Coleman, *Diplomacy by Deception: An Account of the Treasonous Conduct by the Governments of Britain and the United States,* P. 118.

Chapter Nine: Occult Nazi Beginnings

1. Dee Zahner, *The Secret Side of History: Mystery Babylon and the New World Order*, P. 98. LTAA Communications Publishers, Hesperia, California, 1994.

2. Des Griffin, *Descent into Slavery*, P. 119. Emissary Publications, Colton, OR, 1980. 2009 Edition.

3. Jim Marrs, *Rule by Secrecy*, P. 146. Harper Collins Publishers Inc. New York, 2001.

4. Ibid, P. 153

5. Ibid, P. 155

6. Ibid, P. 157

7. David Allen Rivera, *Final Warning: A History of the New World Order*, P. 190. Edited and Published by ProgressivePress.com. 2010.

8. Jim Marrs, *Rule by Secrecy*, P. 163.

9. Ibid, P. 145

10. Antony C. Sutton, *Wall Street and the Rise of Hitler*, P. 27, Buccaneer Books, Cutchogue, New York. 1976.

11. Ibid, P. 33-34

12. Ibid, P. 33

13. Ibid, P. 28

14. Ibid, P. 67

15. Ibid, P. 28

16. Carroll Quigley, *Tragedy and Hope: A History of the World in Our Time*, P. 308. First Published in 1966 by The Macmillan Company. GSG and Associates, San Pedro, California.

17. Ibid, P. 324

18. Antony C. Sutton, *Wall Street and the Rise of Hitler*, P. 27.

19. Ibid, P. 51

20. Ibid, P. 55

21. Ibid, P. 165

22. Jim Marrs, *Rule by Secrecy*, P. 163.

23. Tony Paterson, *'Historians find 'proof' that Nazis burnt Reichstag'*, Telegraph.co.uk, 15th, April 2001. http://www.telegraph.co.uk/news/worldnews/europe/germany/1310995/Historians-find-proof-that-Nazis-burnt-Reichstag.html

24. Antony C. Sutton, *Wall Street and the Rise of Hitler,* P. 37.

Chapter Ten: *World War Two*

1.   A. Ralph Epperson, *The Unseen Hand: An Introduction to the Conspiratorial View of History,* P. 261. Publius Press, Tucson, Arizona, 2006.

2.   Captain Archibald. H. Maule Ramsay, *The Nameless War*, P. 3. Britons Publishing Company, London 1952.

3.   William Guy Carr, *Pawns in the Game*, P. 162. (No Publishing Information).

4.   Des Griffin, *Descent into Slavery*, P. 139. Emissary Publications, Colton, OR, 1980. 2009 Edition.

5.   William Guy Carr, *Pawns in the Game*, P. 163.

6.   Captain Archibald. H. Maule Ramsay, *The Nameless War*, P. 44.

7.   William Guy Carr, *Pawns in the Game*, P. 163.

8.   Ibid, P. 164

9.   Des Griffin, *Descent into Slavery*, P. 145.

10. Captain Archibald. H. Maule Ramsay, *The Nameless War,* P. 48.

11. William Guy Carr, *Pawns in the Game*, P. 166.

12. Captain Archibald. H. Maule Ramsay, *The Nameless War,* P. 48.

13. William Guy Carr, *Pawns in the Game*, P. 167.

14. Ibid, P. 167

15. Ibid, P. 168

16. John Toland*, Infamy: Pearl Harbor and Its Aftermath*, New York: Doubleday, 1982, P.115-18. Cited – James Perloff, *The Shadows of Power: The Council on Foreign Relations and the American Decline*, P. 65. Published by The John Birch Society Through Western Islands, Appleton, Wisconsin, 2008.

17. James Perloff, *The Shadows of Power: The Council on Foreign Relations and the American Decline*, P. 67.

18. Dan Smoot, *Invisible Government*, P. 22. Western Islands Publishers, Boston/Los Angeles, 1965.

19. William Stevenson, *A Man Called Intrepid,* New York: Harcourt Brace Jovanovich, 1976. Cited - James Perloff, *The Shadows of Power: The Council on Foreign Relations and the American Decline,* P. 65.

Chapter Eleven: *Tower of Babel*

1.   Senator William Jenner, *Congressional Record*, February 23th, 1954 – Cited G. Edward Griffin - *The Fearful Master: A Second Look At The United Nations*, P. 67. Western Islands, Belmont, Massachusetts. Fourth Printing, January 1965.

2. Dee Zahner, *The Secret Side of History: Mystery Babylon and the New World Order*, P. 147. LTAA Communications Publishers, Hesperia, California, 1994.

3. Robert W. Lee, *The United Nations Conspiracy,* P. 33. Western Islands Publishers, Boston/ Los Angeles, 1981.

4. David Allen Rivera, *Final Warning: A History of the New World Order*, P. 263. Edited and Published by ProgressivePress.com. 2010.

5. Dan Smoot, *The Invisible Government*, P. 7-8. Western Islands Publishers, Boston/Los Angeles, 1965.

6. James Perloff, *The Shadows of Power: The Council on Foreign Relations and the American Decline*, P. 71. Published by The John Birch Society Through Western Islands, Appleton, Wisconsin, 2008.

7. Dr John Coleman, *Diplomacy by Deception: An Account of the Treasonous Conduct by the Governments of Britain and the United States*, P. 7.

8. David Allen Rivera, *Final Warning: A History of the New World Order*, P. 265.

9. Dr John Coleman, *Diplomacy by Deception: An Account of the Treasonous Conduct by the Governments of Britain and the United States*, P. 13.

10. Ibid, P. 14

11. G. Edward Griffin, *The Fearful Master: A Second Look At The United Nations*, P. 158.

12. V. Orval Watts, *The United Nations: Planned Tyranny*, P. 100. The Devin-Adair Company, New York, 1955. Third Printing January 1956.

13. Ibid, P. 103

14. *Christian Century,* August 11th, 1965. Cited – Robert W. Lee, *The United Nations Conspiracy,* P. 33.

15. Dr John Coleman, *Diplomacy by Deception: An Account of the Treasonous Conduct by the Governments of Britain and the United States*, P. 137.

16. Ibid, P. 138

17. V. Orval Watts, *The United Nations: Planned Tyranny*, P. 37.

18. Eustace Mullins, *The World Order: A Study in the Hegemony of Parasitism*, P. 180. Ezra Pound Institute of Civilization, Staunton, VA, 1985.

19. G. Edward Griffin, *The Fearful Master: A Second Look At The United Nations,* P. 160

20. Ibid, P. 160

21. Daily Worker, Oct 28th, 1953, P. 6, Cited – G. Edward Griffin, *The Fearful Master: A Second Look At The United Nations*, P. 161.

22. Des Griffin, *Fourth Reich of the Rich*, P. 148. Emissary Publications, Clackamas, OR, 1998 Edition, 1998 Edition.

23. David Allen Rivera, *Final Warning: A History of the New World Order*, P. 276.

24. Dee Zahner, *The Secret Side of History: Mystery Babylon and the New World Order*, P. 157.

25. David Allen Rivera, *Final Warning: A History of the New World Order*, P. 276.

26. V. Orval Watts, *The United Nations: Planned Tyranny*, P. 7.

27. Ibid, P. 8

Chapter Twelve: *Katanga: The Untold Story*

1. *46 Angry Men,* American Opinion Reprints Published by Robert Welch, Inc., Belmont, Massachusetts 02178. 1962.

2. *Katanga: The Untold Story*, Documentary Video Narrated by Congressman Donald L. Jackson (Member House Foreign Affairs Committee 1947-1960) Produced and Directed by Stanford-Stuart, Executive Producer D. B. Lewis.

3. Ibid, P. 10

4. Ibid, P. 11

5. Ibid. P. 15

6. Philippa Schuyler, *Who Killed The Congo?* P. 238. New York, The Devin-Adair Company, 1962. Cited – G. Edward Griffin, *The Fearful Master: A Second Look At The United Nations,* P. 16.

7. *Situation in the Republic of the Congo*, report of the UN Conciliation Commission for the Congo, UN document A/4711/ADD 2, P. 42-46. March 20th, 1961. Cited – G. Edward Griffin, *The Fearful Master: A Second Look At The United Nations*, P. 19-20.

8. *Katanga: The Untold Story*, Documentary Video Narrated by Congressman Donald L. Jackson (Member House Foreign Affairs Committee 1947-1960)

9. *"Lumumba Gets Pledge of U.S. Aid,"* Los Angeles Examiner (July 28th, 1960), sec. 1, P. 16. Also, *"Added U.S. Funds Voted for Congo,"* Los Angeles Examiner (August 17th, 1960), sec. 1, P. 7. Also, *Department of State Bulletin* (October 3[rd,] 1960), P. 510, 530; and (October 10th, 1960), P. 588. Cited – G. Edward Griffin, *The Fearful Master: A Second Look At The United Nations*, P. 20.

10. G. Edward Griffin, *The Fearful Master: A Second Look At The United Nations*, P. 16.

11. Senator Thomas Dodd, *Congressional Record* (August 3rd, 1962). Cited – G. Edward Griffin, *The Fearful Master: A Second Look At The United Nations*, P. 24.

12. Smith Hempstone, *Rebels, Mercenaries and Dividends*, P. 134. New York, Frederic A. Praeger, Inc., 1962. Cited – G. Edward Griffin, *The Fearful Master: A Second Look At The United Nations*, P. 36.

13. Philippa Schuyler, *Who Killed The Congo?* P. 260. New York, The Devin-Adair Company, 1962. Cited – G. Edward Griffin, *The Fearful Master: A Second Look At The United Nations*, P. 29.

14. *Katanga: The Untold Story,* Documentary Video Narrated by Congressman Donald L. Jackson (Member House Foreign Affairs Committee 1947-1960)

15. G. Edward Griffin, *The Fearful Master: A Second Look At The United Nations,* P. 36.

16. *Katanga: The Untold Story*, Documentary Video Narrated by Congressman Donald L. Jackson (Member House Foreign Affairs Committee 1947-1960)

17. Ibid

18. *46 Angry Me*n, American Opinion Reprints Published by Robert Welch, Inc., Belmont, Massachusetts 02178. 1962.

19. *Katanga: The Untold Story*, Documentary Video Narrated by Congressman Donald L. Jackson (Member House Foreign Affairs Committee 1947-1960)

20. *World Press*, December 6th, 1961. Cited – *46 Angry Men,* P. 14.

21. *New York Times*, west. Ed. (January 22[nd,] 1963) P. 1. Cited – G. Edward Griffin, *The Fearful*

Master: A Second Look At The United Nations, P. 64.

22. *46 Angry Men*, American Opinion Reprints Published by Robert Welch, Inc.

Chapter Thirteen: *Looting the World*

1. *The Independent*, 'Johann Hari: It's not just Dominique Strauss-Kahn. *The IMF itself should be on trial*,' http://www.independent.co.uk/opinion/commentators/johann-hari/johann-hari-its-not-just-dominique-strausskahn-the-imf-itself-should-be-on-trial-2292270.html

2. Bruce Rich, *Mortgaging the Earth: The World Bank, Environmental Impoverishment, and the Crisis of Development*, P. 5. Beacon Press, Boston. 1999.

3. *Wall Street Journal*, New York, 18th July and 27th September 1985. Cited - Graham Hancock, *Lords of Poverty: The Free-Wheeling Lifestyles, Power, Prestige and Corruption of the Multi-Billion Dollar Aid Business*, P. 40. MacMillan London Limited, 1989.

4. Graham Hancock, *Lords of Poverty: The Free-Wheeling Lifestyles, Power, Prestige and Corruption of the Multi-Billion Dollar Aid Business*, P. 38. MacMillan London Limited, 1989.

5. German NGO's published an extensive illustrated account of the 1988 meeting and the German and International alternative activities. Cited-Bruce Rich, *Mortgaging the Earth*, P. 9.

6. Bruce Rich, *Mortgaging the Earth: The World Bank, Environmental Impoverishment, and the Crisis of Development*, P. 9.

7. *"Watching 'Angels' from the edge of the slum,"* Nation, 9th, October 1991, 2. Cited - Bruce Rich, *Mortgaging the Earth*, P. 6.

8. Bruce Rich, *Mortgaging the Earth*, P. 10

9. Walt Rainboth, professor of biology, University of California at Los Angeles, letter to Dr. George Davis, Department of Malacology, Academy of Natural Sciences of Philadelphia, 4th, December, 1991, 6. Cited - Bruce Rich, *Mortgaging the Earth*, P. 12

10. Bruce Rich, *Mortgaging the Earth*, P. 11

11. Sanitsuda Ekachai, *"Is It Growth or Decline?"* Bangkok Post, 3rd, October, 1991, 27. Cited - Bruce Rich, *Mortgaging the Earth*, P. 14

12. Ann Danaiya Usher, *"Forum Raps 'Green Revolution,'"* Nation, 10th, October, 1991, A2. Cited - Bruce Rich, *Mortgaging the Earth*, P. 14.

13. Suda Kanjanawanawan, "Shrimp Farms Spoiling Ecosystems," Nation, 10th, October, 1991, A1. Cited - Bruce Rich, *Mortgaging the Earth*, P. 14.

14. Bruce Rich, *Mortgaging the Earth*, P. 25.

15. Testimony of Bruce Rich, Senior Attorney, Environmental Defense Fund, before the House Subcommittee on International Development Institutions and Finance. Hearing on the Environmental Performance of Multilateral Development Banks, Washington, DC, 8th April 1987. Cited - Graham Hancock, *Lords of Poverty*, P. 130.

16. Graham Hancock, *Lords of Poverty: The Free-Wheeling Lifestyles, Power, Prestige and Corruption of the Multi-Billion Dollar Aid Business*, P. 130. MacMillan London Limited, 1989.

17. Testimony of Bruce Rich, Senior Attorney, Environmental Defense Fund, before the House Subcommittee on International Development Institutions and Finance. Hearing on the Environmental Performance of Multilateral Development Banks, Washington, DC, 8th April 1987. Cited - Graham Hancock, *Lords of Poverty*, P. 131.

18. Special Report by John Pilger, *The New Rulers of the World,* Carlton Television Documentary Film, 2001. Produced by John Pilger, Alan Lowery, Polly Bide.

19. Byron Richards, *Fight for Your Health: Exposing the FDA's Betrayal of America,* P. 74. Published by Truth in Wellness LLC, Tucson, Arizona, 2006.

20. *1985 – And Towards the 1990's,* United Nations Development Programme, New York, October 1986. Cited – Graham Hancock, *Lords of Poverty,* P. 115.

21. Ibid, P. 115.

22. Adrian Adams, 'An Open Letter to a Young Researcher,' *African Affairs,* 78, No. 313, London, October 1979. Cited – Graham Hancock, *Lords of Poverty,* P. 125.

23. Graham Hancock, *Lords of Poverty,* P. 125.

24. Ibid, P. 127.

25. Ibid, P. 116.

26. V. S. Baskin, *Western Aid: Myth and Reality, Progress Publishers, Moscow,* 1985. Cited – Graham Hancock, *Lords of Poverty,* P. 116.

27. Graham Hancock, *Lords of Poverty,* P. 113.

28. *Sunday Times Magazine,* London, 3rd, April 1988. Cited – Graham Hancock, *Lords of Poverty,* P. 113.

29. *Survival International Urgent Action Bulletin,* London, 3rd January, 1985. Cited – Graham Hancock, *Lords of Poverty,* P. 114.

30. Graham Hancock, *Lords of Poverty,* P. 113.

31. Bruce Rich, *Mortgaging the Earth,* P. 26.

32. Bruce Rich, *Mortgaging the Earth,* P. 27.

33. Ibid, P. 27

34. Ibid, P. 28

35. Ibid, P. 26

36. Linda Greenbaum, "*The Failure to Protect Tribal Peoples: The Polonoroeste Case in Brazil,*" Cultural Survival Quarterly, Vol 8 (December 1984), 76-77. Cited - *Mortgaging the Earth,* P. 28.

37. Bruce Rich, *Mortgaging the Earth,* P. 28.

38. Ibid, P. 29

39. Ibid, P. 30

40. G. Edward Griffin, *The Creature from Jekyll Island: A Second Look at the Federal Reserve.* P. 100. American Media, Westlake Village, California, 1999.

41. Ibid, P. 99.

42. Graham Hancock, *Lords of Poverty,* P. 119-120.

43. G. Edward Griffin, *The Creature from Jekyll Island: A Second Look at the Federal Reserve.* P. 100.

44. Ibid, P. 100.

45. Ibid, P. 98.

46. Ibid, P. 98.

47. Stephanie Soechtig, *Tapped [DVD],* Atlas Films, Executive Producers Michael Walrath and Michelle Walrath, 2010.

48. Ruth Caplan, NAT. COORD., *Defending Water for Life Alliance for Democracy.* Cited - Stephanie Soechtig, *Tapped [DVD],* Atlas Films, Executive Producers Michael Walrath and Michelle Walrath, 2010.

49. http://www.indiaresource.org/issues/water/2003/lessonsfrombolivia.html

50. Bovard, *"The World Bank and the Impoverishment of Nations,"* in Perpetuating Poverty, op. Cit., P. 59. Cited – William F. Jasper, *The United Nations Exposed: The Internationalist Conspiracy to Rule the World,* P. 224. The John Birch Society, Appleton, Wisconsin. Third Printing 2001.

Chapter Fourteen: *Eugenic Beginnings*

1. Dr. Thomas Roder, Volker Kubillus, Anthony Burwell, Psychiatrists - *The Men Behind Hitler: The Architects of Horror,* P. 10-11. English Edition by Freedom Publishing, Los Angeles. 1995.

2. Edwin Black, *War Against the Weak: Eugenics and America's Campaign to Create a Master Race,* P. 12. Four Walls Eight Windows, New York / London, First Printing September 2003.

3. Margaret Sanger, *The Pivot of Civilization,* P. 105. Brentano's Publishers, New York, Second Printing, October, 1922.

4. Edwin Black, *War Against the Weak: Eugenics and America's Campaign to Create a Master Race,* P. 5.

5. Dr. Thomas Roder, Volker Kubillus, Anthony Burwell, *Psychiatrists - The Men Behind Hitler: The Architects of Horror,* P. 44.

6. Edwin Black, *War Against the Weak: Eugenics and America's Campaign to Create a Master Race,* P. 55.

7. Ibid, P. xv.

8. Ibid, P. 22.

9. Ibid, P. 18.

10. Ibid, P. xvi.

11. Ibid, P. 248.

12. Margaret Sanger, *The Pivot of Civilization,* P. 81.

13. Edwin Black, *War Against the Weak: Eugenics and America's Campaign to Create a Master Race,* P. 32.

14. Ibid, P. 47.

15. Ibid, P. 57.

16. http://www.eugenicsarchive.org

17. First Eugenics Congress, *'Four Hundred Delegates in London – Americans to Read Papers,'* New York Times, July 25th, 1912.

18. Stefan Kuhl, *Nazi Connection: Eugenics, American Racism, and German National Socialism,* P. 15. Oxford University Press, Inc., 2002.

19. Edwin Black, *War Against the Weak: Eugenics and America's Campaign to Create a Master Race* P. 73.

20. Ibid, P. 75

21. Lombardo, Paul A. *"The Black Stork: Eugenics and the Death of 'Defective' Babies in American Medicine and Motion Pictures Since 1915."* The Hastings Center Report. The Hastings

Center. 1997. HighBeam Research. 22 May. 2011.

22. Ibid, Lombardo, Paul A.

23. Edwin Black, *War Against the Weak: Eugenics and America's Campaign to Create a Master Race,* P. 257.

24. John Russell M. A. T*he Eugenic Appeal In Moral Education; Reprinted from the "Eugenics Review,"* July, 1912, Eugenics and Education, Eugenics Education Society, Kingsway House, Kingsway, W.C.

25. Edwin Black, *War Against the Weak: Eugenics and America's Campaign to Create a Master Race*, P. 125.

26. Margaret Sanger, *The Pivot of Civilization,* P. 81.

27. Ibid, P. 80.

28. Edwin Black, *War Against the Weak: Eugenics and America's Campaign to Create a Master Race*, P. 127-128.

29. See Roswell H. Johnson, *"The Eugenic Aspects of Population Theory,"* Birth Control Review, September 1930, P. 256-258. See Eleanor Dwight Jones, "Practical Race Betterment," *Birth Control Review*, July, 1928, P. 203-204. See American Medicine, "Intelligent or Unintelligent Birth Control?" *Birth Control Review,* May 1919, P. 12. See Sanger, "Address," P. 3. See Perry, P. 176.

30. Margaret Sanger, *The Pivot of Civilization*, P. 101.

31. Edwin Black, *War Against the Weak: Eugenics and America's Campaign to Create a Master Race*, P. 129.

32. Margaret Sanger, *The Pivot of Civilization*, P. 281.

33. 'Want More Babies In Best Families, Major Darwin Sees It Patriotic Duty of Better Classes to Increase Their Offspring. Limitation Also Needed, Danger of Best Types Disappearing and the Inferior Multiplying, He Tells Eugenists.' *The New York Times*, Sept 25th, 1921.

34. Ibid, Sept 25th, 1921.

35. Edwin Black, *War Against the Weak: Eugenics and America's Campaign to Create a Master Race* P. 238.

36. *The New York Times,* 23rd Aug, 1932.

37. Edwin Black, *War Against the Weak: Eugenics and America's Campaign to Create a Master Race,* P. 296.

38. Stefan Kuhl, *Nazi Connection: Eugenics, American Racism, and German National Socialism,* P. 37.

39. Dr. Thomas Roder, Volker Kubillus, Anthony Burwell, *Psychiatrists - The Men Behind Hitler: The Architects of Horror,* P. 44.

40. Stefan Kuhl, Nazi Connection: *Eugenics, American Racism, and German National Socialism,* P. 39

41. Ibid, P. 47

42. Ibid, P. 46

43. Ibid, P. 30

44. Dr. Thomas Roder, Volker Kubillus, Anthony Burwell, *Psychiatrists - The Men Behind Hitler: The Architects of Horror*, P. 49

45. Edwin Black, *War Against the Weak: Eugenics and America's Campaign to Create a Master Race*, P. 7-8

46. Claire Chambers, *The SIECUS Circle: A Humanist Revolution*, P. 5. Published by Western Islands, Belmont Massachusetts 02178, 1977.

47. 1961: *Birth control pill 'available to all,'* http://news.bbc.co.uk/onthisday/hi/dates/stories/december/4/newsid_3228000/3228207.stm

48. http://www.popcouncil.org/who/history.asp

49. Frederick Henry Osborne, *Future of Human Heredity: An Introduction to Eugenics in Modern Society*, P. 104. Weybright and Talley, New York 1968.

50. "*A Family Planning Perspectives Special Supplement*" published by Planned Parenthood-World Population, NYC, NY, 1970.

51. William F. Jasper, *Global Tyranny... Step by Step: The United Nations and the Emerging New World Order*, P. 166-167. Published by Western Islands, Appleton, Wisconsin, Second Printing March 1993.

52. Claire Chambers, *The SIECUS Circle: A Humanist Revolution*, P. 8.

53. http://www.population-security.org/rockefeller/001_population_growth_and_the_american_future.htm#The%20Commission

54. http://thepragmaticprogressive.blogspot.com/2003/05/this-article-printed-in-its-entirety.html

55. http://www.sott.net/articles/show/182359-UNICEF-Nigerian-Polio-Vaccine-Contaminated-with-Sterilizing-Agents-Scientist-Finds

56. http://web.archive.org/web/19991008043627/http://www.africa2000.com/INDX/bbchorizon.html

57. http://ncbi.nlm.nih.gov/pmc/articles/PMC1537571

58. http://gavialliance.org/media_centre/press_releases/2000_04_11_en_press_release.php

59. http://guttmacher.org/about/alan-bio.html

60. Jacqueline Kasun, *The War Against Population: The Economics and Ideology of World Population Control*, P. 237. Ignatius Press, San Francisco, Second Edition 1999.

61. http://www.gavialliance.org/resources/global_strategy_commitments.pdf

62. Billionaire club in bid to curb overpopulation: '*America's richest people meet to discuss ways of tackling a 'disastrous' environmental, social and industrial threat'* The Sunday Times, May 24th, 2009 http://www.timesonline.co.uk/tol/news/world/us_and_americas/article6350303.ece

63. http://examiner.com/celebrity-charity-events-in-national/hilary-clinton-and-melinda-gates-launch-saving-lives-at-birth

64. http://commdocs.house.gov/committees/intlrel/hfa27067.000/hfa27067_0f.htm

65. http://foreignaffairs.house.gov/111/kad061009.pdf

66. A. Ralph Epperson, *The Unseen Hand: An Introduction to the Conspiratorial View of History*, P. 227. Publius Press, Tucson, Arizona, 2006.

67. *New York Times* 8-10-1973.

68. http://www.prolife.org.au/election

Chapter Fifteen: *War on the Family*

1. Dennis Laurence Cuddy, Ph. D., *A Chronology of Education with Quotable Quotes*, P. 3. Published by Pro Family Forum Inc., Highland City, Florida, Third Printing 1994.

2. A. Ralph Epperson, *The Unseen Hand: An Introduction to the Conspiratorial View of History*, P. 382. Publius Press, Tucson, Arizona, 2006.

3. Claire Chambers, *The SIECUS Circle: A Humanist Revolution*, P. 6. *Published by Western Islands*, Belmont Massachusetts 02178, 1977.

4. "The Climate of Freedom," *The Saturday Review*, July 19th, 1952, P. 22. Cited – William Norman Grigg, *Freedom on the Altar: The UN's Crusade Against God and Family*, P. 36. American Opinion Publishing, Inc., Appleton, Wisconsin. First Printing 1995.

5. John Stormer, *None Dare Call It Education: The Documented Account of How Education "Reforms" are Undermining Academics and Traditional Values*, P. 69. Liberty Bell Press, Florissant, Missouri. Second Printing – December 1998.

6. Ibid, P. 70.

7. Ibid, P. 70.

8. "*The Communist Pattern in the UN*," speech by Joseph Z. Kornfeder before the Congress of Freedom, Veterans War Memorial Auditorium (San Francisco, April 1955. Cited - G. Edward Griffin, *The Fearful Master: A Second Look At The United Nations*, P. 141. Western Islands, Belmont, Massachusetts. Fourth Printing, January 1965.

9. Jim Keith, *Mass Control: Engineering Human Consciousness*, P. 23. Published by Adventures Unlimited Press, Kempton, Illinois 60946. 2003.

10. Ibid, P. 23.

11. Ibid, P. 10.

12. Paolo Lionni, *The Leipzig Connection: The Systematic Destruction of American Education*, P. 9. Heron Books, Sheridan, Oregon. Fourth Printing: January 1993.

13. Dennis L. Cuddy, Ph. D., *A Chronology of Education with Quotable Quotes*, P. 3.

14. Paolo Lionni, *The Leipzig Connection: The Systematic Destruction of American Education*, P. 56. Published by Heron Books, Sheridan, Oregon, Fourth Printing, 1993.

15. Ibid, P. 57

16. Dennis L. Cuddy, Ph. D., *A Chronology of Education with Quotable Quotes*, P. 11.

17. Ibid, P. 10

18. John Stormer, *None Dare Call It Education: The Documented Account of How Education "Reforms" are Undermining Academics and Traditional Values*, P. 32.

19. Ibid, P. 32.

20. Rene A. Wormser, *Foundations: Their Power and Influence*, P. 157. Covenant House Books, Sevierville, TN. Third Printing 1993.

21. Ibid, P. 160.

22. Ibid, P. 161.

23. John Stormer, *None Dare Call It Education: The Documented Account of How Education "Reforms" are Undermining Academics and Traditional Values*, P. 69.

24. Ibid, P. 31

25. Dennis L. Cuddy, Ph. D., *A Chronology of Education with Quotable Quotes*, P. 1.

26. William F. Jasper, *The United Nations Exposed: The Internationalist Conspiracy to Rule the World*, P. 271. Published by The John Birch Society, Appleton, Wisconsin Third Printing October 2001.

27. Phyllis Schlafly Report, in the *Utah Independent*, (December 23rd, 1976) Cited – A. Ralph Epperson, *The Unseen Hand: An Introduction to the Conspiratorial View of History*, P. 383.

28. Claire Chambers, *The SIECUS Circle: A Humanist Revolution*, P. 22. Published by Western Islands, Belmont Massachusetts 02178, 1977.

29. John Stormer, *None Dare Call It Education: The Documented Account of How Education "Reforms" are Undermining Academics and Traditional Values*, P. XV.

30. Claire Chambers, *The SIECUS Circle: A Humanist Revolution*, P. 12.

31. Ibid, P. 40

32. Ibid, P. 138

33. Ibid, P. xiii

34. Ibid, P. 105-106

35. John Stormer, *None Dare Call It Education: The Documented Account of How Education "Reforms" are Undermining Academics and Traditional Values*, P. 50-51.

36. Valerie Riches, *Sex Education or Indoctrination: How Ideology Has Triumphed Over Facts*, P. 27. Family Youth Concern, Printed in Great Britain by Cromwell Press, Trowbridge, Wiltshire, 2004.

37. Harry Conn, *Four Trojan Horses* (Van Nuys, CA., reprinted with permission of Bible Voice, Inc., 1978), P. 65. Cited – Homer Duncan, *Secular Humanism: The Most Dangerous Religion in America*, P. 18. Missionary Crusader, Lubbock, Texas Ninth Printing August 1979.

38. Barbara Morris, *The Religion of Humanism in the Public Schools*, P.O. Box 756, Upland, CA., 91786. Cited - Homer Duncan, *Secular Humanism: The Most Dangerous Religion in America*, P. 8.

39. Allyn and Bacon, *Inquiries in Sociology*, 1978, P. 45. Cited – John Stormer, *None Dare Call It Education: The Documented Account of How Education "Reforms" are Undermining Academics and Traditional Values*, P. 61.

40. William Norman Grigg, *Freedom on the Altar: The UN's Crusade Against God and Family*, P. 47. American Opinion Publishing Inc., Appleton, Wisconsin. First Printing March 1995.

41. John Stormer, *None Dare Call It Education: The Documented Account of How Education "Reforms" are Undermining Academics and Traditional Values*, P. 63.

42. Karl Marx, *Economie Politique et Philosophie*, Vol. I, Pages 38-40. Cited - Claire Chambers, *The SIECUS Circle: A Humanist Revolution*, P. 104.

43. Valerie Riches, *Sex Education or Indoctrination: How Ideology Has Triumphed Over Facts*, P. x

44. Ibid, P. 2

45. Select Committee on Science and Technology (1969-70), Minutes of Evidence on Population, HMSO, 1970. Cited - Valerie Riches, *Sex Education or Indoctrination: How Ideology Has Triumphed Over Facts*, P. 29.

46. Valerie Riches, *Sex Education or Indoctrination: How Ideology Has Triumphed Over Facts*, P. 20.

47. Dr. Richard Farson, Western Behavioural Sciences Institute: http://wbsi.org/ilf

48. Richard Farson, *Birthrights: A Bill of Rights for Children*, P. 42. Macmillan Publishing Co., Inc., New York. 1974.

49. Ibid, P. 42

50. Ibid, P. 135

51. Ronald and Beatrice Gross, eds., *The Children's Rights Movement: Overcoming the Oppression of Young People* (Garden City, New York: Anchor Press/Doubleday, 1977): 321-322. Cited - Ingrid J. Guzman, *Parent Police: The U.N. Wants Your Children*, P. 11. Huntington House Publishers, Lafayette, Louisiana 1995.

52. Ingrid J. Guzman, *Parent Police: The U.N. Wants Your Children*, P. 5. Huntington House Publishers, Lafayette, Louisiana 1995.

53. Douglas Phillips, "*The United Nations Convention on the Rights of the Child*," National Center for Home Education Special Report. Cited – Ingrid J. Guzman, *Parent Police: The U.N. Wants Your Children*, P. 6.

54. Ingrid J. Guzman, *Parent Police: The U.N. Wants Your Children*, P. 14.

55. Ibid, P. 14.

56. Ibid, P. 16.

57. *The Daily Mail*, 23rd, April, 2010, *Mother's fury as children as young as EIGHT are being offered free condoms*. http://dailymail.co.uk/news/article-1268291/Mothers-fury-children-young-EIGHT-offered-free-condoms.html

58. Ingrid J. Guzman, *Parent Police: The U.N. Wants Your Children*, P. 17

59. http://www.examiner.com/x-17320-Sex-Education-Examiner~y2009m9d3-Condomsmasturbation-abortion-content-provoke-controversy-in-UNESCO-sex-education-draftguidelines

60. http://c-fam.org/publications/id.1798/pub_detail.asp

61. http://www.guardian.co.uk/commentisfree/2008/oct/26/sex-education-relationships?

62. http://www.dailymail.co.uk/news/article-1364360/Sex-education-Do-want-5-year-old-child-given-explicit-lessons.html

63. http://www.unol.org/rms/wcc.html

Chapter Sixteen: *United Nations of Religion*

1. Kathy Newburn, *A Planetary Awakening: Reflections on the Teachings of the Tibetan in the Works of Alice A. Bailey*, P. 3. Blue Dolphin Publishing, Nevada City, California, 2007.

2. Ibid, P. 9

3. Howse, Brannon, *Reclaiming a Nation at Risk: The Battle for Your Faith, Family and Freedoms*, P. 190, Bridgestone Multimedia Group, 1995

4. Kathy Newburn, *A Planetary Awakening: Reflections on the Teachings of the Tibetan in the Works of Alice A. Bailey,* P. 9.

5. Marilyn Ferguson, *The Aquarian Conspiracy, Personal and Social Transformation in the 1980's*, P. 36. J. P. Tarcher, Inc., Los Angeles, 1980.

6. William Norman Grigg, *Freedom on the Altar: The UN's Crusade Against God and Family,* P. 158. American Opinion Publishing Inc., Appleton Wisconsin. First Printing March 1995.

7. Ibid, P. 159

8. Blavatsky, *The Secret Doctrine*, P. 24. Cited - William Norman Grigg, *Freedom on the Altar: The UN's Crusade Against God and Family*. P. 166.

9. Bailey, Alice A (nne) (LaTrobe-Bateman) (1880-1949). *Encyclopedia of Occultism and Parapsychology*. Latin Trade

10. Alice A. Bailey, *Externalization of the Hierarchy*, P. 278. Lucis Publishing Co. 1957.

11. Constance Cumbey, *The Hidden Dangers of the Rainbow: The New Age Movement and our Coming Age of Barbarism*, P. 49. Huntington House, Inc., Lafayette, Los Angeles, 1983.

12. Ibid, P. 50

13. Ibid, P. 109

14. Ibid, P. 110

15. Ibid, P. 110

16. http://ngws.org/service/Articles/AABailey.htm

17. http://lucistrust.org/en/service_activities/world_goodwill/purposes_objectives

18. Constance Cumbey, *Hidden Dangers of the Rainbow*, P. 16.

19. Ibid, P. 67

20. Ibid, P. 24

21. William F. Jasper, *Global Tyranny... Step by Step: The United Nations and the Emerging New World Order,* P. 219. Published by Western Islands, Appleton, Wisconsin. Second Printing March 1993.

22. Executive Intelligence Review, Dope Inc. *The Book that Drove Henry Kissinger Crazy,* P. 540. Executive Intelligence Review, Washington D. C. 1992.

23. Ibid, P. 536

24. Jim Keith, *Mass Control: Engineering Human Consciousness*, P. 106. Published by Adventures Unlimited Press, Kempton, Illinois 60946. 2003.

25. Executive Intelligence Review, Dope Inc. *The Book that Drove Henry Kissinger Crazy,* P. 537

26. Ibid, P. 539

27. Jim Keith, *Mind Control, World Control, The Encyclopedia of Mind Control*, P. 104. Adventures Unlimited Press, Kempton, Illinois. Second Printing, 1998.

28. Alex Constantine, *The Covert War Against Rock,* P. 28. Feral House, Los Angeles 2000.

29. Marilyn Ferguson, *The Aquarian Conspiracy, Personal and Social Transformation in the 1980's,* P. 90.

30. Ibid, P. 51

31. David Hunt, T. A. McMahon, *America, The Sorcerer's New Apprentice: The Rise of New Age Shamanism,* P. 47. Harvest House Publishers, Eugene, Oregon 1988.

32. Ibid, P. 48

33. *The Sunday Times* (UK), "*Maharishi Mahesh Yogi, Guru of transcendental meditation who used his association with the Beatles to create a hugely profitable global movement,*" February 7th, 2008. http://timesonline.co.uk/tol/comment/obituaries/article3320882.ece

34. Caryl Matrisciana, *Yoga Uncoiled: From East to West, A Look Into The Practice of Yoga in the Church*, Caryl Productions, LLC, Menifee, California, 2007.

35. Ibid,

36. Kathy Newburn, *A Planetary Awakening: Reflections on the Teachings of the Tibetan in the Works of Alice A. Bailey*, P. XV.

37. David Hunt, T. A. McMahon, *America, The Sorcerer's New Apprentice: The Rise of New Age Shamanism*, P. 52.

38. Caryl Matrisciana, *Yoga Uncoiled: From East to West, A Look Into The Practice of Yoga in the Church.*

39. David Hunt, T. A. McMahon, *America, The Sorcerer's New Apprentice: The Rise of New Age Shamanism*, P. 49.

40. Marilyn Ferguson, *the Aquarian Conspiracy, Personal and Social Transformation in the 1980's*, P. 62.

41. Executive Intelligence Review, *Dope Inc. The Book that Drove Henry Kissinger Crazy*, P. 548.

42. David Hunt, T. A. McMahon, America, *The Sorcerer's New Apprentice: The Rise of New Age Shamanism*, P. 86.

43. Executive Intelligence Review, *Dope Inc. The Book that Drove Henry Kissinger Crazy*, P. 549.

44. http://bookrags.com/research/new-age-movement-eorl-10

45. Constance Cumbey, *Hidden Dangers of the Rainbow*, P. 107.

46. http://lorian.org

47. Constance Cumbey, *Hidden Dangers of the Rainbow*, P. 52.

48. Ibid, P. 22

49. http://lorian.org/aboutlorian.html#gpm1_2

50. David Hunt, T. A. McMahon, America, *The Sorcerer's New Apprentice: The Rise of New Age Shamanism*, P. 33.

51. http://www.hinduwisdom.info/Nature_Worship.htm

52. http://www.udcworld.org

53. 'Unity-and-Diversity World Council.' *Encyclopedia of Occultism and Parapsychology*. 2001. HighBeam Research. (May 8, 2011). http://www.highbeam.com/doc/1G2-3403804651.html

54. William Norman Grigg, *Freedom on the Altar: The UN's Crusade Against God and Family*. P. 163.

55. Shared Vision, Global Forum of Spiritual and Parliamentary Leaders on Human Survival, Volume 3, Number 1, 1989, P. 3. (Note: the address on the publication is 345 East 45th Street, 12th floor, New York, NY 10017, the same address as the UN Global Committee of Parliamentarians on Population and Development.) Cited - http://www.freedom.org/reports/ggreligion.htm

56. James Lovelock, *Gaia: A New Look at Life on Earth*, P. 148. Oxford University Press 1982.

57. http://www.crossroad.to/Books/YourChildNewAge/YCNA-5.htm

58. http://www.geometryofplace.com/gaiagraphy.html

59. Berit Kjos, *Brave New Schools: Guiding Your Child Through the Dangers of the Changing School System*, P. 41-42. Harvest House Publishers, Eugene, Oregon 1995.

60. http://www.sovereignty.net/p/gov/gganalysis.htm

61. Weiss, Alfred, "*Caldwell College Marks United Nations 50th Anniversary: Former.*" The Italian Voice. 1995

62. William Norman Grigg, *Freedom on the Altar: The UN's Crusade Against God and Family*, P. 158.

63. http://www.UNol.org/rms

64. *"Colorado's Spiritual Crossroads; In tiny Crestone, the world's religions coincide with a landscape that inspires believers of all stripes. (TRAVEL)."* Star Tribune, Minneapolis, MN. The Star Tribune Company. 2009 + Diane Daniel, Globe Correspondent. *"In a Scared Valley, a New Age Hub."* The Boston Globe, Boston, MA. International Herald Tribune. 2002

65. http://www.freedom.org/reports/srbio.htm

66. Preston, Julia, *"The Man With the Rio Plan; Summit Organizer Maurice Strong, Seeing Green."* The Washington Post. The Washington Post Company. 1992

67. *'Strong, Hon. Maurice F., P.C., O. C.'* Canadian Parliamentary Guide, 2005

68. Inside Report: *Maurice Strong's new frontman, The New American.* American Opinion Publishing, Inc. 2003

69. http://www.freedom.org/reports/srbio.htm

70. Ibid.

71. http://en.wikipedia.org/wiki/Brundtland_Commission

72. *Report of the World Commission on Environment and Development: Our Common Future*, Chairman's Foreword, xiii. Oxford University Press, 1987.

73. http://www.radioliberty.com/stones.htm

74. *World Environment Day observed by 10,000 at Headquarters*, UN Chronicle. United Nations Publications. 1987

75. *Al Gore, The Earth in the Balance: Ecology and the Human Spirit.* Cited - Berit Kjos, *Brave New Schools*, P. 31.

76. Dave Hunt, *Occult Invasion: The Subtle Seduction of the World and Church*, P. 10. Harvest House Publishers, Eugene, Oregon 1998.

77. Larry Witham, *"Gaia addresses science, faith, new age: Today's event unites man's consciousness with the living Earth. (Culture, Et Cetera)."* The Washington Times (Washington, DC). The Washington Times LLC, 3600 New York Ave. NE, Washington, DC 20002 USA. 1997

78. *Forty-two astronauts and cosmonauts to participate in UN Earth Day.* (NEWS ADVISORY), United Nations, Includes program schedule

79. *"The Declaration of the Sacred Earth Gathering, Rio 92,"* Earth Summit Times, June 3rd, 1992. Cited - William F. Jasper, Global Tyranny: Step by Step, P. 220.

80. Inside Report: *Maurice Strong's new frontman*, The New American. American Opinion Publishing, Inc. 2003

81. Joel Achenbach, *"What on Earth Is Going On? All Kinds of Organisms Plan for the Rio Summit."* The Washington Post. The Washington Post Company. April 27th, 1992

82. Joan Veon, *The United Nations' Global Straightjacket*, P. 164. Hearthstone Publishing, Oklahoma City, 2000.

83. Laurie C. Merrill, *"Environmental Activists See Champion in Gore."* Record Staff Writer.

84. *"Contrary To Will, Al Gore's Book Enlightens,"* Buffalo News. Sun-Times News Group. 1992

85. James Brooke, *"Fair Is Showcase for Lighter Side of the Rio Summit,"* June 3rd, 1992, http://nytimes.com/1992/06/03/world/fair-is-showcase-for-lighter-side-of-the-rio-summit.html

86. Joel Achenbach, *"On the Fringe of Rio; Vikings, Vegetarians and Taoists at the Alternative Summit,"* The Washington Post. The Washington Post Company. 1992

87. The Report of the Commission on Global Governance, *Our Global Neighbourhood*: P. 216. Oxford University Press, 1995.

88. Henry Lamb, "*Meet Maurice Strong*," Eco-Logic, November/December 1995

89. "*The Reorganization of Society*," eco-logic Magazine (Publ. By Environmental Conservation Organization, Hollow Rock, TN), September/October 1995, P. 4.

90. SPECIAL REPORT on, the American Heritage Rivers Project, Biodiversity etc. To the Commissioners of Bonneville County. THE WILDLANDS PROJECT UNLEASHES ITS WAR ON MANKIND, By Marilyn Brannan, Associate Editor, Monetary & Economic Review FAMC, 3500 JFK Parkway, Fort Collins, CO 80525 (1-800-336-7000)

91. http://clinton2.nara.gov/PCSD/Charter/index.html

92. http://clinton2.nara.gov/PCSD

93. The Report of the Commission on Global Governance, *Our Global Neighbourhood*, Oxford: Oxford University Press, 1995, P. 208

94. "*Stronger measures to protect ozone layer, (Includes other environmental topics in which the UN is involved).*" UN Chronicle. United Nations Publications. 1996

95. The Report of the Commission on Global Governance, *Our Global Neighbourhood*, Oxford: Oxford University Press, 1995, P. 208

96. John Elvin, "*Wild-Eyed in the Wilderness. (The Wildlands Project (TWP) will designate areas environmentally unique).*" Insight on the News. The Washington Times LLC, 3600 New York Ave. NE, Washington, DC 20002 USA. 2001

97. http://www.sierraclub.org/sierrasportsmen/people/leaders

98. John Elvin, "*Wild-Eyed in the Wilderness. (The Wildlands Project (TWP) will designate areas environmentally unique).*" Insight on the News. The Washington Times LLC, 3600 New York Ave. NE, Washington, DC 20002 USA. 2001

99. "*Roundup: Mountains worldwide need urgent measures of protection: UNEP.*" Xinhua News Agency, Xinhua News Agency, 2002.

100. "*UNEP launching new initiative to protect world's bio-diversity*," PTI - The Press Trust of India Ltd. The Times of Central Asia. 2008.

Chapter Seventeen: *Greatest Scientific Fraud in History*

1. Alexander King and Bertrand Schneider, *The First Global Revolution: A Report by the Council of the Club of Rome*, P. 115. Pantheon Books, New York 1991.

2. Ibid, P. 108

3. Ibid, P. 115

4. Rene A. Wormser, *Foundations: Their Power and Influence*, P. 39. Covenant House Books, Sevierville, TN. Third Printing 1993.

5. http://www.salon.com/news/feature/2007/03/22/primary_sources

6. Hannah Devlin, Ben Webster, Philippe Naughton in Copenhagen, "*Inconvenient truth for Al Gore as his North Pole sums don't add up,*" December 15th, 2009, http://timesonline. co.uk/tol/news/environment/copenhagen/article6956783.ece

7. Tom Leonard, "*Al Gore's electricity bill goes through the (insulated) roof,*" 18th, Jun, 2008, The Telegraph, http://www.telegraph.co.uk/news/worldnews/northamerica/usa/2153179/Al-Gores-electricity-bill-goes-through-the-insulated-roof.html

8. http://www.heritage.org/Research/Testimony/The-Economic-Impact-of-the-Waxman-Markey-Cap-and-Trade-Bill

9. http://www.inhofe.senate.gov/pressreleases/climateupdate.htm

10. Paul R. Ehrlich, *The Population Bomb*, Ballantine Books, 1968.

11. Mathew Connelly, *Fatal Mis-Conception: The Struggle to Control World Population*, P. X. The Belknap Press of Harvard University Press, Cambridge, Massachusetts/London, England, 2008.

12. http://blogs.telegraph.co.uk/news/jamesdelingpole/100035928/today-is-earth-day-apparently

13. Claire Chambers, *The SIECUS Circle: A Humanist Revolution*, P. 9. Published by Western Islands, Belmont Massachusetts 02178, 1977.

14. *Boston Globe*, August 10th, 1968. Cited - Claire Chambers, *The SIECUS Circle: A Humanist Revolution,* P. 9.

15. http://reason.com/archives/2000/05/01/earth-day-then-and-now/1

16. James Delingpole, *"Today is Earth Day, Apparently,"*22nd, April, 2010, http://blogs.telegraph.co.uk/news/jamesdelingpole/100035928/today-is-earth-day-apparently

17. http://earthday.envirolink.org/history.html

18. Brian Sussman, *ClimateGate: A Veteran Meteorologist Exposes the Global Warming Scam*, P. 10. Published by World Net Daily, Washington, D. C., 2010.

19. http://earthday.envirolink.org/history.html

20. Ibid

21. Brian Sussman, *ClimateGate: A Veteran Meteorologist Exposes the Global Warming Scam*, P. 14.

22. James Delingpole, *"Today is Earth Day, Apparently,"*22nd, April, 2010, http://blogs.telegraph.co.uk/news/jamesdelingpole/100035928/today-is-earth-day-apparently

23. Claire Chambers, *The SIECUS Circle: A Humanist Revolution*, P. 339.

24. *Newsweek*, April 25th, 1975

25. Stephen Glover, *"50 days to save the world? I might listen to the doomsayers if they weren't such ludicrous hypocrites,"*15th, December, 2009, http://www.dailymail.co.uk/debate/article-1236497/STEPHEN-GLOVER-50-days-save-world-I-listen-doomsayers-werent-ludicrous-hypocrites.html

26. Time Magazine, *"Another Ice Age?"* Monday, June. 24th, 1974, http://time.com/time/magazine/article/0,9171,944914,00.html

27. James Delingpole, *"Today is Earth Day, Apparently,"* 22nd, April, 2010, http://blogs.telegraph.co.uk/news/jamesdelingpole/100035928/today-is-earth-day-apparently

28. UK Channel 4 documentary, *"The Green Conspiracy,"* Aired on SBS Television in Australia, 1990.

29. Ibid.

30. William F. Jasper, *The United Nations Exposed: The Internationalist Conspiracy to Rule the World,* P. 97. Published by The John Birch Society, Appleton, Wisconsin Third Printing October 2001.

31. Dixie Lee Ray, *Environmental Overkill,* P. 205. Washington D. C. Regnery Gateway, 1993. Cited - William F. Jasper, *The United Nations Exposed: The Internationalist Conspiracy to Rule the World*, P. 97.

32. William F. Jasper, *The United Nations Exposed: The Internationalist Conspiracy to Rule the World*, P. 97.

33. http://msnbc.msn.com, *"Al Gore, U.N. climate panel win Nobel Peace Prize,"* 10/12/2007

34. http://www.his.com/~sepp/Archive/controv/ipcccont/Item05.htm

35. Quotation from Christopher Booker, *The Real Global Warming Disaster*, P. 1, the Continuum International Publishing Group, 2009.

36. http://unfccc.int/files/kyoto_protocol/status_of_ratification/application/pdf/kp_ratification.pdf

37. http://www.cato.org/pubs/pas/pa-307es.html

38. Professor Richard Lindzen, as quoted in the *'Daily Mail,'* online edition, December 2nd, 2009.

39. http://naturalclimatechange.us/notes on _global warming or global governance_.htm

40. http://msnbc.msn.com, *"Al Gore, U.N. climate panel win Nobel Peace Prize,"* 10/12/2007

41. The Daily Mail, *"Schools must warn of Gore climate film bias,"* 3rd, October, 2007, http://dailymail.co.uk/news/article-485336/Schools-warn-Gore-climate-film-bias.html

42. Brian Sussman, *ClimateGate: A Veteran Meteorologist Exposes the Global Warming Scam*, P. 68.

43. http://co2science.org/articles/V2/N4/EDIT.php

44. http://sovereignindependent.com/?p=17314

45. http://newsletter.co.uk/news/local/yes_global_warming_quot_is_just_propaganda_quot_1_1876258

46. Stephen Glover, *"50 days to save the world? I might listen to the doomsayers if they weren't such ludicrous hypocrites,"*15th, December, 2009, http://www.dailymail.co.uk/debate/article-1236497/STEPHEN-GLOVER-50-days-save-world-I-listen-doomsayers-werent-ludicrous-hypocrites.html

47. Adam Vaughan, *"Global media unite over Copenhagen climate change conference editorial,"* The editorial, calling on rich countries to commit to deep cuts, appeared on the Guardian front page and ran in 56 newspapers in 45 countries, 7th, December, 2009.

48. http://good-cop15.org/blogs/climate+thinkers+blog

49. Prince Charles Copenhagen speech: *"The eyes of the world are upon you,"* 15th, December, 2009. http://www.guardian.co.uk/environment/2009/dec/15/prince-charles-speech-copenhagen-climate

50. Stephen Glover, *"50 days to save the world? I might listen to the doomsayers if they weren't such ludicrous hypocrites,"*15th, December, 2009, http://www.dailymail.co.uk/debate/article-1236497/STEPHEN-GLOVER-50-days-save-world-I-listen-doomsayers-werent-ludicrous-hypocrites.html

51. http://w.wnd.com/index.php?pageId=116882

52. *"Climategate: was Russian secret service behind email hacking plot?"* 6th, December, 2009. http://www.telegraph.co.uk/earth/copenhagen-climate-change-confe/6746370/Climategate-was-Russian-secret-service-behind-email-hacking-plot.html

53. http://news.bbc.co.uk/1/hi/sci/tech/8399252.stm

54. BBC Breakfast TV: "*Carbon Ration Card Proposal*," 20th, July, 2006. http://www.Youtube. com/watch?v=U7HF-ANJLXk

55. http://www.eci.ox.ac.uk/research/energy/downloads/paragstrickland09pcbudget.pdf

56. http://www.eci.ox.ac.uk/research/energy/downloads/40house/background_doc_l.pdf

57. "*Everyone in Britain could be given a personal 'carbon allowance*," 9th, November, 2009. http://www.telegraph.co.uk/earth/environment/carbon/6527970/Everyone-in-Britain-could-be-given-a-personal-carbon-allowance.html

58. "*NYT Environment Reporter Floats Idea: Give Carbon Credits to Couples That Limit Themselves to One Child*," 16th, October 2009. http://cnsnews.com/news/article/55667

59. http://www.energy.gov/8216.htm

60. "*UK reveals roll-out plans to install 53 million smart meters*," 30th, March, 2011. http://www. clickgreen.org.uk/news/national-news/122099-uk-reveals-roll-out-plans-to-install-53-million-smart-meters.html

61. http://www.silverspringnet.com/resources/flashdemo-english.html

62. http://www.forbescustom.com/EnergyPgs/utilipoint/SmartGridNewProductsP1.html

www.ingramcontent.com/pod-product-compliance
Lightning Source LLC
Chambersburg PA
CBHW070802270326
41927CB00010B/2258